Cape Canaveral, Cocoa Beach & Florida's Space Coast Great Destinations

A COMPLETE GUIDE

1ST EDITION

Cape Canaveral, Cocoa Beach & Florida's Space Coast Great Destinations

Dianne Marcum

The Countryman Press
Woodstock, Vermont

Suggestions and comments are welcome. Please email the publisher at
countrymanpress@wwnorton.com or visit www.DianneMarcum.com.

ISBN 978-1-58157-079-3

Cover photo © Gregg Newton/Corbis

Interior photos by the author unless otherwise specified

Book design Bodenweber Design

Page composition by Opaque Design & Print Production

Maps by Mapping Specialists, Ltd., Madison, WI © The Countryman Press

Published by The Countryman Press, P.O. Box 748, Woodstock, Vermont 05091

Distributed by W. W. Norton & Company, Inc., 500 Fifth Ave., New York, NY 10110

Printed in the United States of America

10 9 8 7 6 5 4 3 2 1

GREAT DESTINATIONS TRAVEL GUIDEBOOK SERIES

Recommended by *National Geographic Traveler* and *Travel & Leisure* magazines.

[A] CRISP AND CRITICAL APPROACH, FOR TRAVELERS WHO WANT TO LIVE LIKE LOCALS.
— *USA Today*

Great Destinations™ guidebooks are known for their comprehensive, critical coverage of regions of extraordinary cultural interest and natural beauty. The authors in this series are professional travel writers who have lived for many years in the regions they describe. Each title in this series is continuously updated with each printing to ensure accurate and timely information. All the books contain more than one hundred photographs and maps.

Current titles available:

THE ADIRONDACK BOOK
ATLANTA
AUSTIN, SAN ANTONIO & THE TEXAS HILL COUNTRY
THE BERKSHIRE BOOK
BIG SUR, MONTEREY BAY & GOLD COAST WINE COUNTRY
CAPE CANAVERAL, COCOA BEACH & FLORIDA'S SPACE COAST
THE CHARLESTON, SAVANNAH & COASTAL ISLANDS BOOK
THE CHESAPEAKE BAY BOOK
THE COAST OF MAINE BOOK
COLORADO'S CLASSIC MOUNTAIN TOWNS: GREAT DESTINATIONS
THE FINGER LAKES BOOK
GALVESTON, SOUTH PADRE ISLAND & THE TEXAS GULF COAST
THE HAMPTONS BOOK
HONOLULU & OAHU: GREAT DESTINATIONS HAWAII
THE HUDSON VALLEY BOOK
LOS CABOS & BAJA CALIFORNIA SUR: GREAT DESTINATIONS MEXICO
THE NANTUCKET BOOK
THE NAPA & SONOMA BOOK
PALM BEACH, MIAMI & THE FLORIDA KEYS
PHOENIX, SCOTTSDALE, SEDONA & CENTRAL ARIZONA
PLAYA DEL CARMEN, TULUM & THE RIVIERA MAYA: GREAT DESTINATIONS MEXICO
SALT LAKE CITY, PARK CITY, PROVO & UTAH'S HIGH COUNTRY RESORTS
SAN DIEGO & TIJUANA
SAN JUAN, VIEQUES & CULEBRA: GREAT DESTINATIONS PUERTO RICO
THE SEATTLE & VANCOUVER BOOK: INCLUDES THE OLYMPIC PENINSULA, VICTORIA & MORE
THE SANTA FE & TAOS BOOK
THE SARASOTA, SANIBEL ISLAND & NAPLES BOOK
THE SHENANDOAH VALLEY BOOK
TOURING EAST COAST WINE COUNTRY

If you are traveling to, moving to, residing in, or just interested in any (or all!) of these enchanting regions, a Great Destinations guidebook is a superior companion. Honest and painstakingly critical, full of information only a local can provide, Great Destinations guidebooks give you all the practical knowledge you need to enjoy the best of each region. Why not own them all?

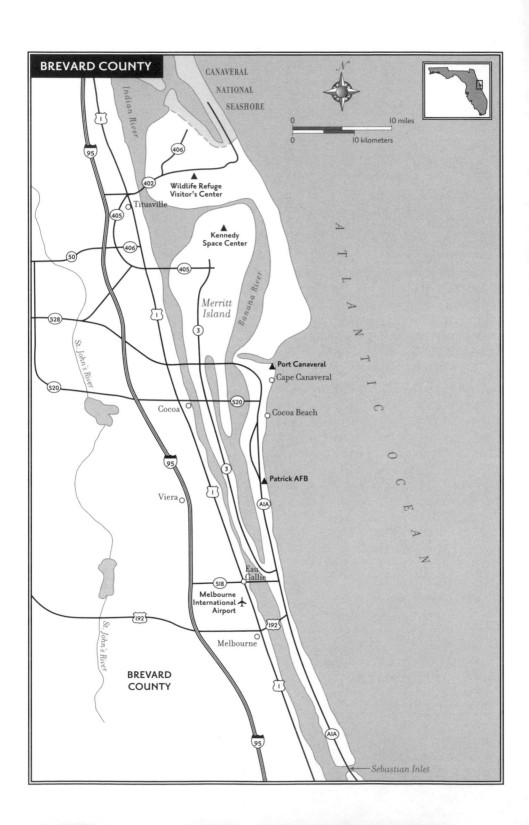

BREVARD COUNTY

CANAVERAL
NATIONAL
SEASHORE

Indian River

95

406

402

Wildlife Refuge
Visitor's Center

Titusville

405

406

50

405

Kennedy
Space Center

Banana River

Merritt
Island

528

3

1

St. John's River

520

520

Cocoa

520

Port Canaveral

Cape Canaveral

Cocoa Beach

ATLANTIC OCEAN

95

3

1

Patrick AFB

Viera

A1A

Eau
Gallie

518

Melbourne
International
Airport

192

St. John's River

192

192

Melbourne

1

BREVARD
COUNTY

95

A1A

Sebastian Inlet

10 miles

10 kilometers

Contents

ACKNOWLEDGMENTS

It takes a community to write a travel book. The stories and enthusiasm of the people who live and love Brevard County are woven through every page of this book. Thank you all.

The Cocoa Beach Writer's Workshop has been my support system as I've stretched my wings as a writer. Mary Mae Burruss is the heart of this literary family and has generously shared her advice and talent. Eileen Callen and I became friends and partners through the group. She contributed to the challenging task of visiting and reviewing many of the establishments included in the Restaurants and Food Purveyors and Shopping chapters.

Many local organizations and individuals offered information, photographs, and references. My appreciation to the Space Coast Tourism Development Commission, particularly to Bonnie King, who included me as part of the sales team meetings. JaNeen Smith, Director of the Brevard Museum of History and Natural Science, checked my facts and made great suggestions for the history narrative. Businessman Roger Dobson is a Brevard County pioneer. His encouragement and direction were invaluable. Laurilee Thompson, a recreational and environmental guru, inspired me with her love for the natural resources of the area.

Two talented photographers contributed to the images that illustrate the beauty and diversity of the county. Renowned wildlife photographer Jim Angy shared his work as well as the picture-taking tips included in the Recreation chapter. Roger Scruggs captures the people and places of Brevard County. He shot the powerful photograph of Space Shuttle Atlantis included at the start of this book.

Thank you to everyone at the Countryman Press, especially Kermit Hummel for this opportunity, and Jennifer Thompson and Justine Rathbun for patiently guiding me through the landscape of travel writing.

My heartfelt gratitude goes to my friends and family, who intuitively knew when to help and when to give me time and space to complete a task or meet a deadline. My dear friends Maggie Megee and John Anderson accompanied me on field trips, reviewed drafts, and celebrated every small success. Cassidy Dianne Neary researched activities suited to younger visitors, checked facts, and—as she has for thirteen years—made me smile.

Introduction

"How would you like to live in a place like this?" writes a visitor describing the beauty and wildlife of the Indian River on the back of a postcard. The message was penned nearly a century ago but could just have easily been sent yesterday. Brevard County is one of those rare vacation spots where people picture themselves living one day, an extraordinary blend of sunshine, beaches, pristine natural resources, and space-age technology.

Many visitors base their stay in the shoreside communities of Cocoa Beach and Cape Canaveral, which are centrally located for easy access to the airport and theme parks in Orlando, all major Florida highways and other areas of Brevard County. The towns offer wide beaches and a variety of lodging and dining choices. Most hotels are directly on the coast or just a short walk away. Wood crossovers lead down to the beach at almost every block. A buffer of sand dunes, sea grapes, and palms creates a natural and pretty look.

Port Canaveral, the second busiest cruise port in the world, is a working seaport bustling with marinas, parks, a 1,200-foot fishing pier, and waterside restaurants and bars. Guided fishing boats head offshore each morning and return to the docks in the afternoon with their catch. Mega-sized cruise ships passing through the channel on their way to sea are almost close enough to touch.

The Space Coast moniker is not just hyperbole. Brevard County is the birthplace of America's space program and the world's most active spaceport. From along the coast or across the river in north Brevard, the sight and sound of a launch is breathtaking. A tour at Kennedy Space Center Visitor Complex takes you right onto NASA property and close to all their facilities. You can even have lunch with an astronaut. (See the Culture chapter for a summary of aerospace offerings that explore that past, present, and future of space exploration.)

The waterways of the Indian River Lagoon estuary flow the entire length of the county and host an abundance of marine life, birds, plants—and, of course, manatees and dolphins. The mix of fresh and salt water creates an idyllic spot for wildlife and a wonderful recreational playground. This book includes profiles and photographs to help you identify the most visible and popular birds and marine mammals.

Planning should be the easiest part of your vacation. This book is designed to provide all the information you need to have fun along Florida's Space Coast. In addition to suggestions on where to stay, eat, and shop, you'll find listings for cultural and recreational activities. Everybody can enjoy outdoor adventures—novices and experts, children and adults.

So come visit. Bask in the sun, ride a wave, dive in the pool, paddle through quiet waters, reel in a fish, laugh at pelicans, marvel at dolphins, be mesmerized by manatees. Just don't forget to drop a line to friends back home: "How would U like 2 live IA place like this? L8RG8R."

Dianne Marcum
Cape Canaveral Florida
www.DianneMarcum.com

THE WAY THIS BOOK WORKS

Florida's Space Coast is long and narrow, with 76 miles of Atlantic beachfront. Eastbound travelers cross several bridges that span intracoastal waterways flowing like liquid ribbons down the length of the county. This guide is divided into nine chapters, each ready to be explored independently but connected by thematic bridges across a total vacation journey.

Information in each chapter is listed first for "Cape Canaveral & Cocoa Beach," which includes Port Canaveral and a nearby section of Merritt Island. Entries for other areas of Brevard County are categorized geographically, to easily locate restaurants, shops, and activities in proximity to each other. "Central Brevard" includes historic Cocoa Village and the newer community of Viera; "North Brevard" is anchored by the city of Titusville; and "South Brevard" stretches from Eau Gallie and Melbourne to Sebastian Inlet.

Overnight visitors might start with chapter 3, Lodging, and settle on a place to stay. Most of the properties are in the Cape Canaveral and Cocoa Beach area, but some unique offerings in other parts of the county are included. A lodging index at the end of the book sorts all accommodations by price.

Listings within each chapter and area are in alphabetical order. In general, most facilities and activities have some degree of wheelchair accessibility, and this is noted. However, the specifics vary considerably, and those with special needs should call ahead.

The information in this book is as timely and accurate as possible, but like a beach landscape, the terrain is always shifting. Dining prices are based on the cost of a dinner entrée with appetizer and dessert. Lodging prices are a per-room, double occupancy rate, during the peak season. Rates usually drop 20 percent or more during nonpeak times. Not included is a 6 percent Florida sales tax on dining and lodging and a 5 percent countywide resort tax on lodging.

Pricing Codes

	Lodging	Dining
Inexpensive	Up to $100	Up to $15
Moderate	$100 to $150	$15 to $25
Expensive	$150 to $200	$25 to $35
Very Expensive	More than $200	More than $35

Credit cards are abbreviated as follows:

AE:	American Express	DC:	Diner's Club
CB:	Carte Blanche	MC:	MasterCard
D:	Discover Card	V:	Visa

Brevard County has one area code, and it's easy to remember: 321—blast off!

©1993 V. Zimmerman

History

The Edge of the Universe

Dreams are written in the sands of Florida's Space Coast.

On what may have been the first official spring break, Spanish explorer Juan Ponce de León led a flotilla of ships away from the safe harbors of Puerto Rico. The crisp sails of the *Santa Maria, Santiago,* and *San Cristobal* rose tall against the vast baby blue sky. Two hundred dreamers were on a quest for gold and the mythological fountain of youth. In a serendipitous twist, Ponce de León and his men discovered instead a land of natural riches and warm, flowing waters. On April 2, 1513, near the time of the Pascua de Florida or Feast of Flowers, La Florida was claimed for the kingdom of Spain.

The fleet first made landfall near a cape halfway up the east coast of Florida. Surprised natives, who had not yet grasped the value of tourism, sent the explorers rowing quickly back to the mother ship amid a barrage of arrows made from natural canes that grew near the beach. Back home, mapmakers dubbed the place Cabo de Canaveral, Place of the Cane Bearers, as a warning to future sailors. At the time many different Native American tribes populated the eastern coast of Florida, but it was probably the Ais (Eye-es), fierce and unfriendly warriors, who discouraged the Spanish visitors from coming ashore. Their victory was short-lived; they would not survive the relentless waves of weapons and germs brought onshore by European explorers. For more than three hundred years the Spanish, French, and British colonists took turns flying their flags. Florida became a territory of the young and growing United States in 1822; in 1845 it became the 27th state. "Not until the year 2055 will the American flag have flown over Florida as long as did the flag of Spain," points out Michael Gannon in his book *Florida, A Short History.*

Fast-forward nearly five hundred years from Ponce de León's landing. Visitors traveling by car, bus, motorcycle, and sometimes by boat follow in his wake, searching for a golden tan and a dip in the restorative waves of the fountain of youth that is the Atlantic Ocean. The natives are much friendlier and more likely to offer a fruity drink overflowing a cane mug. The sharp spit of land jutting from these sandy shores was once a welcome landmark for weary sailors after a long journey across a seemingly endless ocean. Today, new-age explorers embark from the same distinctive cape, climbing aboard shiny rockets and blasting off on a voyage into the infinity of space. One tourism tagline labeled this stretch of paradise "the edge of the universe." Settle your chair in the shallow water at low tide, look out toward the sun-speckled horizon, and you'll agree.

NATURAL HISTORY

A Kinder, Gentler Evolution

In the millennia of time, as continents shifted and oceans spilled into rocky crevices, Florida was an afterthought. Small and disconnected islands dotted the shallow waters circling the southern coast of North America. The canvas changed as soft strokes from the artist's brush slowly connected the dots into a peninsula, a finishing touch that dangled from the continent like an emerald teardrop earring.

Surrounded by ocean, the width of Florida's exposed land grew and shrank every one hundred thousand years or so as ocean temperatures fluctuated. Today the state is half the size it was when the first settlers migrated here more than twelve thousand years ago. Scientists believe American Indians descended from wanderers who crossed the Bering Strait. We can only imagine that with each harsh winter they moved just a little farther south, eventually discovering Florida, the edge of their known world. The temperate climate and abundance of flora, fauna, and sea life offered an attractive alternative to these nomadic hunters and gatherers.

An archaeologist's treasure trove found in the midst of Florida's Space Coast yielded solid evidence of the existence and lifestyle of Florida's early inhabitants. In 1982, during a brush-clearing excavation, skulls and skeletons were spotted embedded in the ground. Bulldozers were lowered and engines shut down. Researchers unearthed a world buried under the sands of time. Eight thousand years ago a community existed in this idyllic spot situated between saltwater lagoons stocked with mollusks and green turtles, and the crystal clear, fish-filled currents of the St. Johns River. A hammock (an Indian word meaning shady place or little island) covered with oak, pine, dogwood, and ash supplied more than enough wood for shelter and fires. Palms and palmettos were stripped and woven into fabrics and baskets. During most of the year trees and bushes offered an abundance of berries and nuts. The people were healthy—some living into their 60s. When they died, their bodies were carefully wrapped in a blanket and anchored to the bottom of what today is Windover Pond, just outside Titusville. One young girl, perhaps three years old, was discovered thousands of years later with her arms still tenderly wrapped around her favorite toys. Under a protective cocoon of peat and muck, the remains of these early settlers bear witness to their remarkably ordinary lives.

Nature's Theme Park

Every architectural plan begins with a footprint, the basic design of the project. As oceans receded during the last cooling period, the landscape of Florida's central east coast evolved into a primordial patchwork of water and land—the Indian River Lagoon.

When is a river not really a river? Because of the length and width of the waters bordering Florida's Atlantic coast, early settlers incorrectly labeled them as rivers. In fact, the Indian River Lagoon is an ecosystem of three separate estuaries stretching 156 miles from New Smyrna in the north to Jupiter in the south. The Indian River is the longest and most inland of the lagoons. Mosquito Lagoon sits just east of the northern section of the Indian River—originally connected to it by a shallow ditch. The wide, waist-deep Banana River is an offshoot of the Indian River and separates the barrier island from Merritt Island.

The Indian River Lagoon is a unique type of estuary, a fluid mixture of fresh and salt water. Breezes, not tides, create current and motion. Originally, ocean access was limited to natural openings at each end of the barrier island. Today, six inlets act as revolving doors connecting the lagoon and the ocean, keeping the brackish mix in place and moving marine life between the two systems. The living conditions are stressful—salinity levels frequently change, coastal sediments limit visibility, and the usually warm waters are intermittently cooled as ocean tides rise. Resilient marine creatures able to acclimate to this dynamic locale don't just survive. They thrive.

At the river's edge a graceful blue heron stands tall and still as a statue. A parade of pelicans swoops overhead. Suddenly one bird breaks from the formation and nose-dives below the blue-gray surface to snag a surprised fish. Mullet flip into the air, slow-moving manatees graze in thick grasses, and dolphins arc gracefully across the horizon. You'd never guess that beneath the surface a vibrant community flourishes. According to biologist Kathy Hill, with the St. Johns Water Management District, "The Indian River Lagoon is the most biologically diverse estuary in the continental United States. The lagoon spans both temperate and subtropical zones, creating a unique and welcoming environment for over 4,300 species of animals, plants, and birds."

Florida scrub jay |Jim Angy

Wildlife Profile: Sea Turtle

Sea turtles have been around for more than 100 million years and certainly qualify as the earliest visitors to Florida's Atlantic beaches. Three species of the ancient marine creatures return to this coast each year, making this the busiest turtle-nesting site in the world. The most common of the three is the 300-pound loggerhead, whose strong jaws crunch shellfish and crustaceans. Full-grown greens are about the same size but are vegetarians. The leatherback is a 1-ton giant who dines on jellyfish. Sea turtles are similar to their land-locked cousins except their limbs are flippers and their heads no longer retract. With one exception, they never leave the water.

In the dark of night a female turtle lumbers from the surf, crawls to the sandy dune line, and digs a deep hole with her flippers. After depositing more than one hundred Ping-Pong-ball-size eggs into the nest, the exhausted mom refills the opening—almost dancing as she sways and turns, creating a sandy swirl that makes the nest invisible to predators and beachgoers. Finished with her task, the turtle returns to the ocean, leaving telltale flipper tracks that are usually erased by waves and wind before sunrise.

Loggerhead sea turtle (Caretta caretta) |Jim Angy

Hatchlings incubate for about eight weeks and then pop to the surface en masse, usually at night. Following prehistoric programming, the babies, about the size of a toddler's hand, scramble toward water aglow with shimmering whitecaps. The trip is treacherous. Some never make it to water's edge—pulled off course by artificial light or eaten by predators such as raccoons or ghost crabs. Those that get to the water face a 15-mile swim through a sea teeming with hungry marine life. The lucky ones make it to the security of the weedy Sargasso Sea and remain there until grown. Adult female turtles mate and instinctively return home to familiar beaches to carry on the cycle of life.

Space Coast Sightings: Sea turtles are an endangered species, and it's illegal to interfere with nesting mothers or hatchlings. The Beaches and Surfing chapter has information on approved organizations that conduct nightly turtle walks during the active nesting season.

The lagoon is also the largest marine nursery in North America. Many inhabitants, like shrimp, are spawned at sea and then travel to the estuary, where they settle in a soft cradle of grass and take their place near the beginning of the food chain. Vegetation lines the river bottom and offers refuge to small newcomers. Young fish wander in for a meal and end up playing hide-and-seek with fast-moving tarpon. A sharp-eyed osprey patiently circles the sky waiting for a chance to clutch the larger fish in its talons and carry it away. The Banana River is fringed by mangroves, their thick roots a secure home for small fish and crabs. When their protein-rich leaves fall, larger animals and crustaceans munch on them. What about those babies? The ones that survive and mature return to the ocean, reproduce, and the cycle begins again.

Nature protects this fragile ecosystem with the barrier islands, soft sand blankets buffering the powerful waves of the Atlantic Ocean. Long ago, ocean breezes nudged sand, shells, and natural debris into protective embankments. Marine hammocks blossomed into islands of lush vegetation and a beachside habitat for wildlife. This beautiful and diverse community, with residents like primrose, wild coffee, and cabbage palms, is an irresistible draw for birds and small animals—a chance to frolic under a canopy of live oaks and furry, gray-green moss.

The isolated and scrubby Indian River Lagoon was among the last settled areas of Florida, but a century of technology has made this paradise more approachable. Walt Disney may have been inspired by nature when he talked about his dream of a family theme park. "It's something that will never be finished . . . It will be a live, breathing thing that will need change," he said. On the evolutionary teeter-totter, plants, animals, birds, fish, and all other manner of creatures adapt and adjust to maintain a symbiotic balance. Human beings are welcomed to the game, invited to enjoy the abundance of the area while respecting the fragile resources that are the magic and wonder of nature's theme park.

SOCIAL HISTORY

The Forgotten Frontier

Florida was not easily conquered. Panthers, mosquitoes, rattlers, alligators, and black bears instinctively defended their territory. In his prize-winning book of historical fiction, *A Land Remembered,* Patrick Smith writes of "too much palmetto" and "snakes as thick as skeeters." The Ais Indians may have been the first tribe to plant deep roots along the central east coast, where an abundance of resources helped offset their difficult struggle against the elements. The tribe dominated the area by the time European sailors discovered Florida. Many of their settlements sat near the banks of the large inland river, so the Spanish called the waterway *Río de Ais.*

Traveler Jonathan Dickinson was taken captive by the Ais when his ship wrecked off the Atlantic coast in 1696. His journal gives us a look at this Native American culture that fished with spears, cooked in clay pots, and drank from conch shells. Small round huts with poles tied together and covered with thatch provided shelter. Gatherings were held in the *cacique,* or chief's house, a wood frame covered on the sides and top with palmetto fronds and that accommodated as many as three hundred attendees. Benches along the sides provided seating during the day and beds at night. By the start of the eighteenth century the noble warriors had disappeared from the area—memories of them lingering in the early mist of a river that once carried their name, now known simply as the Indian River.

Under European rule, settlement of La Florida concentrated along the waterfront, including St. Augustine and Jupiter at either end of the Indian River Lagoon. Foreign adventurers were encouraged to come and help populate the new territory. Many emigrated from the new country to the north, the United States, and when they were here in sufficient numbers they banded together to claim part of Florida for themselves. Spain settled the rebellion by ceding Florida to the United States in 1822. The new government immediately engaged in the Indian Wars, and for two decades Floridians lived in a land of uprisings and skirmishes. When a truce was finally called, the Seminoles were the only Native Americans remaining in the state. They were ordered to move south, but a few stayed in Brevard—living, trading, marrying, and surviving alongside their neighbors.

Florida was growing, but only a few hardy souls pushed through to the wild and desolate Indian River Lagoon. In his book *History of Brevard County,* historian J. H. Shofner describes them as "persons with limited means but enterprising spirits and indomitable courage." To reach the area, newcomers sailed from the New Smyrna inlet to a small body of water identified early on as Mosquito Lagoon; then they hauled their vessel and cargo over a short strip of land to reach the Indian River, where they continued their journey south. It would be 1854 before the aptly named Haulover Canal was cut across upper Merritt Island to create a continuous water path from the Atlantic Ocean to the Indian River.

In 1847, the U.S. government commissioned a lighthouse on the cape at Canaveral, a coastal landmark for an ever-growing number of ships that plied the coast. Seven years later Capt. Mills Burnham, who had migrated to Florida a decade earlier to improve his health, moved in to man the tower. A few miles inland Burnham discovered citrus trees planted and abandoned by the Spanish. Soon his 15-acre grove produced basketfuls of juicy, sweet oranges. It was Burnham who gave the Banana River its name, suggested by the wild bananas growing along its banks.

Gradually, a sprinkling of folks found their way to what was first called Mosquito County. Settlers built crude houses and made a living from cattle, citrus, and water delicacies, like the green turtles found throughout the lagoon. Isolated homesteads grew into trading posts that also served as regional gathering spots for picnics and parties. Titusville, closest to the Haulover Canal, was a bustling town in 1877 when Capt. T. J. Lund piloted the steamboat *Pioneer* into the city docks—blowing her whistle and proudly announcing the start of a new era. An area that once thrived on fishing and agriculture now had a new business, tourism. The word was coined by the French, meaning a turn or circuit, as in *Tour de France*. Welcome to the *Tour de Indian River.*

Old Haulover Canal, circa 1854 Courtesy Brevard County Historical Commission

Soon two hundred boats navigated the river every day, carrying passengers and freight. Cruisers stayed in small cabins during the two-day trek from Titusville to Jupiter. Or they could disembark along the way at towns like Cocoa, Rockledge, Eau Gallie, and Melbourne, where hotels and merchants waited to host them. The first luxury liner was christened the *Cinderella*. Tourists crossed the gangplank and set out on a journey through an enchanted land. Letters sent home brought to life a wilderness teeming with unusual and colorful birds, never-before-seen flowers and greenery, and exotic animals. Alligators sunned along riverbanks; manatees bobbed alongside the boat. Egrets and ibises dotted mangrove islands, and majestic white pelicans swept across a blueberry horizon. Days were spent sportfishing for trout, snapper, and redfish. Nights offered card games and dancing. On deck, passengers were mesmerized as the boat churned through dark water tipped with bright, phosphorescent sparkles. One traveler wrote, "On our left a new moon hung its crescent in the sky, and above it shone the evening star. One by one the stars came out, 'til the firmament was all aglow with the celestial fires."

The Merchant *delivered supplies along the Indian River in Cocoa.* Courtesy S. F. Travis Company

The frenzy peaked in 1888 when President Grover Cleveland and his new bride, Frances, cruised south from Titusville on the *Rockledge*. This sleek and fast-moving lady (the ship, not the President's wife) was dubbed "queen of the Indian River steamboats."

By the turn of the 20th century, steamboats were passé. The railroad was the new kid in town. The gilded age tumbled onto the shores of the Indian River as America's northeastern upper class packed their trucks, donned their plumed hats, and headed south. Guests lunched on the verandas of modern, waterside hotels. In the evening drinks flowed and music filled the air. Business was booming, and Brevard County's population accelerated like a slow train gradually picking up speed and barreling down the tracks.

Indian River Hotel, Rockledge Courtesy Joe Carbone

Real Estate and Rocket Science

In 1917, the first bridge to span the Indian River was built to connect Cocoa and Merritt Island. Those wishing to cross the 1-mile wide waterway could now choose between a ferry and a horse-drawn carriage. Then came the automobile! Imagine the first brave soul who got behind the wheel of his Ford Model A Roadster and puttered slowly across rickety wooden planks. Soon a parade of cars was headed east. Businessman Gus Edwards spotted an opportunity, purchased land on the barrier island, and christened the "smooth wide beach stretching for miles" Cocoa Beach. Day-trippers streamed across the 3-mile-long wooden toll bridge built across the shallow Banana River and then followed a short road to an oceanside boardwalk and casino. On the Fourth of July in 1922, more than two thousand folks picnicked on the shore while enjoying car races and fireworks. Though hurricanes, the Depression years, and World War II stalled growth for a while, the barrier island was on the map.

In 1935, the U.S. Navy established the Banana River Naval Air Station on a long strip of land south of Cocoa Beach. It was a good thing they did. Ten weeks after the Pearl Harbor bombings in 1941, a German submarine fired upon and sank a U.S. tanker just 20 miles off the coast of Cape Canaveral. During World War II German subs armed with torpedoes routinely cruised offshore, sometimes sinking as many as three freighters a night. The more than two hundred families living along the coast went beachcombing for shipwreck treasures during the day and hid behind blacked-out windows at night. One ship, the *La Paz,* was towed to shore after being disabled by the Germans. Residents pitched in to aid with the salvage operation. Local lore says that the cargo, cases of Johnny Walker Scotch whisky, quickly and mysteriously disappeared.

The Cocoa Beach Resort was located on the beach at the end of what is today known as the Minuteman Causeway. Courtesy City of Cocoa Beach

The sheltered Banana River was used as a watery runway for seaplanes landing at the U.S. Naval Air Station south of Cocoa Beach. Courtesy Brevard County Historical Commission

The Price of Freedom

African Americans were among the original pioneers of Brevard County, first as slaves and later as free citizens struggling alongside their neighbors to carve out a living in the hostile environment. As settlements grew into communities, blacks gravitated to their own neighborhoods, schools, and churches. In 1925, Harry Moore, a well-educated black man from Jacksonville, arrived in rural, segregated Brevard County. For two decades he served as teacher, principal, and mentor to students at the "colored" schools. After he founded the Brevard County NAACP and lobbied to equalize teacher salaries and integrate the schools, Harry and his wife, Harriette—also a teacher—were fired from their jobs.

When three young black men were unjustly convicted of raping a white woman in nearby Groveland, the activist couple teamed with the NAACP and pursued the case all the way to the U.S. Supreme Court. The justices overturned the convictions and death sentences, but the victory was short-lived. The boys were shot and killed by Sheriff Willis McCall while "trying to escape" when being transported to a new hearing. An outraged Moore called for McCall's arrest.

A few months later, on Christmas night 1951, a bomb exploded under the Moore's small wood home and shattered the peace of a quiet neighborhood surrounded by orange groves. Harry died that night, Harriette nine days later. More than 55 years passed before now-deceased Klansmen were publicly identified as the assailants.

The first assassination of a civil rights leader spurred outrage throughout the country and the world. Harry Moore once said, "Freedom never descends upon a people. It is always bought with a price." Eventually justice came home. Today, Brevard County citizens receive equal treatment under the law at the Harry T. and Harriette V. Moore Justice Center.

Following the war, the United States selected the east coast of Florida as home for the business of rockets and missiles, commandeering the north end of Merritt Island and the Canaveral seashore. A large piece of land, preserved as the Merritt Island National Wildlife Refuge, continues to provide the military operations with a secure and impenetrable barrier of thick palmetto trees, snake-filled bogs, and alligators. On July 24, 1950, *Bumper 8,* the first rocket launched from the Air Force Station at Cape Canaveral, broke through gravity's hold and successfully soared 15 miles up and out. Crowds lined the beaches and cheered for the first small step on an endless path through the cosmos.

Almost overnight, two beach communities, sandwiched between Cape Canaveral Air Force Station to the north and Patrick Air Force Base to the south, rose like sand castles along the water's edge. Engineers and rocket scientists thronged to the tiny island, and Brevard County had a new moniker—Florida's Space Coast. As America raced to the moon, Cocoa Beach raced to keep up with the growth, quickly building dozens of motels, restaurants, and bars—and gaining a reputation as a space-age party town. Cape Canaveral evolved into a more domestic community for space workers and their families. News stories about rocket launches aired around the world, and then came the market exposure tourism-development money can't buy: a hit TV show. In it, astronaut Tony Nelson found a genie-named-Jeannie in a bottle and brought her home to Cocoa Beach.

Discussions of a canal joining the ocean to the intracoastal waterways of central Brevard County took on a new urgency. The U.S. Army Corps of Engineers carved out a channel just south of the protruding cape. When it opened in 1951, the new inlet not only facilitated essential shipping of goods to the space center but also laid the foundation for Port Canaveral, a busy marine community and economic anchor for the area.

"We go not because it's easy, but because it's hard" said President John F. Kennedy in May 1961 about America's race to the moon. Less than a year later, John Glenn became the first American to orbit Earth.
Courtesy NASA

By 1971, when Walt Disney World opened its gates in nearby Orlando, a multilane, high-speed expressway called the Beeline (recently renamed the Beachline) carried visitors directly to the coast. For a while it was the road-seldom-taken. When NASA cancelled the Apollo program the local economy crashed, and the stream of visitors to the area slowed to a trickle. There was a resurgence during the 1980s and '90s, as shuttles replaced rockets and more theme parks opened in central Florida. Word began to spread about the "smooth, wide beaches" (as promoted 50 years earlier by Gus Edwards), and the area was back in business.

One longtime resident put the area on the map in a different way. In *The Book Lover's Guide to Florida* author Kevin McCarthy writes of a gathering at the Cocoa Beach home of journalist Al Neuharth in February 1980. The group designed a national newspaper, *USA Today*, and McCarthy describes its impact on the world of print media as "a moon shot in its own right." The prototype, *Florida Today*, is still the Space Coast newspaper.

On a clear, cool January day, more than half a century after Bumper 8 soared 15 miles into the sky, residents and visitors again gathered along the beach and scanned the heavens. The hammers of workers constructing three new hotels paused as *Atlas 5* rose from the launch pad. With a blaze of fire and a roar of thunder, the powerful spacecraft broke through the clouds and set a course for Pluto, three billion miles away. Brevard County is still a community immersed in real estate and rocket science.

Time flies: The 1970 Atlas Centaur soars skyward just 67 years after the historic Wright brothers flight.
Courtesy NASA

The Dream Continues

Dreamers and doers settled Brevard County, helping themselves to the abundant offerings of the land—first for survival, later for sport. Today mature communities appreciate the need to balance development with conservation and protect the environment while pursuing economic growth. Ecotourism demonstrates that economic profit and environmental protection can work in tandem.

Port Canaveral has become the second busiest cruise port in the world. Towering liners navigate alongside cargo ships, military vessels, and small pleasure craft; restaurants and recreation facilities host millions of visitors each year. At the same time, more than 50 acres of protected parks, beachfront, and marshes remain an environmental playground.

During the 1960s' rush of development, land along the Banana River was dredged to help control the mosquito population. In hindsight the solution wasn't the best, but one positive outcome was enhancement of nearby islands from the dumping of the dredged mud. Mangroves claimed the new ground, and today the Thousand Islands are one of the jewels of the area, a vibrant habitat for fish and wildlife. They don't number a thousand, but several create narrow and winding paths for explorers in kayaks, canoes, and slow-moving boats.

Port Canaveral is an ideal spot for viewing space launches. Courtesy Canaveral Port Authority

Dreams continue to be written in the sands of Florida's Space Coast. Within a few years, the space shuttle fleet will be retired. Powerful craft designed for frequent travel to the moon and beyond will move from the drawing board to the launch pads at Kennedy Space Center—poised for ignition at the edge of the universe.

Melbourne Causeway Roger Scruggs

2

TRANSPORTATION

Follow the Sun

Brevard County stretches along the eastern edge of Florida like a long, lean, lazy cat napping in the sun. The Indian River, running north to south the length of the county, was the earliest transportation thoroughfare. Communities formed along its banks, and docks protruding from the shore were as common as driveways are today. People, supplies, and mail arrived by boat. At St. Michaels in Cocoa, families attending Sunday services arrived by water and tied up at the pier near the back of the church. By the beginning of the 20th century, railroads were gaining in popularity. Trains chugged through the area on tracks built parallel to the river, and stations were set up near the already established towns.

The mule train to Titusville, circa 1880   Courtesy Brevard County Historical Commission

While steamers and luxurious rail cars transported America's wealthy to the wilds of Florida, the automobile brought the working class to the Sunshine State. Roads crisscrossing America connected first to the Dixie Highway and then to modern US 1 extending down the peninsula from Jacksonville to Miami. In his book *Land of Sunshine, State of Dreams,* history professor Gary Mormino gives easy directions. "Every tourist knows the way to Florida: when you hit the East coast, turn south."

Development spread eastward as bridges and causeways opened up the barrier island. All roads led to folkloric Highway A1A, a scenic coastal alternative to US 1. During boom times, land developers promoted A1A as a yellow brick road leading straight to the home of your dreams. Connie Francis and her girlfriends hit the strip in the 1960 movie *Where the Boys Are* and began an exodus of spring breakers in search of crowded beaches and Coppertone tans—convertibles cruising, radios blaring, ponytails blowing in the breeze, and surfboards propped in the back seat. Astronaut John Glenn celebrated his space milestones—in 1962 as the first American astronaut to orbit the earth, and 36 years later in 1998 as the oldest man in space—with parades down the Cocoa Beach stretch of A1A. A drive along this colorful highway still leads directly to fun in the sun.

Mean Temperatures (Month Max/Min.)

January 71.7°/50.0° **February** 72.9°/50.8° **March** 77.2°/55.2° **April** 80.5°/ 60.1°
May 85.0°/66.3° **June** 88.6°/71.2° **July** 90.5°/71.9° **August** 90.0°/72.7°
September 88.1°/71.9° **October** 83.3°/67.4° **November** 78.3°/60.0° **December** 73.3°/53.0°
Source: National Weather Service, Melbourne, Florida

Getting to Cape Canaveral & Cocoa Beach

Traveling to the Space Coast should be as relaxing as, well, a day at the beach. Pack for pleasant weather and casual dress. Temperatures average in the 80s during the summer, and a comfortable 60s in the winter. When rain falls, it often arrives in a deluge. After an hour or so the downpour stops as suddenly as it began, and beachgoers return outside to bask in the warm rays of the sun. Travel to the area is heaviest during the winter months, over holidays and school breaks, and when a shuttle or rocket launch is scheduled, so reservations for those times should be made as early as possible. Visit in late spring or in the fall for a triple treat of small crowds, remarkable weather, and bargains.

By Plane

Travelers consistently select **Orlando International Airport** (MCO) as one of the best airports in the world. More than 50 airlines fly to Orlando, so there are usually plenty of options around timing and fares. From the moment passengers deplane, the airport decor and landscaping create a tropical ambience. Shuttle trains connect outlying gates to a central terminal, so walking is kept to a minimum (relative to other major airports). Signs direct arriving passengers to baggage claim and ground transportation, both on the ground level. Unless an airline has several planes arriving at the same time, luggage arrives promptly at the claim turntables. Departing passengers should allow extra time to check in and pass through security. The large number of families juggling small children, strollers, and other paraphernalia slows the lines. An array of restaurants and shops offers great food, and a chance to purchase some last-minute souvenirs before heading home. Information and facility maps are on the airport's Web site, www.orlandoairports.net.

Wildlife Profile: Bald Eagle and Osprey

Looking skyward, the bald eagle resembles an airplane—wide wings, outstretched and flat, soaring effortlessly on currents of air. Like many area visitors, they fly into Brevard County in the fall and stay until spring. The eagle is an opportunistic feeder, and during this period the area teems with migratory birds and waterfowl that make for easy prey. Eagles mate for life and will return together to upgrade an old nest and roost. They prefer to settle in live trees. One nest along a Kennedy Space Center tour route has been there for at least 45 years and is the size of a queen-sized bed. The eagle has piercing yellow eyes and, like most raptors, can see much farther than humans.

Osprey (Pandion haliaetus) Jim Angy

The osprey is smaller than the eagle but has the same yellow eyes, curved talons to grab prey, and a strong, hooked bill. The brown and white birds fly with their wings bent at the ends. This fish hawk also has a few unique features that ensure it catches a regular diet of fish. Reversible toes let the osprey grab a fish and turn it the same direction as the body for improved aerodynamics. Also, the talons have spiny pads that make it easier to hold on to slippery marine life. Ospreys are year-round residents. They nest in the spring and prefer to use dead trees, platforms, or navigational buoys.

Spend any time at all on the water, and you're likely to spot an osprey flying about with a fish in tow. Occasionally an eagle will happen by and make the same observation, then fly below the osprey until it pushes the bird so high that it drops the fish—right into the grasp of the waiting eagle. Both birds are memorable to see.

Space Coast Sightings: Black Point Wildlife Drive at the Merritt Island National Wildlife Refuge, Cocoa Beach Thousand Islands, Wild Florida exhibit at Brevard Zoo.

The Space Shuttle has a first-class seat for the trip home to the Kennedy Space Center. Courtesy NASA

Melbourne International Airport (MLB), located off US 1, 26 miles south of Port Canaveral, may be a more convenient arrival point for some travelers. Delta Airlines has direct flights each day from Atlanta and Washington, D.C. For more information log on to the airport's Web site, www.mlbair.com.

By Rental Car

Unless a trip is very limited, visitors to Florida's Space Coast need a car. Almost all car rental companies serve travelers to Orlando International Airport. Avoid last-minute surprises by asking beforehand about extra charges for insurance, taxes, a second driver, a young driver, or child safety seats. Families will find plenty of minivans available to rent. Florida law requires that car drivers, front-seat passengers, and all riders under 18 years of age wear a seat belt. Children age three and under must be secured in an approved safety seat; children ages four and five should be in an approved safety seat or wear a seat belt. Five car rental companies maintain lots at Cape Canaveral or Cocoa Beach, which might be helpful to visitors staying in these areas who encounter problems with their car rental. These firms also have locations at Melbourne International Airport.

Avis: 1-800-831-2847; www.avis.com
Budget: 1-800-257-0700; www.budget.com
Hertz: 1-800-654-3131; www.hertz.com
National: 1-800-227-7368; www.nationalcar.com
Thrifty: 1-800-367-2277; www.thrifty.com

By Ground Transportation

Several businesses specialize in transportation from the airports to locations in Brevard County, including the cruise terminals at Port Canaveral. Reservations should be made at least 48 hours in advance. If you need special equipment like a wheelchair or car seat, be sure to let them know. Prices vary but generally run about $80 each way for a party of four traveling from Orlando International Airport to hotels in the Cape Canaveral and Cocoa Beach area.

A1A Ocean Drive Transportation & Limo: 386-226-1111, 1-866-356-2326; www.ocean-drivetransandlimo.com.
Art's Shuttle: 321-783-2112, 1-800-567-5099; www.artsshuttle.com
Beachline Transportation: 321-453-9660, 1-877-382-3224; www.beachlinetransportation.net
Blue Dolphin Shuttle: 321-433-0011, 1-888-361-0155; www.gobluedolphinshuttle.com
Busy Traveler Transport: 321-453-5278, 1-800-496-7433; www.abusytraveler.com (also provides service to and from Melbourne International Airport)

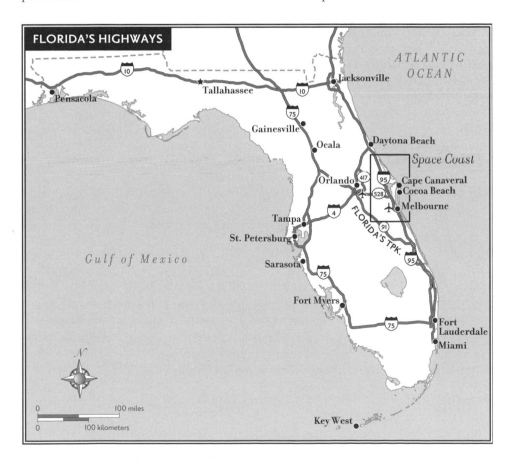

By Car

Most major roadways in the state intersect in central Florida and connect to Florida Highway 528 (FL 528), the Beachline. Previous visitors might remember this road as the Beeline, an apt name given because of the straight path it makes from Orlando to the coast. Florida's interstate highways have gas, food, and restrooms at frequent and multiple exits; the Florida Turnpike has service plazas about every 45 miles. Some highways, including the Beachline, are toll roads. It's always good to have a map, but these are the most-traveled routes for reaching Cape Canaveral and Cocoa Beach: (Travelers to other parts of the county will usually exit to the east or west on US 1 or I-95.)

From Orlando International Airport: Exit the airport heading east on FL 528, and follow signs to Cocoa and the Kennedy Space Center. Travel time from the airport is about 35 minutes.

From Orlando-area attractions: Follow signs to FL 417 and the airport, and then continue past the airport to FL 528 eastbound. Travel time from Walt Disney World is just over an hour.

From I-95: Travelers from the north or south take exit number 205, FL 528. Travel distance is about 150 miles from Jacksonville, 200 miles from Miami.

From the north on I-75: Switch to the Florida Turnpike at exit 328 (Wildwood), and then just past Orlando pick up FL 528 eastbound.

From the southwest on I-75: Take I-4 east from Tampa. Exit at FL 417. FL 528 eastbound is just beyond the airport. Travel time from the I-4/I-75 intersection to the beach is about two hours.

By Bus

Greyhound Bus Lines (1-800-231-2222; www.greyhound.com) operates a terminal at Melbourne International Airport.

By Train

The closest **AMTRAK** (1-800-872-7245; www.amtrak.com) station is in Orlando. Busy Traveler Transportation (1-800-496-7433) provides service from the station to Brevard County.

By Boat

Arriving by water is an alternative way to travel to Brevard County. Enter from offshore, or via the Intracoastal Waterway (ICW). The Canaveral Barge Canal crosses the Indian River/ICW just north of FL 528 and is a direct eastbound route to Port Canaveral. This entire section is designated as a no wake zone for protection of manatees, so you'll need to maintain a low speed. Full-service marinas at Port Canaveral provide dockage facilities on a short or long-term basis, but space is limited, so be sure to secure reservations, especially during the busy season. All the marinas monitor channel 16 on VHF.

Cape Marina: 321-783-8410; www.capemarina.com
Sunrise Marina: 321-783-9535; www.sunrisemarina.com

A Banana River traffic sign

GETTING AROUND CAPE CANAVERAL & COCOA BEACH

By Car

After crossing the Banana River, the speed limit slows from expressway to browsing speed as FL 528 curves to the right and exits onto FL A1A (commonly just called A1A), the primary axis road running north and south through the communities. Port Canaveral has two exits at the end of FL 528, and signs mark the appropriate exit for the cruise terminals. Almost every road crossing A1A goes east to the ocean, but parking may sometimes be limited or unavailable. Day visitors will find free or low-cost spots at several beach parks. (For details see the Beaches and Surfing chapter.) Overnight guests will discover that most hotels are within easy walking distance of the beach or provide a shuttle service.

By Space Coast Area Transit

The beach trolley operated by **Space Coast Area Transit** (www.ridescat.com) offers an affordable ride along A1A and through Port Canaveral. Every trolley has a wheelchair lift and accommodates surfboards and bicycles. Standard fare is $1.25, but seniors, veterans, the disabled, and students pay just 60 cents. Children five and under are free. In general, routes run from 7 in the morning until 9 at night. Pick up a brochure at your hotel or stop by the central stop on the northeast side of the intersection of Atlantic Avenue and E. Cocoa Beach Causeway.

By Taxicab or Shuttle

Taxis are almost always available on short notice, and they line up outside venues at busy times, such as when guests are disembarking from cruise ships or ending an evening at the more popular nightspots.

AAT Beachside Taxi: 783-0809
Checker Cab: 449-1000

By Local Car Rental

Several rental firms have local lots and rent cars by the day. Many allow a one-way rental to the Orlando and Melbourne airports without an additional drop-off fee, so renting a car may be more convenient and economical than taking a shuttle when there are just one or two passengers.

Avis Rent A Car: 783-3643; 6650 N. Atlantic Ave., Cape Canaveral
Budget Car Rental: 784-0634; 8401 Astronaut Blvd., Cape Canaveral
Hertz: 783-7771; 8963 Astronaut Blvd., Cape Canaveral
National Car Rental: 783-7575; 1675 N. Atlantic Ave., Cocoa Beach
Thrifty Rent A Car: 783-2600; 6799 N. Atlantic Ave., Cape Canaveral

EXPLORING BREVARD COUNTY

Central Brevard

Brevard County is 76 miles long but less than 20 miles wide in most spots. Three major roadways run north and south: A1A along the beaches, US 1 on the mainland and paralleling the shore of the Indian River, and I-95 close to the western border of the county. Seven bridges and causeways run east and west across the water-rich landscape: FL 406 in Titusville, FL 405 near Kennedy Space Center, FL 528—the Beachline—leading from Orlando to Cape Canaveral, FL 520 at Cocoa, FL 404 near Patrick Air Force Base, FL 518 at Eau Gallie, and FL 192 in Melbourne. Throughout this guide, most directional references use these major thoroughfares and intersections as a point of reference.

The town of **Cocoa**, reportedly named after a can of chocolate powder sitting on the shelf at a general store, is just a short drive from Cocoa Beach. Originally a trading post alongside the Indian River, it has evolved into one of the county's major communities. Visitors will enjoy strolling down the tree-lined streets of **Cocoa Village**, where buildings

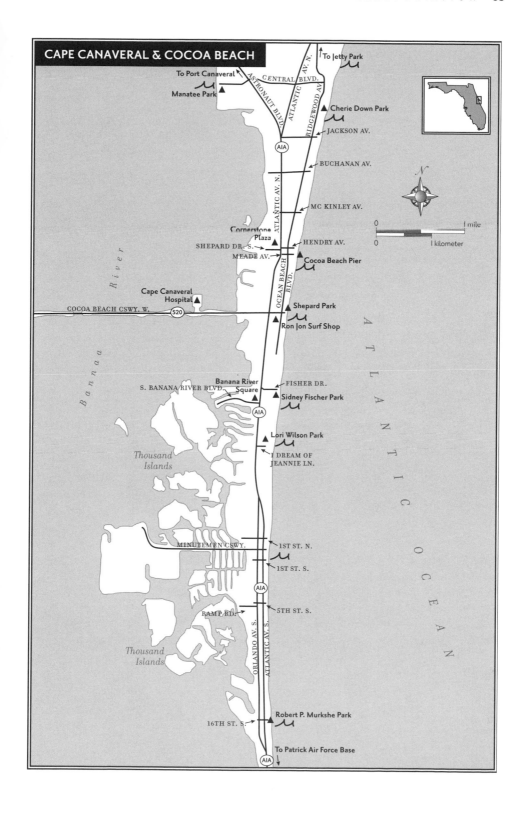

CAPE CANAVERAL & COCOA BEACH

To Jetty Park

To Port Canaveral
CENTRAL BLVD.
Manatee Park

ATLANTIC AV. N.
ASTRONAUT BLVD.
RIDGEWOOD AV.

Cherie Down Park

JACKSON AV.

A1A

BUCHANAN AV.

ATLANTIC AV. N.

MC KINLEY AV.

N

Cornerstone
Plaza
SHEPARD DR. S.
MEADE AV.
HENDRY AV.

OCEAN BEACH BLVD.
Cocoa Beach Pier

River

Cape Canaveral
Hospital
COCOA BEACH CSWY. W. 520
Shepard Park

Ron Jon Surf Shop

0 ____ 1 mile
0 ____ 1 kilometer

B a n a n a

Banana River
Square
S. BANANA RIVER BLVD.
FISHER DR.
Sidney Fischer Park

A1A

A T L A N T I C

Lori Wilson Park

Thousand
Islands
I DREAM OF
JEANNIE LN.

MINUTEMEN CSWY.
1ST ST. N.

1ST ST. S.

A1A

O C E A N

RAMP RD.
5TH ST. S.

ORLANDO AV. S.
ATLANTIC AV. S.

Thousand
Islands

Robert P. Murkshe Park

16TH ST. S.

To Patrick Air Force Base

A1A

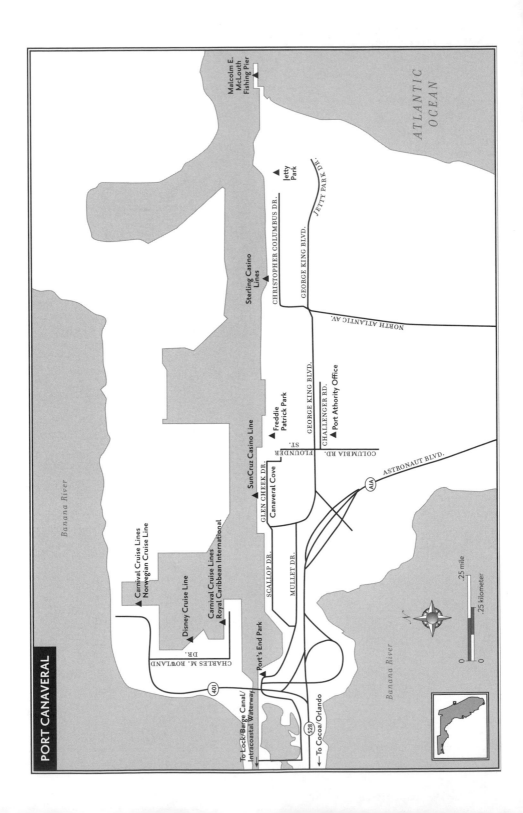

PORT CANAVERAL

Malcolm E. McLouth Fishing Pier

ATLANTIC OCEAN

Jetty Park

JETTY PARK DR.

CHRISTOPHER COLUMBUS DR.

Sterling Casino Lines

GEORGE KING BLVD.

NORTH ATLANTIC AV.

GEORGE KING BLVD.

Port Athority Office

Freddie Patrick Park

CHALLENGER RD.

SunCruz Casino Line

FLOUNDER ST.

GLEN CHEEK DR.

Canaveral Cove

COLUMBIA RD.

ASTRONAUT BLVD.

A1A

Banana River

Carnival Cruise Lines
Norwegian Cruise Line

Disney Cruise Line

Carnival Cruise Lines
Royal Caribbean International

SCALLOP DR.

MULLET DR.

CHARLES M. ROWLAND DR.

Port's End Park

To Lock/Barge Canal/
Intracoastal Waterway

401

528

To Cocoa/Orlando

Banana River

25 mile
.25 kilometer
0
0

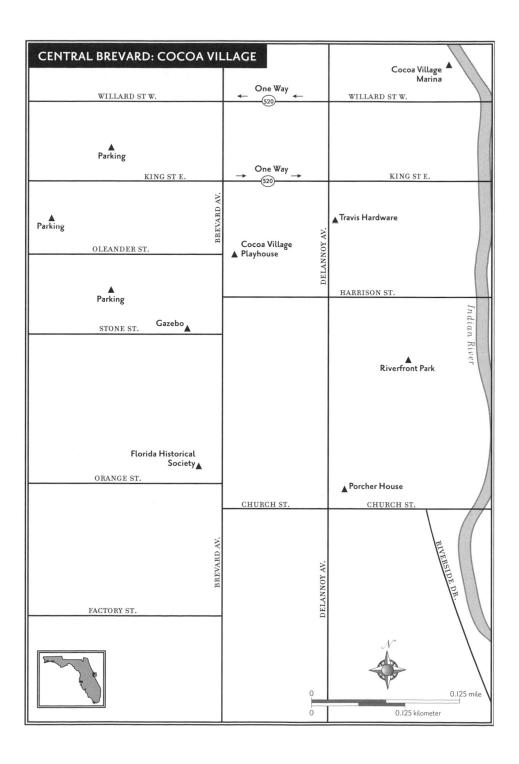

CENTRAL BREVARD: COCOA VILLAGE

Cocoa Village Marina ▲

WILLARD ST W.   ← One Way ← (520)   WILLARD ST W.

▲ Parking

KING ST E.   → One Way → (520)   KING ST E.

▲ Parking

BREVARD AV.

▲ Parking

OLEANDER ST.   Cocoa Village ▲ Playhouse

▲ Travis Hardware

DELANNOY AV.

HARRISON ST.

▲ Parking

STONE ST.   Gazebo ▲

Riverfront Park ▲

Indian River

Florida Historical Society ▲

ORANGE ST.

▲ Porcher House

CHURCH ST.   CHURCH ST.

BREVARD AV.

DELANNOY AV.

RIVERSIDE DR.

FACTORY ST.

N

0   0.125 mile

0   0.125 kilometer

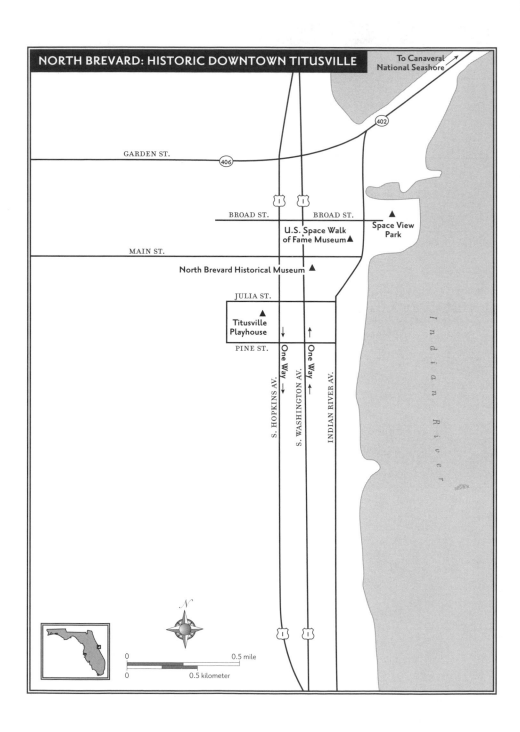

NORTH BREVARD: HISTORIC DOWNTOWN TITUSVILLE

To Canaveral
National Seashore

402

GARDEN ST.   406

BROAD ST.   BROAD ST.

U.S. Space Walk
of Fame Museum ▲

Space View
Park ▲

MAIN ST.

North Brevard Historical Museum ▲

JULIA ST.

▲
Titusville
Playhouse

PINE ST.

One Way →   One Way ↑

S. HOPKINS AV.

S. WASHINGTON AV.

INDIAN RIVER AV.

Indian River

N

0   0.5 mile
0   0.5 kilometer

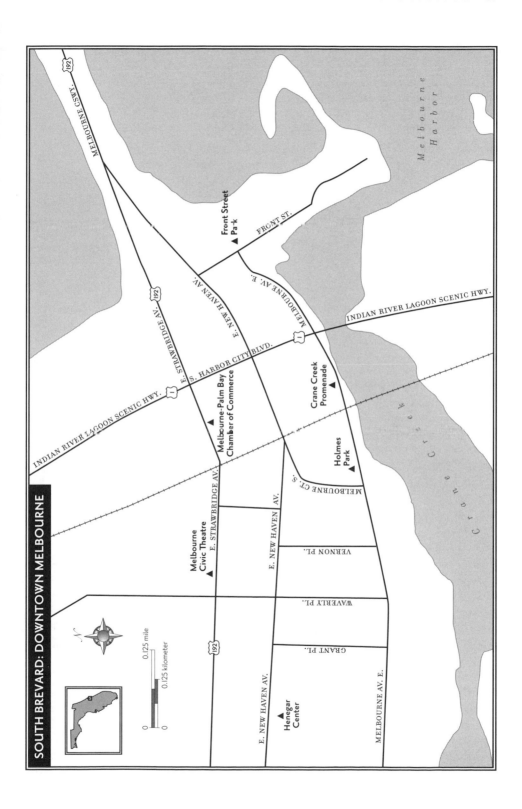

SOUTH BREVARD: DOWNTOWN MELBOURNE

Melbourne Harbor

Crane Creek

MELBOURNE CSWY.

192

Front Street Park

FRONT ST.

MELBOURNE AV. E.

INDIAN RIVER LAGOON SCENIC HWY.

E. NEW HAVEN AV.

E. STRAWBRIDGE AV. 192

S. HARBOR CITY BLVD.

INDIAN RIVER LAGOON SCENIC HWY.

1

Melbourne-Palm Bay Chamber of Commerce

Crane Creek Promenade

Holmes Park

S. MELBOURNE CT.

Melbourne Civic Theatre

E. STRAWBRIDGE AV.

E. NEW HAVEN AV.

VERNON PL.

WAVERLY PL.

GRANT PL.

MELBOURNE AV. E.

E. NEW HAVEN AV.

Henegar Center

192

0.125 mile
0.125 kilometer

from the steamboat era now house a quaint collection of restaurants, shops, and art galleries. **Riverfront Park** is a gathering spot for events and celebrations. **Brevard Community College** has a campus in Cocoa, and the world-class **Astronaut Memorial Planetarium and Observatory** is located there. The **Brevard Museum of History and Natural Science** is right next door.

Century-old homes lining the river road in **Rockledge,** to the south of Cocoa, reflect the golden age of this community. **Viera** is a new, planned community west of I-95. The **Avenue Viera** is the county's largest entertainment, retail, and dining complex. The **Brevard Zoo** and **Space Coast Stadium**—featuring the Washington Nationals during baseball's spring training season and the minor league Brevard Manatees in the summer—are located nearby.

To get to Cocoa Village, take FL 520 west from Cocoa Beach for 7.5 miles, crossing over the Banana River and Indian River. Turn left at Brevard Avenue, 2 blocks west of the Indian River. To reach Viera, continue on FL 520 to I-95 southbound. Space Coast Stadium is at exit 195/Fiske Boulevard; the Avenue Viera and the Brevard Zoo are near exit 191/Wickham Road.

North Brevard

The old, the new, and the natural converge in north Brevard County. The city of **Titusville** on the Indian River Lagoon is the oldest settlement in the county. It flourished as a docking site for 19th-century sailing vessels. Today, **Space View Park** along the river faces **Kennedy Space Center.** Crowds gather by a giant countdown clock to watch the space shuttle soar into the vast waters of the universe. The original downtown area is restored with shops, eateries, and galleries. The **North Brevard Historical Museum** talks of a deep-rooted past, while around the corner the **U.S. Space Walk of Fame Museum** shares the successes of America's space adventures.

More than 50 years ago, the government purchased thousands of acres of scrubland at the north end of Merritt Island (just across the Indian River) for military and space programs. NASA owns the land and operates on about one-third of it. The remainder is protected and maintained by the Department of the Interior. How ironic that space-age technology, which brought significant and sometimes unwelcome development to the area, also ensured that two large adjacent parks, **Merritt Island Wildlife National Refuge** and **Cape Canaveral National Seashore,** would remain in much the same pristine condition as when the Ais Indians roamed the area.

Plan on a drive time of 30 to 60 minutes to reach most of the attractions in this area. Kennedy Space Center is about 30 miles from Cape Canaveral. To get there, follow FL 528 west and exit north on US 1. FL 405 eastbound leads directly over the NASA Parkway to Kennedy Space Center. To reach historic downtown Titusville, continue a few miles north to the intersection of US 1 and Main Street. Garden Street, FL 406, is 3 blocks north of Main Street. Go east over the bridge to reach the Merritt Island National Wildlife Refuge and Canaveral National Seashore.

South Brevard

South Brevard is a technology hub—home to the Florida Institute of Technology and cutting-edge corporations like Harris, Rockwell Collins, and Northrop Grumman. Many of the county's largest communities, including **Melbourne** and Palm Bay, are in the south. Along the south Brevard coast are the quieter towns of Melbourne Beach and Indialantic. **Sebastian Inlet** defines the southern boundary of the county. The 40-mile drive down A1A to Sebastian Inlet is one of the most scenic drives in the county.

Eau Gallie was one of Brevard County's earliest river ports, but it has struggled to maintain a unique identity since being incorporated into the city of Melbourne. The **Brevard Art Museum** is the centerpiece of an eclectic and creative district featuring galleries, antiques shops, and cafés. Just south, Melbourne was built at the strategic waterway intersection of the Indian River and Crane Creek. New Haven Avenue, alongside the Crane Creek promenade, is now a shopping and dining center with most of the old buildings still in use.

Eau Gallie is about 20 miles from Cocoa Beach. Take A1A south to FL 518 at Indian Harbour Beach. Go west across the Indian River. Highland Avenue is the second street after the bridge and the focal point of old Eau Gallie. To get to downtown Melbourne, continue on FL 518 to US 1 (S. Harbor City Boulevard) and turn left. Continue 1 block past US 192 and turn right onto New Haven Avenue.

Welcome

This Hotel was first owned by the original seven Astronauts in the U.S. Mercury space programs' *"Race for Space"*

Alan Shepard, Jr.	*"Freedom 7"*	May 5, 1961
Virgil "Gus" Grissom	*"Liberty Bell"*	July 21, 1961
John Glenn, Jr.	*"Friendship 7"*	February 20, 1962
Scott Carpenter	*"Auroura 7"*	May 24, 1962
Walter Shirra	*"Sigma 7"*	October 3, 1962
Gordon Cooper, Jr.	*"Faith 7"*	May 15, 1963
Donald "Deke" Slayton	*"Apollo Soyez"*	July 15, 1975

Home of the Original 7 Astronauts

La Quinta Inn

3

LODGING

Dream a Little Dream of Sea

In Hans Christian Andersen's tale of the little mermaid, she longs to have legs instead of a tail so she can step from the water and experience all the wonders of living on land. Perhaps she was just worn out from all those years in the surf and sun and was dreaming of cool linens, a soft mattress, and a fluffy pillow for her petite head. A day at the beach is both invigorating and exhausting, so it's important to find just the right place to call home, whether visiting for a night, a week, or a season.

Early motel development in Cocoa Beach was fast and furious, trying to keep pace with the overnight demand created by space workers, media, and curious tourists. Expectations were simple—clean, comfortable, and affordable. Over the years modern, spacious chain hotels have replaced most of the small motels. Surprisingly, many of the new facilities are owned and operated by the same families who built the original motels. They love it here and want you to feel the same way.

Cape Canaveral and Cocoa Beach are the closest beaches to airports and highways, so most of the recommended lodging is in that corridor. Expect friendly small-town service and affordable rates. Pay attention to definitions when you make your booking: Oceanfront rooms face the ocean, some with a balcony. Beach view suggests that the property is on the beach, but the windows may point north or south—which often offers a great panoramic look at the coast. Beachside properties are on the east side of A1A and within a block of the ocean, but not directly on the beach. Prime real estate is upper floors, oceanfront.

In this chapter, properties are divided into Hotels & Motels and Vacation & Condo Rentals categories. In general, condominiums are more appropriate for longer stays and family groups, where the per person, per day rate will be lower. They are more spacious and have fully equipped kitchens, but sometimes they lack expected amenities like daily housekeeping, restaurants, and on-site management. Because this is a family beach community, a lot of the hotels and motels stock standard rooms with microwaves and minirefrigerators. Unless noted otherwise, the facilities have free Internet access and do not permit smoking or pets.

Most properties have ADA-accessible common areas and a small number of rooms with limited or full wheelchair accessibility. Roll-in showers are not common. Each information block provides basic information, but if you have special needs, it's best to inquire when you make your reservation.

Rates are for a standard room, double occupancy during the December–April peak season. If you upgrade to a premium room or best view, the cost will increase. Rates drop by about 20 percent during less busy times. Inquire about discounts for AAA, AARP, Florida residents, and Internet bookings.

Rates are broken down into the following categories:

Inexpensive	Up to $100
Moderate	$100 to $150
Expensive	$150 to $200
Very Expensive	More than $200

The following abbreviations are used for credit card information:

AE:	American Express
CB:	Carte Blanche
D:	Discover Card
DC:	Diner's Club
MC:	MasterCard
V:	Visa

CAPE CANAVERAL & COCOA BEACH

Hotels & Motels

Beach Island Resort

Managers: Wayne and Fran Henderson
321-784-5720
www.beachislandresort.com
1125 S. Atlantic Ave., Cocoa Beach 32931
Price: Moderate
Credit Cards: AE, D, MC, V
Wheelchair Access: No

This charming, older motel has 20 units that circle around a courtyard looking directly out on the Atlantic Ocean. All the colorful rooms have one or two bedrooms, a living area, and fully equipped kitchen. Updated facilities like a hot tub, pool, and wireless Internet enhance the property. Families will enjoy this very affordable spot that is out of the mainstream but just blocks away from the restaurants and action of downtown Cocoa Beach.

Beach Place Guesthouses

Owners: Joseph Paulus and Hernando Posada
321-783-4045, fax 321-868-2492
www.beachplaceguesthouses.com
1445 S. Atlantic Ave., Cocoa Beach 32931
Price: Expensive
Credit Cards: AE, D, MC, V
Wheelchair Access: Yes
Special Features: On-site Quique's Gallery

Happy hour at Beach Place Guest Houses

If you've dreamed of living on the beach, this is your chance. Two motels from the '60s have been combined and renovated in warm, tropical tones, decorated inside and out with original art. Sixteen one- and two-bedroom guest houses each have a separate living room and a full kitchen. Some have courtyard views, while others look out at the ocean, but every room is just steps away from a quiet stretch of beach. A small gallery featuring local artists is in the center of the well-landscaped grounds. Rocking and Adirondack chairs are plentiful and inviting. Beachside decks offer grills, tables, and chairs so guests can take full advantage of the outdoors. There's no pool, but there are plenty of complimentary towels, beach chairs, and umbrellas—as well as volleyball, bocce ball, and croquet equipment. The location is on the main drag, but away from the more crowded hubs of restaurants and shops. The intimate size and design make it perfect for family reunions, small weddings, and other gatherings.

Best Western Ocean Beach Hotel

General Manager: Ron Gulasa
321-783-7621, 1-800-962-0028
fax 321-799-4576
www.bestwesterncocoabeach.com
5600 N. Atlantic Ave., Cocoa Beach 32931
Price: Moderate–Expensive
Credit Cards: All major cards accepted
Wheelchair Access: Yes
Special Features: Eight rooms with full ADA accessibility and roll-in shower

At the Best Western oceanfront hotel neighborhood, several buildings in shades of sunrise yellow and ocean blue provide accommodations to fit every price range, from standard rooms to oceanfront suites. Many rooms adjoin to accommodate families and groups traveling together. Two pools, an upper-deck bar and grill, barbecue grills, benches, and gardens weave through the grounds. The newly remodeled lobby area has a sundry store and business center. A continental breakfast is part of each stay, or sample one of the many restaurants within walking distance. The Cocoa Beach Pier is next door, and the beach is close enough to hear the surf and feel the salt air. Meet the neighbors at the manager's reception every Tuesday evening. This hotel campus has successfully blended being conveniently located in the middle of everything with a quiet, peaceful ambience. A limited number of smoking rooms are available; some rooms are pet-friendly.

Best Western Oceanfront Hotel Courtesy Best Western Oceanfront Hotel

Comfort Inn & Suites

General Manager: David Nimmo
321-783-2221, 1-800-247-2221
fax 321-783-0461
www.comfortinncocoabeach.com
3901 N. Atlantic Ave., Cocoa Beach 32931
Price: Moderate
Credit Cards: All major cards accepted
Wheelchair Access: Yes

With a ballroom able to accommodate up to 450 guests, this hotel, centrally located in Cocoa Beach, is a popular spot for business events and wedding receptions. Guests can choose from a standard room with two double beds, an efficiency that adds a full kitchen, or a suite with a living area, kitchen, bedroom, and private balcony or patio. A standard and efficiency can be adjoined to provide even more space for a family or group. The hotel is a short walk to the beach; the tower rooms have a great view. The tropical courtyard is a gathering spot with a playground, shuffleboard courts, swimming pool, hot tub, and a snack bar and grill. Enjoy karaoke in the Lagoon Lounge, or join the kids in the game room. A host of restaurants and other conveniences are an easy walk. Smoking rooms are available.

Country Inns & Suites by Carlson

General Manager: Shawn Townsend
321-784-8500, 1-888-201-1746,
fax 321-784-8544
www.countryinns.com/capecanaveralfl
9009 Astronaut Blvd., Cape Canaveral 32920
Price: Moderate
Credit Cards: All major cards accepted
Wheelchair Access: Yes

This member of the Carlson family is a new arrival in Cape Canaveral and has quickly found a niche among cruisers and business travelers. Every room comes with a refrigerator, microwave, and coffeemaker. Select from several different guest room options, including an in-room Jacuzzi or a second room that sleeps three children. One Executive Suite provides a huge living, dining, and kitchen area adjoining two other rooms and makes an ideal gathering spot for groups. The hotel is on the riverside of A1A, but the beach is just a few blocks away. On-site enjoy the regular pool, a kids' pool with a mushroom waterfall, Jacuzzi, arcade, and health center. A complimentary breakfast buffet is served every morning; fresh-baked cookies are always available in the lobby.

Courtyard by Marriott Cocoa Beach

General Manager: Tom Williamson
321-784-4800, 1-800-321-2211
fax 321-784-4812
www.courtyardcocoabeach.com
3435 N. Atlantic Ave., Cocoa Beach 32931
Price: Moderate–Expensive
Credit Cards: All major cards accepted
Wheelchair Access: Yes
Special Features: Chlorine-free mineral swimming pool

Leisure guests at this oceanside hotel share in a long list of amenities designed around business travelers. Every room has a coffeemaker, minirefrigerator, microwave,

high-speed Internet access, desk with ergonomic chair, and bathtub with spray jets. Families will appreciate the pullout sofa bed and self-serve laundry facilities. Stroll to the beach or grab lunch by the pool. Beach chairs, umbrellas, and other beach paraphernalia are available to rent. Top floors have a water view. From east-facing rooms you can sip coffee and watch day break over the ocean; others can enjoy a glass of wine and a sunset over the Banana River. The restaurant serves three meals a day, including a full buffet breakfast, and room service is available during the dinner hours. On Wednesday join the hotel manager at an evening reception in the lounge. This site is a multiple winner of the Chairman's Award, Marriott's most prestigious guest service recognition.

Every room has a private balcony at Courtyard by Marriott.

Days Inn Cocoa Beach

General Manager: Ron Gulasa
321-784-2550, 1-800-245-5225
fax 321-868-7124
www.daysinncocoabeach.com
5500 N. Atlantic Ave., Cocoa Beach 32931
Price: Moderate
Credit Cards: All major cards accepted
Wheelchair Access: Yes

The Days Inn brand promises a clean, comfortable room; great value; and "sunsational" service, and this conveniently located property delivers, having consistently been awarded the top honor of five sunbursts. Choose a standard room with a king or two queen beds, or efficiency with queen bed and sofa or two queens. There is a pool and sundeck, and the beach is one block away. Every room includes a complimentary breakfast, or head next door to the Omelet Station. The property is pet-friendly, and smoking rooms are available.

Discovery Beach Resort

General Manager: John Fahnestock
321-868-7777, 1-800-352-4874
fax 321-868-0086
www.discoverybeachresort.com
300 Barlow Ave., Cocoa Beach 32931
Price: Very Expensive
Credit Cards: MC, V
Wheelchair Access: Yes
Special Features: Full-service activities desk

At this impressive complex, decorated with tropical turquoise touches, every spacious one-, two-, and three-bedroom apartment has a balcony and oceanfront view, as well as a full kitchen, laundry facilities, and a sleeper sofa. The ground floor is all common area and includes an expansive lobby, exercise room, library and computer area, arcade and pool room, and sauna. Open the outside door to a pool, hot tub, and direct path to the beach, as well as tennis and basketball courts. The resort has a restaurant, café, and lounge; music, meals, and drinks are served poolside during busy times. The Cocoa Beach Pier is just 3 blocks south, chair and umbrella rentals are handy, and plenty of restaurants are nearby. Advance deposit is required to hold reservations. The front desk is staffed from 7 AM to 11 PM. There is 24-hour security.

Dolphin Inn

Owners: Duane and Deborah Griffith
321-868-3701

www.dolphininncocoabeach.com
2902 S. Atlantic Ave., Cocoa Beach 32931
Price: Inexpensive
Credit Cards: MC, V
Wheelchair Access: No

The courtyard of the Dolphin Inn

Adults looking for a simple, inexpensive, clean, and quiet place to stay will love the tropical feel and friendly style of this small motel situated on the banks of the Banana River. The island is only about 500 feet wide at this spot, so the beach is just steps away. Imagine a road trip in the '50s, and finding a spot where you can paddle a kayak down the river, catch and grill a fresh seafood dinner, or watch dolphins swim by while sipping a morning cup of coffee on the dock. Each room is a small efficiency with living area, refrigerator, stove, and a king or queen bed. There's no pool. Weekly and monthly rates are available.

Doubletree Oceanfront Hotel

General Manager: Christy Galzerano
321-783-9222, 1-800-222-8733
fax 321-799-3234
www.cocoabeachdoubletree.com
2080 N. Atlantic Ave., Cocoa Beach 32931
Price: Expensive
Credit Cards: All major cards accepted
Wheelchair Access: Yes

Welcome to one of the more luxurious hotels on the beach. Arriving guests are greeted by valets, treated to a fresh-baked chocolate chip cookie, and escorted to a spacious ocean-view room, perhaps with a private balcony. Stay on the club level for larger accommodations and a private lounge with complimentary breakfast and evening receptions. Grab a thick, terry towel from the towel bar and relax by the pool and sundeck while enjoying music and refreshments at the bar. Dine in the elegant 3 Wishes restaurant or at one of the outside tables overlooking the beach. The hotel has private access to the beach; chairs, umbrellas, cabanas, and beach gear are available to rent. A small sundry shop has a few gift items and other essentials you may have forgotten to pack. Guests have 24-hour access to the fitness room and business center. End your day tucked into an extra comfortable bed, with a plush-top mattress, jumbo down pillows, and high-count linens. Sweet dreams.

The pool deck of the Doubletree Oceanfront Hotel

Fawlty Towers Resort Motel
Manager: Jeff Robertson
321-784-3870, 1-800-887-3870
fax 321-799-1694
www.fawltytowersresort.com
100 E. Cocoa Beach Cswy., Cocoa Beach 32931
Price: Moderate
Credit Cards: AE, DC, MC, V
Wheelchair Access: Partial
Special Features: Complimentary access to Boom Fitness Center

This pastel pink building with a sky blue roof is a calm oasis right in the middle of a bustling seaside neighborhood. The property, one of the oldest at the beach, was acquired by anglophiles Paul and Terrie nearly 20 years ago and renamed for their favorite British television show. The theme continues with amenities like current copies of the *Union Jack* newspaper, European beers and ciders at the Tiki Bar, and a teakettle in every room. From the tiny lobby, enter into a lush courtyard with pool where guests gather for a pint or two each evening. Comfortable and clean rooms enter onto the gardens. Choose a regular room with king or two double beds, an efficiency with a kitchen, or a minisuite. Some rooms are pet-friendly. Smoking rooms and on-site coin laundry are available.

Four Points by Sheraton
General Manager: Melanie Rodriquez
321-783-8717, 1-866-225-0145
fax 321-783-8719
www.fourpoints.com/cocoabeach
4001 N. Atlantic Ave., Cocoa Beach 32931
Price: Moderate
Credit Cards: All major cards accepted
Wheelchair access: Yes
Special Features: Surf shop

Families with tweens and teens might consider riding a wave into this new, bright hotel located inside the Cocoa Beach Surf Company. In addition to the huge merchandise shop, surf rentals and lessons are available. The hotel is not on the beach, but it's located just one block away. The rooms are decorated in the colors of the ocean, and surf art hangs on the walls. In addition to a traditional room with one king or two queen-sized beds, there are suites (with and without a whirlpool) that have a separate living area separated by a half-wall from the bedroom. Some of the rooms overlook the surf shop, but the windows are soundproof, and the noise from shoppers and the piped music doesn't filter into the rooms. Dine at the Shark Pit Bar & Grill or grab a treat at Starbucks. There is a pool, but it is very small and enclosed next to the parking garage; it's probably most suited to a quick dip after an afternoon spent at the beach. Small, well-behaved pets are welcome.

Hampton Inn

General Manager: Tom Williamson
321-799-4099, 1-877-492-3224
fax 321-799-4991
www.hamptoninncocoabeach.com
3425 N. Atlantic Ave., Cocoa Beach 32931
Price: Moderate–Expensive
Credit Cards: All major cards accepted
Wheelchair Access: Yes
Special Features: Complimentary use of Boom Fitness Center

The rooms are comfortable and the staff helpful at this attractive hotel, conveniently located a few blocks south of FL 520 and Shepard Park. A 200-yard landscaped walkway leads directly to the beach. Standard rooms have one king or two queen-sized beds. Some add a sofa bed for extra capacity; others have a private balcony with a view of the ocean or intracoastal waters. Every room includes a refrigerator, microwave, and coffeemaker. Start your day with a complimentary hot breakfast. Smoking rooms are available.

Hilton Cocoa Beach Oceanfront

General Manager: Debra Green
321-799-0003, fax 321-799-0344
www.hiltoncocoabeach.com
1550 N. Atlantic Ave., Cocoa Beach 32931
Price: Moderate–Expensive
Credit Cards: All major cards accepted
Wheelchair Access: Yes
Special Features: Largest oceanfront pool deck on the Space Coast

Cocoa Beach's most prestigious hotel has welcomed world leaders, Oscar winners, and space superstars, and it promises roomy, comfortable accommodations and exceptional hospitality for every guest at this full-service Hilton resort.

The ocean view from the Hilton's Presidential Suite
Courtesy Hilton Cocoa Beach Oceanfront

The newly renovated modern and bright hotel offers a standard room with city and coastline view at a surprisingly reasonable rate; or upgrade to a junior suite, or executive room with ocean view and concierge-level service. No matter what room you pick, all resort amenities are at your disposal. Every room is fitted with luxury bedding, coffee set-up, and pay-per-view movies and video games. Dine inside or on the deck at Atlantis Bar & Grill, open for all meals; room service is available from dawn to late night. Settle in by the pool, or step down the walkway to the beach and easy access to chair and umbrella rentals, surf lessons, hair braiding, and a volleyball court. Valet service and baggage storage, a business center, fitness room, and activity desk are also at your disposal, ensuring a first-class vacation experience. A small number of smoking rooms are available.

Holiday Inn Cocoa Beach–Oceanfront Resort

General Manager: Shay Baranowski
321-783-2271, 1-800-972-2590
fax 321-784-8878
www.ichotels.com

1300 N. Atlantic Ave., Cocoa Beach 32931
Price: Expensive
Credit Cards: All major cards accepted
Wheelchair Access: Yes

Families will have a blast at this full-service
hotel, located directly on the beach and
packed with amenities and special features.
Choose from five hundred rooms, including standard rooms, suites, two-level ocean
lofts, three-room ocean villas, and accommodations that include a separate sleeping
area for the kids with a TV, video/cassette
player, and game station. The lofts and villas have sitting rooms and kitchenettes.
Captain's Grill restaurant serves all meals,
there is a snack bar by the pool, or dine at
Mambos Beachside Bar & Grill. Room service is also available. Outside, enjoy the
Olympic-sized pool and sundeck while the
children play in a special pirate-ship pool.
Other amenities include tennis and sand
volleyball courts, shuffleboard, a fitness
center, and a whirlpool spa. With so many
choices, don't forget to head to the beach.
On-site concessionaires provide chair and
umbrella rentals, hair braiding, and surf
lessons. Smoking rooms are available.

*Kids can walk the plank at the Holiday Inn Cocoa
Beach–Oceanfront pirate pool.*

Holiday Inn Express Hotel & Suites
General Manager: Denzil Noronha
321-868-2525, fax 321-868-6302
www.hiexpress.com/es-cocoabeach
5575 N. Atlantic Ave., Cocoa Beach 32931
Price: Moderate
Credit Cards: AE, MC, V
Wheelchair Access: Yes

The location is convenient but not scenic at
this recognizable property located just off
A1A, within walking distance of the beach,
restaurants, and a supermarket. The bright,
attractive property is comfortable and
clean. Choose from smoking and nonsmoking rooms. There's a small pool and
most of the common amenities, such as a
fitness center, complimentary breakfast
bar, and a microwave and minirefrigerator
in every room.

The Inn at Cocoa Beach
Innkeeper: Larry York
321-799-3460, 1-800-343-5307
fax 321-784-8632
www.theinnatcocoabeach.com
4300 Ocean Beach Blvd., Cocoa Beach 32931
Price: Expensive
Credit Cards: AE, D, MC, V
Wheelchair Access: Yes
Special Features: Early-evening wine and
cheese gathering

This European-style adult resort is perfect
for a peaceful retreat or a romantic inter-
lude. With 50 rooms, it's too big to qualify
as a bed & breakfast, but it has all the same
luxuries and amenities, and the staff works
hard to make you feel like a guest in their
home. Outside, one of the busiest strips of
the beach is just steps away, with plenty of
choices for recreation and concessions.
Inside the inn, the mood is quiet and
relaxed. Every room is uniquely decorated
with king, double, or twin beds, and many
have an oceanfront view. Deluxe rooms
have a private balcony and sofa sitting area;
a few are Jacuzzi suites. Relax in common

areas like the salon and library, or settle in a chair next to the pool and spa. A complimentary breakfast is served inside or on the patio. Coffee and an honor bar are always available. Be prepared for a wonderful experience. The most common comment in the guest book is a wish to stay another night.

La Quinta Inn

General Manager: Don Terzieff
321-783-2252, 1-800-795-2252
fax 321-323-5045
www.622.lq.com
1275 N. Atlantic Ave., Cocoa Beach 32931
Price: Inexpensive–Moderate
Credit Cards: All major cards accepted
Wheelchair Access: Yes.

Although this inn is on the west side of A1A and surrounded by concrete and city noise, it all fades away when you step into the yard. A large pool and garden are at the center of the property; the tiki bar opens with drinks and snacks when things get busy. Start off the day with an upscale continental breakfast with hot and cold foods. Guests enjoy great service and comfortable, value-priced rooms. A traffic signal makes it easy to cross the street to the beach and Lori Wilson Park. The property is pet-friendly, and smoking rooms are available.

Luna Sea Bed & Breakfast Motel

General Manager: Joanne Farnham
321-783-0500, 1-800-586-2732
fax 321-784-6515
www.lunaseacocoabeach.com
3185 N. Atlantic Ave., Cocoa Beach 32931
Price: Inexpensive–Moderate
Credit Cards: AE, DC, MC, V
Wheelchair Access: Partial

For more than 30 years this small, family-owned motel has provided guests with value and service. The beach is a short walk away after crossing A1A, but the location is very convenient to dining, fast food, and shops.

Wildlife Profile: Bottlenose Dolphin

Dolphins capture our imagination: There is ample evidence they are intelligent, and without a doubt, they are curious and social. Several hundred bottlenose dolphins make their home in the Indian River Lagoon, and because they breathe from a blowhole every couple of minutes, they're easy to spot. Just keep an eye out for their long, sleek bodies gracefully breaking the surface of the water.

The bottlenose dolphin takes its name from the distinctive shape of its snout. The lagoon dolphins are a nonmigratory coastal ecotype that has adapted to life in the shallow, warm waters of the lagoon. Their bodies are a little smaller than the average of 10 feet long and 500 pounds. They gather in smaller pods than their ocean-swimming cousins, perhaps because the enclosed setting is better protected. Their tastes have adapted to include mullet, a prevalent fish in the lagoon waters. While dolphin usually swim about 5 miles per hour, sometimes they seem to come from nowhere in a burst of speed and circle around as they feed on prey.

Bottlenose dolphin (Tursiops truncatus) Courtesy NASA

Female dolphins gestate for about 12 months. Calves are born in the water with an umbilical cord that snaps during or shortly after birth. Newborns are about 4 feet long and weigh around 44 pounds. They'll nurse for at least a year but will begin eating fish after six months. In the Indian River Lagoon, most births occur in April and August.

Boaters and anglers tell tales of playful interludes with dolphins that seem to be showing off for a captive human audience. They jump, dive, and catch rides in the waves around a boat. Like people, dolphins sleep about one-third of each day—but it is still unclear to scientists how they do this. One thing is certain; children of all ages will have sweet dreams after an encounter with these fascinating creatures.

Space Coast Sightings: Throughout the length of the Indian River Lagoon; on most boat and kayak tours; near the Port Canaveral locks; Haulover Canal.

Standard rooms are available with king or two double beds, and there are larger rooms that also come with a pullout sofa and small kitchen; some are smoking. Tropical landscaping surrounds the pool and the backyard garden, which feature lawn chairs and barbecues. Guests enjoy a complimentary full breakfast at either of two nearby restaurants, both locally owned and famous for a great breakfast: Sunrise Diner or Roberto's Little Havana Restaurant.

Oceanside Inn

Owner: David McGee
321-784-3126, 1-800-874-7958
fax 321-799-0883
www.cocoabeachoceansideinn.com
1 Hendry Ave., Cocoa Beach 32931
Price: Moderate–Expensive
Credit Cards: All major cards accepted
Wheelchair Access: Yes

The Oceanside Inn is an appropriate name for this tropical-themed beachfront property located next door to the Cocoa Beach Pier. Standard rooms have one king or two double beds, plus a small refrigerator and private balcony. Some of the rooms face the ocean; others face the pier. Ground-floor views are obstructed, so ask for an upper

floor if having a view is important. The top floor has a honeymoon penthouse suite designed for two, and a studio suite that accommodates six. The hotel doesn't have any food service, but there are lots of choices in the area. Smoking rooms are available.

Pelican Landing Resort

Manager: Lace Howard
321-783-7197
www.vrbo.com
1201 S. Atlantic Ave., Cocoa Beach 32931
Price: Inexpensive–Moderate
Credit Cards: AE, MC, V
Wheelchair Access: No

This small, oceanside motel is a two-story complex of individually owned efficiency units, each sleeping four, with a king and convertible bed. The setting is well kept but not fancy. Linen is provided, and there are laundry facilities on-site. A wood deck overlooks the ocean. This is a nonsmoking property. Rates are reduced for weekly bookings.

Radisson Resort at the Port

General Manager: Joe Panackia
321-784-0000, 1-800-333-3333
fax 321-784-3737
www.radisson.com/capecanaveralfl
8701 Astronaut Blvd., Cape Canaveral 32920
Price: Moderate–Expensive
Credit Cards: All major cards accepted
Wheelchair Access: Yes
Special Features: Stunning pool, waterfall, and gardens

With color, decor, and landscaping reminiscent of a tropical resort, this luxury facility provides guests with first-class accommodations, an award-winning restaurant, and a helpful staff to ensure you enjoy your stay. The hotel is not on the beach, but it is just minutes from the cruise ships, dining, and nighttime entertainment at Port Canaveral. The rooms are large and spacious, and each includes a king bed or two doubles with sleep-number mattresses and plush bedding, ceiling fans, coffeemakers, microwave, full-sized desk, and in-room movies and games. Two-room minisuites with whirlpool tubs and a small dining table are also available. In addition to the free-form pool, there's a children's pool, Jacuzzi, and tennis court. The Flamingo Restaurant, lounge, and poolside tiki bar provide meals and refreshments. The resort caters to groups for business, weddings, or reunions. One suite has an expansive living, dining, and kitchen area and adjoins to rooms on either side, making it a great spot for receptions or gatherings.

The tropical gardens at Radisson Resort at the Port

Residence Inn by Marriott

General Manager: Pat Looney
321-323-1100, 1-800-331-3131
fax 321-323-1029
www.marriott.com
8959 Astronaut Blvd., Cape Canaveral 32920
Price: Expensive
Credit Cards: All major cards accepted
Wheelchair Access: Yes

Families and travelers staying several days will appreciate having significantly more space at this all-suite hotel. Every accommodation includes a separate living, eating, and sleeping area and has a fully equipped kitchen. During the week they provide a complimentary hot breakfast and late-afternoon snacks and drinks. While this property is not located on the beach, it is very convenient to the restaurants, clubs, and cruise ships at Port Canaveral. Relax by the pool, or get some exercise on the multifunctional sports court or in the fitness center.

The Resort on Cocoa Beach

General Manager: Sandi Thompson
321-783-4000, 1-866-469-8222
fax 321-799-0272
www.theresortoncocoabeach.com
1600 N. Atlantic Ave., Cocoa Beach 32931
Price: Expensive
Credit Cards: All major cards accepted
Wheelchair Access: Yes
Special Features: Fitness center and spa

A stay at the Resort on Cocoa Beach is not just a room for the night; it's a total vacation experience. Imagine a cruise ship anchored to land, and with bigger rooms. Two-bedroom, two-bath apartments have a full kitchen, laundry facilities, and a balcony—and host up to six guests. The complex is right on the water, and every room is oceanfront or ocean view.

Every unit at the Resort on Cocoa Beach is a spacious apartment.

Leave your room, and you'll find: a supersized swimming pool, water splash pad, an arcade, fitness center and sauna, indoor and outdoor play center for kids, basketball and tennis courts, a theater with 24-hour running movies, and—last but certainly not least—the beach! There are events for every age, including supervised activities for children ages 4 to 12. The Moo Cafe opens at 6 AM for coffee and pastries, and the Aztecta II restaurant is open for dinner. A large outdoor tiki bar provides meals and refreshments around the pool. Pack a small bag with a bathing suit and change of clothes, and use the locker room to extend your stay for a few hours on the day you check out.

Ron Jon Cape Caribe Resort

General Manager: Launa Young
321-784-4922, 1-888-933-3030
fax 321-783-2021
www.ronjonresort.com
1000 Shorewood Dr., Cape Canaveral 32920
Price: Very Expensive
Credit Cards: All major cards accepted
Wheelchair Access: Yes
Special Features: Exclusive water park for guests and unit owners

More than just a place to stay, this newcomer to the area is a one-of-a-kind Caribbean vacation experience. More than two hundred rooms are available to rent by the night or week, or to purchase as a vacation ownership property. Choose a studio that sleeps four, standard and deluxe one- and two-bedroom units, or the spacious three-bedroom villa that sleeps up to 12 and includes a living room, full kitchen, sitting room, separate kitchenette, laundry facilities, and a whirlpool tub.

All rooms, except for the studio, have a balcony, but only a few are oceanfront. This all-inclusive resort has a slew of amenities, most at no cost. Especially impressive is the water park, with a huge pool, waterfalls, water features for play, hot tub, Lazy River Ride, and a four-story-high water slide. Guests also enjoy a children's play center, theater, game room, fitness center, miniature golf, tennis, basketball, and shuffle

The water park at Ron Jon Cape Caribe Resort

board. A daily activity schedule includes special events like the Safari Todd Wildlife Show, line dance lessons, face painting, and a Relaxation Spa Escape. The sundry shop has food, necessities, and, of course, Ron Jon Surf Shop merchandise and beach paraphernalia. Dine inside or out, from 11 AM to 10 pm, at the Ron Jon Surf Grill; a full bar is inside. Plan to stay at least a couple of days just to learn your way around!

Sea Aire Motel

Resident Manager: Gary Jenkins
321-783-2461, 1-800-319-9637
fax 321-783-2461
www.l-n.com/seaaire
181 N. Atlantic Ave., Cocoa Beach 32931
Price: Inexpensive—Moderate
Credit Cards: AE, D, MC, V
Wheelchair Access: Partial

For 50 years this intimate, family-owned motel has been hosting Cocoa Beach visitors. Of the 16 rooms, 8 front directly on the ocean. Located a block from downtown, the motel offers guests the advantage of low prices, a clean and comfortable place to stay, and amenities typical of a public beach, including rentals, restaurants, bars, and entertainment. Rooms circle around a well-kept lawn, and the beach really is just steps away. Every room includes two double beds, a fully equipped kitchenette, a small dining table, and cable TV. Boogie boards, sand pails, and beach toys are available for children, as well as lawn games like croquet, badminton, and horseshoes. The flowery landscape, wide yard, and oceanfront setting make this a popular spot for beach weddings.

South Beach Inn

Innkeeper: Dave Sauder
321-784-3333, 1-877-546-6835
fax 321-784-9486
www.southbeachinn.com
1701 S. Atlantic Ave., Cocoa Beach 32931
Price: Inexpensive–Moderate
Credit Cards: AE, D, MC, V
Wheelchair Access: No

This small, older motel might be a good choice for travelers looking for less-expensive accommodations for a few nights. Each of the 18 units in this two-story building is an apartment with a fully equipped kitchen and small dining area. The two-bedroom units sleep six. There is a sundeck but no pool, and daily maid service is not provided. Smoking is permitted, and pets are welcome. Murkshe Park, one of the more popular surfing spots, is located right next door.

Surf Studio Beach Resort

Owners: Greg Greenwald and Gina Greenwald
321-783-7100
www.surf-studio.com
1801 S. Atlantic Ave., Cocoa Beach 32931
Price: Inexpensive–Moderate
Credit Cards: All major cards accepted
Wheelchair Access: Yes

Owners and siblings Greg and Gina grew up at this small beachfront motel built by their father 60 years ago, and their love for the property is evident in the well-maintained and modernized facilities. Eleven ground-floor units circle around an immaculately groomed courtyard. Sundecks furnished with chairs and umbrellas sit at sand's edge and overlook the surf. Cool off with a dip in the pool or a breezy swing in a hammock.

Choose an efficiency room or a one-bedroom apartment that sleeps six. Families are welcome, and many visitors have been returning for years, feeling like part of the family. This is a nonsmoking facility. Pets are welcome.

Wakulla Suites

Hotel Manager: Ruby Daniel
321-783-2230, 1-800-992-5852
fax 321-783-0980
www.wakullasuites.com
3550 N. Atlantic Ave., Cocoa Beach 32931
Price: Expensive
Credit Cards: All major cards accepted
Wheelchair Access: Yes
Special Features: Flat-screen televisions, hookups for DVD players and games

Guests mingle at Wakulla Suites's courtyard pool.

Suites in this friendly and comfortable hotel encircle a lengthy courtyard, landscaped with more than one hundred varieties of tropical plants. Interspersed are benches, picnic tables, grills, shuffleboard courts, and pools for adults and children. A walk through the gardens is like a stroll through the neighborhood, with guests mingling, playing cards, or sharing a meal. The Polynesian motif continues in the recently renovated, spacious, and modern units. Each includes living room, complete kitchen, and two bedrooms, one with a king bed and the other with a full and twin bed. A short walk away, a large oceanfront deck leads down to the sand. A few oceanfront rooms are available in a separate beachside building. Parking is limited, but most amenities are within walking distance, so once you find a space you may not need to move your car.

Vacation & Condo Rentals

Canaveral Towers Resort
Manager: Cyndi Shaffer
321-784-4311, 1-877-773-2866
fax 321-799-2676
www.resortreservations.cc
7520 Ridgewood Ave., Cape Canaveral 32920
Price: Expensive–Very Expensive
Credit Cards: All major cards accepted
Wheelchair Access: No

This nine-story building is the tallest on the Cape Canaveral beaches, and every unit has a direct or angled view of the ocean. The apartments are individually owned and furnished, but all are well maintained and roomy, with two or three bedrooms, two baths, a full kitchen, large living room, and sliding doors that open to a patio or balcony. A minimum stay of a week is required. No housekeeping service is provided, but there is a great pool and sauna, and a putting green for golf aficionados. The Cocoa Beach Country Club course is about 6 miles south. Pictures of rental units are available on the Web site. Smoking is allowed in most units. (A cleaning and processing fee is added to the rental.)

Cape Winds Resort
Manager: Cyndi Shaffer
321-784-4311, 1-800-248-1030
fax 321-799-2676
www.resortreservations.cc
7400 Ridgewood Ave., Cape Canaveral 32920
Price: Expensive–Very Expensive
Credit Cards: All major cards accepted
Wheelchair Access: No

This upscale property, situated along the beach at the halfway point between the Cocoa Beach Pier and Port Canaveral, is an upscale condo with many hotel touches, such as daily housekeeping service and high-speed Internet access in each unit. The one- and two-bedroom units are comfortably furnished with an overstuffed sofa and recliner in the living room, marble countertops in the full-sized kitchen, and a table and chairs on the oceanfront patio or balcony. Relax in the pool, hot tub, or sauna; work out on the tennis or basketball courts; or enjoy the beach waiting right outside the door. Smoking is permitted on the balconies.

Cocoa Beach Club Condominiums
Property Manager: Joyce Hebert
321-784-2457, fax 321-783-3019
www.cocoabeachclub.com
5200 Ocean Beach Blvd.
#214, Cocoa Beach 32931
Price: Expensive
Credit Cards: None
Wheelchair Access: Partial

The design and exterior of this 1970s property is a little dated, but the location is ideal, and Joyce, manager since opening, ensures everything is well maintained. The apartment units are roomier than the newer facilities, and the 60-foot-long pool is perfect for swimming laps. Choose from mostly two- and three-bedroom individually owned and decorated condos, some with an oceanfront setting. You can request a digital image before finalizing the booking. A deposit is required to hold your reservation.

Ocean Landings Resort & Racquet Club

General Manager: Rod Ressler
321-783-9430, 1-800-323-8413
fax 321-783-1339
www.oceanslanding.com
900 N. Atlantic Ave., Cocoa Beach 32931
Price: Moderate–Expensive
Credit Cards: All major cards accepted
Wheelchair Access: Partial
Special Features: Gregory's Comedy Club
upstairs on Thursday nights

This well-managed time-share resort is all
about choices. Select a one- or two-bedroom unit, oceanfront or off-ocean, for a
daily or weekly stay. There are two pools,
four courts each for tennis and racquetball,
a playground for the kids, and a fitness
center for adults. Social activities such as
wine and cheese parties and barbecue picnics add to the enjoyment. Every unit has a
fully equipped kitchen and living area with
a pullout couch. The off-ocean suites sleep
six in the one-bedroom (two queens and
the sofa) and eight in the two-bedroom
(king, two queens, and the sofa). Smaller
hotel-sized accommodations are available.

Ola Grande Condominiums

Managers: Sam and Rose Dettore
321-783-3101, fax 321-799-4249
www.olagrande.com
5350 Ocean Beach Blvd., Cocoa Beach 32931
Price: Moderate–Expensive
Credit Cards: None
Wheelchair Access: No

Ola Grande, or "big wave," is a fitting name
for the cozy and surprisingly quiet property
located right next door to the Cocoa Beach
Pier. Two-bedroom condominiums are
rented by the week or month, each with a
patio or balcony overlooking the neatly
trimmed lawn, like rowhouses in a friendly
suburban locale. Individual owners furnish
the units, but each is set up for a lengthy
stay with a full kitchen and laundry facilities, and some permit smoking. A private
crossover leads directly to the beach, or
take a refreshing dip in the pool. A deposit
is required to hold your reservation.

Royal Mansions

General Manager: Keith Acker
321-784-8484, 1-800-346-7222
fax 321-799-2907
www.royalmansions.com
8600 Ridgewood Ave., Cape Canaveral 32920
Price: Expensive
Credit Cards: All major cards accepted
Wheelchair Access: Yes
Special Features: Ocean view from pool and
Jacuzzi

This compound of beachside villas claims
one of the best locations along the coast—a
quiet strip just south of Jetty Park and an
easy bike ride to the restaurants and clubs at
the port. Unpack and settle into a one-bedroom atrium or patio unit, or splurge with
the two-bedroom penthouse. For a premium, oceanfront units are available in each
category. The condos are privately owned
and uniquely decorated, and every one
includes a fully equipped kitchen and daily
housekeeping. C & W Hotel Management
Company operates the property with an
emphasis on hospitality and community.
Join other guests around the pool, at social
events, and in the club room for continental
breakfast or a weekly wine reception.

The poolside view of the ocean at Royal Mansions.

Seagull Beach Club

Resort Manager: Cari Jordon
321-783-4441, 1-800-386-6732
fax 321-783-4454
www.seagullbeachclub.com
4440 Ocean Beach Blvd., Cocoa Beach 32931
Price: Moderate
Credit Cards: AE, D, MC, V
Wheelchair Access: Partial

This small complex, conveniently located next to Shepherd Park where FL 520 meets the ocean, offers warm, homey, and affordable accommodations. The pool and deck are a little small, but they are so close to the ocean that you can almost touch the waves at high tide. Select a one- or two-bedroom unit with a separate living and dining space, and a fully equipped kitchen. The staff is friendly and works hard to make your stay enjoyable and entertaining with activities like a group lunch in the park, bingo by the pool, a KidsKamp on Thursday afternoons, and a Friday ice cream social.

CENTRAL BREVARD

Hotels & Motels

Crowne Plaza Melbourne Oceanfront

General Manager: Ghee Alexander
321-777-4100, 1-800-227-6963
fax 321-773-6132
www.cpmelbourne.com
2605 N. FL A1A, Melbourne 32903
Price: Expensive–Very Expensive
Credit Cards: All major cards accepted
Wheelchair Access: Yes
Special Features: Full-service Ocean Reef Spa

The exceptional staff at this eight-story luxury hotel just south of the Eau Gallie Causeway will cater to your every need. Standard rooms, two-room suites, and kitchenette suites are decorated in relaxing tones of deep sky blue, soft sunrise yellow, and rich maroon. Guests receive a delivered newspaper in the morning, in-room movies, coffeemaker, microwave, small refrigerator, and posh bedding at the end of the day. There's a choice of technology options, including high-speed Internet, a wireless data connection, and Internet browser TV. Parents can enroll children in the Kids Club that's open during the day from Monday through Saturday. Settle in a chair by the large pool and oceanside deck, or on a chaise lounge at the beach. Coquina's Seafood Grill serves fine dining indoors and out, and there is room service from early morning until late evening. Languages spoken by hotel staff include English, Hindi, Portuguese, and Spanish. Complimentary transportation is provided to Melbourne International Airport.

Crowne Plaza Melbourne's oceanfront bar and deck
Courtesy Crowne Plaza Melbourne Oceanfront

Holiday Inn & Conference Center
General Manager: Mercedes Diaz
321-255-0077, 1-800-554-5188
fax 321-259-9633
www.ichotels.com
8298 N. Wickham Rd., Melbourne 32940
Price: Moderate
Credit Cards: All major cards accepted
Wheelchair Access: Yes

This comfortable property in Viera has a history of providing affordable, upscale accommodations and exceptional guest service. Room options include a standard, with a king or two double beds, and business suites, which add a seating area, sleeper sofa, workspace, microwave, and refrigerator. The RendezVous Restaurant and Lounge is open for casual dining every evening except Sunday, and several restaurants and fast-food outlets are located close to the hotel. Relax by the pool or take advantage of nearby recreation, including golf courses, shopping, baseball games, and the Brevard Zoo. The King Performing Arts Center is just 5 miles away, and combination room and ticket packages can be booked directly through the hotel.

NORTH BREVARD

Hotels & Motels

Casa Coquina Bed & Breakfast
Owner: Linda Rigo
321-268-4653, 1-877-684-8341
www.casacoquina.com
4010 Coquina Ave., Titusville 32780
Price: Economy–Moderate
Credit Cards: AE, D, MC, V
Wheelchair Access: No

Built as a private home in the 1920s, this very colorful landmark overlooking the Indian River has been recently renovated and provides adult guests with an alternative to more traditional lodging. Seven suites, each named after a jewel, are decorated in the appropriate color scheme and have unique design—pick the passionate Ruby or the more restful Sapphire. An executive suite is available for longer stays. The home is an eclectic mix of angels, flowers, antiques, brocade, and lace. Common areas for guests include a bar, library, gardens, and sundeck. A full breakfast is served each morning. The backyard garden and gazebo are popular spots for weddings and renewing vows. Avoid traffic delays and simply walk across the street to a nearby park for a perfect view of a shuttle launch.

Casa Coquina's breakfast room

The Clarion Inn at Kennedy Space Center
General Manager: Bryan Rafferty
321-269-2121, fax 321-268-1411
www.clarionspacecenter.com
4951 S. Washington Ave., Titusville 32780
Price: Inexpensive–Moderate
Credit Cards: All major cards accepted
Wheelchair Access: Yes

Families looking to enjoy the space attractions and natural outdoors of north Brevard will love the convenience and value of this riverside motel. The rooms have king, queen, or two double beds, along with basic amenities. An on-site restaurant serves breakfast every day and dinner is served Tuesday–Saturday; room service is available when open. Outside there's a large pool and kiddie pool. Next door is Kennedy Point Park, with a paved walkway along the shore of the Indian River and facilities for picnics and grilling. Shuttle launch pads at Kennedy Space Center can be seen on the other side of the river. Small pets are welcomed; a cleaning fee is charged.

Dickens Inn Bed & Breakfast
Innkeepers: Christine and Mark Joyce
321-269-4595, 1-877-847-2067
www.dickens-inn.com
2398 N. Singleton Ave., Mims 32754
Price: Moderate
Credit Cards: MC, V
Wheelchair Access: Partial

Luxuriate in the lap of southern hospitality at this 1860 plantation home, built in the shade of live oaks dripping with Spanish moss and stately pecan trees blowing in the summer breeze. Five rooms are uniquely decorated in a simple style and soothing pastel tones. Each has an en suite bath, television, CD player, and DSL computer connection. Christine and Mark, who spent several years on the cruise ship *Queen Elizabeth 2*, deliver a five-star service level with plush bedding, towels, and robes; coffee, chilled water, and chocolate in each room; and maid service twice a day. Enjoy a full breakfast each morning with fresh-squeezed orange juice from the grove when in season. Visitors looking for a rural retreat or a friendly home close to the North Brevard attractions will enjoy the dickens out of this spot.

Hampton Inn Titusville
General Manager: Dominic Fraticelli
321-383-9191, fax 321-383-9166
www.hamptoninn.com
4760 Helen Hauser Blvd., Titusville 32780
Price: Moderate–Expensive
Credit Cards: All major cards accepted
Wheelchair Access: Yes

One of Titusville's newest properties, the Hampton Inn is conveniently located directly off I-95, about 10 minutes from both downtown Titusville and the Kennedy Space Center. Choose from standard rooms, with one king or two double beds, or suites, which add a sleeper sofa and bar sink. The studio suite includes a small refrigerator and microwave. A complimentary hot breakfast is part of every stay. Smoking rooms are available.

SOUTH BREVARD

Hotels & Motels

Crane Creek Inn Waterfront Bed & Breakfast
Innkeepers: Gillian and Bob Shearer
321-768-6416
www.cranecreekinn.com
907 E. Melbourne Ave., Melbourne 32901
Price: Moderate–Expensive
Credit Cards: AE, CB, DC, MC, V
Wheelchair Access: No

This attractive 1925 home, at the heart of historic downtown Melbourne, provides a haven for adult guests who prefer a more homey and pampered setting. A backyard veranda, pool, hot tub, and hammock overlook picturesque Crane Creek, where manatees, dolphins, and water birds are likely

The Crane Creek Inn was built in 1925.

to come calling. Each of the five rooms is furnished with antiques and includes a private bathroom, television, and wireless Internet. Add romance to your stay with a gift basket, personal massage, or fresh flowers. Continental breakfast is served during the week, a full breakfast on the weekends. Well-behaved pets are welcome, but there is an additional fee.

The Old Pineapple Inn
Innkeepers: Robert and Celeste Henry
321-254-1347, 1-888-776-9864
www.oldpineappleinn.com
1736 Pineapple Ave., Melbourne 32935
Price: Very Expensive
Credit Cards: AE, D, MC, V
Wheelchair Access: No

Step back to another time when you walk through the door of this 1886 three-story Victorian mansion, which was built by William Henry Gleason, the founder of the city of Eau Gallie. Today this stately home, directly across from the Indian River, is a bed & breakfast filled with memories and memorabilia from the past: a porch swing swaying on a breezy veranda, a 1928 baby grand piano, antique furnishings, and a crystal pineapple chandelier. There are also modern touches like a swimming pool, an electronic media center, and Jacuzzi tubs. Three suites are in the main house, and a separate guest house with updated decor and a tropical color scheme has four bedrooms; two baths; kitchen, living, and dining areas; a yard; and a swimming pool. Eau Gallie is ideal for walking and biking; beaches are about 2 miles east.

Shores
Manager: Kim Popp
321-723-3355, 1-800-820-1441
www.tuckawayshores.com
1441 S. A1A, Indialantic 32903
Price: Moderate
Credit Cards: AE, MC, DC, V
Wheelchair Access: Partial

Located on a quiet stretch of beach south of US 192, this charming motel offers the style and hospitality of old Florida, with a few modern twists like wireless Internet and flat-screen televisions in most of the rooms. The decor is clean, crisp, and comfortable. Every accommodation is a two-room suite, oceanfront or ocean view, has a full kitchen, and sleeps four. After a day in the sun, mingle with other guests in the Cabana Room or settle in one of the colorful Adirondack chairs out by the barbecue grille. A perfect choice that's a little off the beaten path and closer to Sebastian Inlet.

Windemere Inn by the Sea
Innkeeper: Elizabeth Fisher
321-728-9334, 1-800-224-6853, fax 321-728-2741
www.windermereinn.com
815 S. A1A, Indialantic 32903
Price: Moderate–Expensive
Credit Cards: D, MC, V
Wheelchair Access: Partial

Discover romance, relaxation, or respite at this luxury bed & breakfast on the south Melbourne beaches. Rooms, furnished in antiques and wicker, with plush linens piled high on four-poster beds, are available in the Main House and the Cottage; or choose the Carriage House Suite with two connecting guest rooms. Some have ocean views and Jacuzzi baths. After a gourmet breakfast (included in the rate), grab a beach chair and towel and settle in for a day of sunshine and swimming on this very quiet stretch of beach. Small weddings can be arranged at the beachside pergola that frames the sunrise on each new day.

4

Culture

Reach for the Stars

Warm, rejuvenating waters nourish the cultural landscape of Brevard County. Acclaimed and prolific writer Nora Zeale Hurston lived on the Indian River in Eau Gallie for several years. When friends asked her why she spent so much time by herself, in a boat, just reading, she mused, "I enjoy it out here. I can concentrate. I can think."

Water was the highway of choice for the county's 19th-century pioneers, a colorful and entrepreneurial lot sailing south, charting a new course in the wet and rustic wilderness. Col. Henry Titus spent years skirting the law and outrunning failed business ventures before landing in Sand Point in north Brevard, where he prospered. True to his risk-taking roots, he won the right to name the town Titusville in a bet on a game of dominoes.

By the turn of the 20th century, enterprising adventurers were transformed into successful and stable town leaders. They built impressive, new age mansions, like the two-story Queen Anne–style home of John and Nannie Lee in Melbourne, and funded ornate playhouses like the Italian Renaissance Aladdin in Cocoa.

The advent of the automobile made the beaches more accessible and reinforced a collective sunny optimism that every opportunity lost would be followed by a wave of new possibility. The space program landed on the shores of Brevard County around midcentury. During the race-to-the-moon 1960s, this narrow strip of land was the fastest growing area in America due to an influx of energetic, creative, and well-educated newcomers. Museums and galleries opened, and groups like the Brevard Symphony Orchestra were formed.

Today's cultural community retains the daring spirit of early settlers and the creative collaboration of space program pioneers. Artists convert small storefronts into vibrant, colorful studios, and musicians perform in coffee shops and beachside bars. Until recently, preserving the heritage of the area has been a grass-roots effort. Now several cities, along with the Brevard Historical Commission, are scrambling to save old properties, collect photographs and memorabilia, and record personal stories.

Half a millennium after the ships of European explorers landed on the sandy coast of Brevard County, astronauts—star sailors—continue the journey, this time across the vast ocean of space. This chapter is your guide to the past and the future, a snapshot of America's space adventures, and a peek into the galleries, museums, and entertainment of Florida's Space Coast—a place where engineers, artisans, musicians, and performers dare to dream, dare to reach for the stars.

Left: *Florida folk musician and songwriter Chris Kahl captures orange blossom memories*

AEROSPACE

In 1919 Brevard County was a community centered around agriculture, cattle, and fishing. Folks took no notice when Robert Goddard, a physics professor from Massachusetts, published *A Method of Reaching Extreme Altitudes*. Goddard had just erased the thin line separating science fiction from science. Until his death 25 years later, this reclusive and determined rocket scientist chased his dream of proving to the world that space travel was more than just a fantasy.

Brevard County was isolated and sparsely populated in 1958 when the newly formed National Aeronautics and Space Administration (NASA) chose Cape Canaveral as the dock from which new-age captains would launch powerful ships skyward. Engineers and technicians enlisted as the crew for this great adventure. "Go for launch" became the Space Coast mantra. The dedicated and spirited men and women of Brevard County continue to build a path from the earth to the sky, transforming vision into works of art that carry explorers to the ever-expanding edge of the universe. There's no better place to tag along on the journey.

Central Brevard

Brevard Community College Astronaut Memorial Planetarium and Observatory

321-433-7373
www.brevardcc.edu/planet
1519 Clearlake Rd, Cocoa 32922
Open: Wed. 1:30–4:30, Fri. and Sat. 6:30–10 PM
Admission: Free for observatory and exhibits; shows: adults $7, seniors and students $6, children under 13 $4, combo tickets available

Glimpse distant galaxies and imagine the adventures awaiting future space travelers. On Friday and Saturday evenings, staff and volunteers help visitors identify key stars through the observatory's state-of-the-art telescope. Discover space memorabilia and meteorites in the exhibit hall. Like the stars in the night sky, show choices in this modern facility are always in motion. Tour the heavens or enjoy a laser show inside the world-class planetarium. View images captured by the Hubble telescope. Follow the constellations to learn the stories of ancient gods and heroes. A concert-level sound system blends rock music with laser effects for a unique musical experience featuring acts like Pink Floyd, the Beatles, and a special Halloween rendition of monster favorites. The Iwerks Movie Theater presents the sights and sounds of nature on a three-story-high screen.

Star Light, Star Bright: Viewing a Space Launch

The best show in town is a thunderous launch of the space shuttle or a rocket from Cape Canaveral. In the daytime a bright light pulling a streamer of white, puffy smoke blazes a trail across a clear blue sky. At night the dark horizon glows as flames propel the craft skyward and then fade in the distance until resembling a single bright star.

Viewing Sites

1　**Port Canaveral** has outstanding views for shuttle and rocket launches at Jetty Park, the restaurants and bars along Glen Cheek Drive, and other parks and docks.

2　The coastline of **Cape Canaveral and Cocoa Beach** is a great spot to watch a shuttle launch and one of the best for rocket launches, especially to the north around Cherie Down Park and the Cocoa Beach Pier.

3 On FL 528, the **Bennett Causeway over the Banana River** has off-road parking space, and several boat tour operators schedule special outings.

4 **US I north and south off FL 50** has several parks right along the Indian River.

5 **US I at FL 406 in Titusville** is ideal for shuttle launches because it is directly across from the launch pads. Sand Point Park and Space View Park make accommodations for crowds, and parking is plentiful in the downtown Titusville area.

6 **Kennedy Space Center Visitor Complex** offers a bus ticket that will get public visitors as close to the shuttle launch as possible. Buy a general admission ticket for a great view of both shuttle and rocket launches.

Other Information

Traffic is very heavy on launch day. Leave early and plan for delays as everyone heads home at the same time.

Hotels and restaurants are usually fully booked. Make reservations as much in advance as possible.

Consider access to refreshments and restrooms, especially if parking at the side of the road.

The roads and waters surrounding Kennedy Space Center and the Cape Canaveral Air Force Station are closed before launches, including parts of the Merritt Island National Wildlife Refuge and Canaveral National Seashore. Boaters should monitor channel 16 VHF-FM for restrictions.

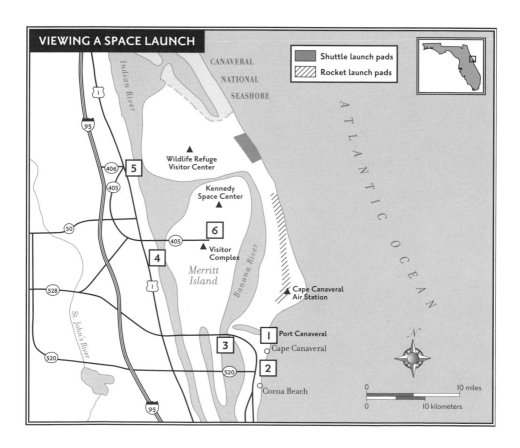

North Brevard

Kennedy Space Center Visitor Complex

321-449-4444
www.kennedyspacecenter.com
NASA Parkway, Merritt Island 32899 (off FL 405, 0.5 mile east of US 1)
Open: Daily at 9; closing times vary. Closed Christmas.
Admission: Adults $38, children ages 3–11 $28

The John F. Kennedy Space Center opened in 1962 as the launch facility for NASA and the last stop on Earth before astronauts headed into space. This all-day theme park, operated by Delaware North Companies Parks & Resorts, Inc. on behalf of NASA, blends entertainment and technology with authentic equipment and operations to tell the story of our nation's past, present, and future space exploration. Learn about each chapter of the manned space program through interactive exhibits, rides and attractions, IMAX movies, and a variety of special tours. Take your time selecting the ticket you want. Regular admission covers most of the center, or you can choose combo tickets that fold in tours and special activities. All attractions are wheelchair accessible, and complimentary strollers and wheelchairs are provided. Whether you're mildly interested in space or over the moon about the topic, a visit to the Kennedy Space Center Visitor Complex is fun, educational, and awe-inspiring for all ages. If you don't get to see it all the first day, a second day is included in the admission price. In addition to life-sized rockets, actual moon rocks, and the largest space merchandise shop on the planet, here are some highlights, most included with the regular ticket.

Guests take a one-of-a-kind ride on the Shuttle Launch Experience at the Kennedy Space Center Visitor Complex.
Courtesy Delaware North Parks & Resorts

SHUTTLE LAUNCH EXPERIENCE

Climb aboard this newest ride, opened in 2007, and come as close as possible to replicating a trip aboard a shuttle as it launches into space. Astronaut testimonials are the heart of this high-tech simulator. Everything is go for launch, so buckle up and prepare for lift-off as your shuttle rumbles, roars, and soars skyward. Once in orbit, the peaceful silence of space settles in, and the payload bay doors slide open to provide a breathtaking look back at planet Earth. The shuttle program is set to retire in 2010, so now the adventure is captured for all time.

THE IMAX EXPERIENCE

Fewer than five hundred men and women have actually traveled into space. Viewers join them through video, special effects, and a wall of sound that moves the audience into the exciting and challenging world of space exploration. Much of the film footage—*Space Station 3D*, narrated by Tom Cruise, and *Magnificent Desolation: Walking on the Moon 3D*, told by Tom Hanks—was shot during actual NASA missions.

The Apollo capsule carried astronauts to the moon.

KENNEDY SPACE CENTER TOUR

A short bus ride takes you to NASA operations while a video explains the sights. Get great photos at the historic Launch Complex 39 observation gantry with a panoramic view of Kennedy Space Center. After a drive by the Vehicle Assembly Building, where shuttles are prepared for launch, the bus tour terminates at the Apollo/Saturn V Center. Here the main attraction is a fully restored, 363-foot-tall *Saturn V* moon rocket lying on its side for an up-close view of how it was assembled and stacked. This 6.5-million-pound engineering marvel roared into the heavens on November 9, 1967. Less than two years later, on July 20, 1969, Neil Armstrong took "one small step for man, one giant leap for mankind" as he planted an American flag on the lunar surface.

ASTRONAUT ENCOUNTER

Check the schedule when you first arrive to plan around this opportunity to visit with an astronaut. For a half hour you'll hear stories and have a chance to ask questions.

LUNCH WITH AN ASTRONAUT

For a more personal experience, join an astronaut for lunch. The buffet is a great midday meal and is accompanied by a video about life in space. Over dessert, an astronaut joins the group, shares personal comments, and answers questions. Each guest gets a signed picture of the host and a few minutes for a personal photo opportunity. The cost is $60.99 for adults and $43.99 for children, and it includes regular park admission.

SPECIAL-INTEREST TOURS

For a more in-depth look at the space program facilities, sign up for one of the guided tours. *NASA Up Close* brings you the closest to the launch pads and swings by the shuttle landing strip—which is so long that it's visible from space. *Cape Canaveral: Then and Now* goes back in time with a visit to **Canaveral Air Station and the Space & Missile Museum**, site of the first successful satellite launch in 1958. Both bus excursions take three to four hours. The ticket price for each is $59 ($43 for children), which includes regular admission. Unless you're a space buff, you may not want to spend the extra time and money.

U.S. ASTRONAUT HALL OF FAME

Part of a foundation created by the seven Mercury astronauts in order to honor space travelers and promote scholarships to strengthen America's position in science and technology, the U.S. Astronaut Hall of Fame shares the human story behind space travel with the largest collection of astronaut artifacts and mementos ever assembled. Those who want to put themselves through the paces that separate NASA's best from the rest can try out the interactive simulators that offer a true taste of space, like the G-Force Trainer, which simulates the pressure of four times the force of gravity. The Hall of Heroes celebrates astronauts inducted into the Hall of Fame. This entertaining and interactive facility is 6 miles from the visitor complex.

ASTRONAUT TRAINING EXPERIENCE (ATX)

Take your space visit to the edge with one- or two-day interactive immersion programs that include education, hands-on training exercises, and a team-based simulated shuttle mission. Special programs are available for individuals, families, and student groups. Check the Web site for more details.

Space Walk of Fame and Astronaut Memorial at Space View Park

321-264-5105
www.brevardparks.com/parks/index.htm
101 N. Washington Ave., Titusville 32796
Open: 7 AM–dark
Admission: Free

This monument at Space View Park honors Mercury 7 *astronauts.*

This expansive waterside park in the heart of historic Titusville honors space workers who built a path to the moon through the Mercury, Gemini, and Apollo programs. Monuments mark the completion of successful missions, and handprint plaques from Hall of Fame astronauts line the walkway. Built on three separate sites, the park is directly across the Indian River from Kennedy Space Center and offers the absolute best off-property spot for viewing shuttle launches. Downtown Titusville has plenty of parking, restrooms are available, and a giant clock counts down to blast-off.

U.S. Space Walk of Fame Museum

321-264-0434
www.spacewalkoffame.com
4 Main St., Titusville 32796
Open: Mon.–Fri. 10–5
Admission: Free

Step behind the scenes at this museum that honors the men and women who made the dream of space travel a reality, along with the astronauts who flew the missions. Retired workers dedicated to preserving America's space history have compiled a collection of authentic artifacts, scale models, rare photos, and other exhibits. Personal tales are woven into the tours by volunteer docents like Sam Beddingfield, who was recruited by Gus Grissom to join NASA as an engineer in 1959, just as the manned space flight program was gearing up. By the time he retired in 1985, 23 shuttle launches had flown. Pint-sized astronaut suits and detailed scale models of rockets and the shuttle are among the unusual offerings found in the gift shop.

An interactive model of the Space Shuttle and rigging at the U.S. Space Walk of Fame Museum

Valiant Air Command Warbird Museum
321-268-1941
www.vacwarbirds.org
6600 Tico Rd., Titusville 23780
Open: Daily 9–5; closed Thanksgiving, Christmas, and New Year's Day
Admission: Adults $12; seniors, military $10; ages 4–12 $5

A warbird is an airplane once used by the armed forces of any country that is now privately owned. At this museum, such aircraft that date from before World War I until today are restored and displayed to preserve aviation history and honor their courageous pilots. A C-47 from the D-Day invasion shares space with a Grumman F-14 like the one shown in the movie *Top Gun*. The museum includes a gift shop and library, and it is located next to Space Coast Regional Airport. Check the Web site for dates of the spring Tico Warbird Airshow, a three-day extravaganza of flying exhibitions, always ending with the Missing Man Formation.

Zero G Weightless Flights
954-756-1000
www.gozerog.com
Price: $3,000 and up

The future of space tourism is here. A modified Boeing 727 flies fifteen parabolic arcs, each one allowing you and a group of family or friends to levitate in weightlessness for up to 30 seconds at a time. Passengers experience about seven minutes of total reduced gravity—about twice as much as on a typical suborbital space flight. Fly across the cabin or do a back flip. This is truly a unique vacation adventure. "Space, here I come," was physicist Stephen Hawking's reaction after his brief flight from Cape Canaveral in April 2007. Call or check the Web site for schedule and booking.

GALLERIES

Along the Space Coast you'll discover works of art ranging from fanciful to elegant. Many of the galleries and studios showcase the incredible talent of local artists, and many works reflect the natural environment or the culture of space exploration. The galleries tend to cluster, so within a few blocks of the same neighborhood you'll find several choices. Pop into the studios that appeal to your taste, or perhaps take a detour and discover something new.

Cape Canaveral & Cocoa Beach

The casual and carefree tone of downtown Cocoa Beach is reflected in the eclectic collection of galleries. The seaside location inspires local artists and influences their work—and sometimes their work ethic. When the waves are good, don't be surprised to discover a GONE SURFING sign on the door. In addition to storefront galleries, many of the area restaurants are decorated with original works of art that are available for purchase.

Beachside Gallery
321-799-9336
133 N. Orlando Ave., Cocoa Beach 32931
Open: Tues.–Sat. 10–5:30

The style and heritage of the 1939 house on Cottage Row in downtown Cocoa Beach is the perfect setting for this fine-arts gallery. The original works of more than 40 talented artists are on display. In addition, owner and resident artist Kate LaDuke specializes in applying natural, gentle methods to restore damaged, aged, and weathered pieces. Full-service custom framing is also available.

Courage Belle Art Studio and Gallery
321-783-5033
38 N. Brevard Ave., Cocoa Beach 32931
Open: Tues. and Thurs. 10–noon and by appointment

In 2002, painters and friends Carolyn Cherry and Susan Tully combined their talent and passion for creating tropical watercolors. Vibrant works credited to each woman are on display, as well as joint paintings signed TouCan (because they believe two can work together to create beautiful

Indian River *by Carolyn Seiler*

pieces). Often you'll see a work in progress on the center table as you browse through originals and prints. *Neptune's Party,* a TouCan watercolor of life under the sea, was selected to appear on posters and T-shirts for the 2006 Space Coast Art Festival.

Quique's Gallery
321-783-4045
www.beachplaceguesthouses.com
1445 S. Atlantic Ave., Cocoa Beach 32931
Open: Varies

Local artists are showcased in a small courtyard gallery at Beach Place Guesthouses, just south of downtown Cocoa Beach. Receptions are held for the opening of each show, and the public is invited to meet the artist and enjoy ocean breezes, wine, appetizers, and music. Check the Web site for information on future events.

Central Brevard
In historic Cocoa Village, art is everywhere: Building murals set a scene of days gone by, colorful signs and decorated benches line the sidewalks, and galleries mimic the personality of the artists. No matter what the medium, expect expressions of nature from studios in this riverside locale.

Boatyard Studio
321-637-0444
118 Harrison St., Cocoa 32922
Open: Tues.–Sat. 10–6, Sun. noon–4

Carolyn Seiler's entryway is easy to find: Just look for a bright yellow-orange sun and WELCOME on the threshold. Step inside to an oasis of whimsical paintings and sketches, some original, others reproduced in posters and notecards. Loys Anne Locklear recently joined Carolyn, adding clay pieces with natural designs. During the holidays, Locklear and Seiler collaborate on ornaments depicting local scenes and seasonal messages.

The Clay Studio
321-636-4160
116B Harrison St., Cocoa 32922
Open: Mon.–Sat. 7–4

This small pottery workshop tucked between two larger buildings is easy to miss. Wrought-iron gates swing open to a brick-lined path winding past a tropical bamboo garden and goldfish pond. A small green turtle peeks over a rock, but this turtle is imaginary. Here, artisan Harry Guthrie Phillips combines his passions for pottery and scuba diving to create nautical sculptures and functional pieces.

Cousins II Gallery
321-632-2326
631 Brevard Ave., Cocoa 32922
Open: Mon.–Fri. 10–5, Sat. 10–3

This working studio and gallery has been a haven for aspiring artists for more than thirty years. Owner Charlotte Griffin teaches and inspires a new generation of talent in art classes for adults and children. Works from accomplished, award-winning artists from throughout the state line the walls. Art supplies are also available.

Kurt Zimmerman Gallery & Studio

321-633-6514
119 Harrison St., Cocoa 32922
Open: Tues.–Sat. 10–noon, 1–2:30

An assignment with the Apollo Moon Project brought Kurt Zimmerman to this area. Today, the works of this nationally renowned folk artist reflect a unique perspective of the universe. In his small upstairs gallery, Zimmerman enjoys challenging the senses and "making viewers aware of the greater dimensionality of life, a view very different from the normal day-to-day reality we perceive."

R. L. Lewis Gallery

321-433-0145
234 W. King St., Suite 105, Cocoa 32922
Open: Tues.–Fri. 10–5, Sat. 10–4

The door of the R. L. Lewis Gallery opens into a world of Florida landscapes and coastal scenes. Lewis, a Cocoa native, was one of the legendary Florida Highwaymen—a group of African-American artists who traveled the state selling art from their cars because they were denied access to galleries. Today this retired art teacher and member of the Florida Artists Hall of Fame sells his own original works, as well as paintings from fellow Highwaymen.

North Brevard

Historic Titusville is a quiet town, reminiscent of a summer afternoon spent sipping sweet tea on a breezy wraparound porch. The old downtown area sometimes seems on the fence, trying to decide whether to roll up the sidewalks or kick up its heels. Most galleries are working studios, and the artists are available to discuss their works and techniques.

Downtown Gallery

321-268-0122
335 S. Washington Ave., Titusville 32796
Open: Mon.–Fri. 10–5, Sat. 11–3

The beauty and wonder of the area is magically captured through the lens of award-winning photographers Jeff and Heidi Thamert, who use the ocean and outdoor landscape for a backdrop and wildlife for their subjects. A majestic blue heron is frozen in time, posing in the shallow surf rippling along the edge of the Atlantic Ocean. A moon rising over the Indian River Lagoon is forever suspended in a muted, purple sky. Pictures in the gallery are matted, and some are framed—either way, a perfect way to take a small slice of Brevard County home in your suitcase. Chose from a variety of sizes and price ranges.

Photographers at work at Downtown Gallery, Titusville

The Greenwood Gallery
321-268-3362
1520 Garden St., Titusville 32796
Open: Tues.–Fri. 10–5:30, Sat. 10–1

German artist Helene Greenwood came to Titusville with her husband when he was recruited as a participant in the build-up of America's space program in 1964. For more than 30 years she has operated a first-class gallery displaying original fine art along with etchings, serigraphs, and limited-edition posters. Custom framing and art supplies are available. Greenwood may close on Saturday during the summer months, so call ahead.

Peggy Gunnerson Studio & Gallery
321-268-3388
www.gunnerson.com/peggy
11 Main St., Titusville 32796 (in the Gaslight Mall)
Open: Mon.–Sat 9–11:30 and 3–5, by appointment

Three artists, Peggy Gunnerson, Jon R. Miller, and Mary Lou Antes, share this space. All work in acrylic but with very different styles. Many of their large paintings are featured as scenery for Titusville Playhouse productions. Displayed works are always changing. Plan to spend time absorbing this array of thought-provoking works. The artists are all in the studio on Thursday afternoons.

R. Merrill Gordon, Artist

321-268-9732
11 Main St., Titusville 32796 (in the Gaslight Mall)
Open: Mon.–Sat 11–5

After just a few minutes in this tiny Art, Inc. gallery, you're inspired to pick up a brush and create. Award-winning artist Rosemary Gordon displays her own works, as well as those of others she coaches in exploring bold new directions in fine arts. The result is poetry and dance captured on the canvas. Natural materials such as seashells, bamboo, and feathers are incorporated into many of the paintings, giving the scenes a three-dimensional perspective.

South Brevard

EAU GALLIE, MELBOURNE

The town center of Eau Gallie is Highland Avenue, the main thoroughfare for a riverside neighborhood that has long been a gathering spot for creative talent. Two galleries provide an outlet for area artists.

Art and Antique Studio

321-253-5553
1419 Highland Ave., Eau Gallie 32935
Open: Mon.–Fri. 10–5:30, Sat. 9–4

Fun things often come in small packages. Sixteen artists cooperatively display and give classes in this working studio and gallery adjoining an open-air courtyard. The garden decor inside includes a unique blend of styles. An antique table doubles as an easel for displaying contemporary art. Watercolors by founder Therese Ferguson hang alongside sketches of historic Eau Gallie homes.

Fifth Avenue Art Gallery

321-259-8261
www.fifthavenueartgallery.com
1470 Highland Ave., Eau Gallie 32935
Open: Tues.–Sat. 10–5 (Mon. in Nov. and Dec.), Sun. 1–5

Together for more than 30 years, this cooperative of local artists has earned a nationwide reputation for exhibiting high-quality and collectible art. The spacious and bright gallery features an impressive and original array of artistic works, as well as one-of-a-kind jewelry and gift items. New exhibitions are introduced at an opening reception held from 5:30 to 8 on the first Friday of each month. Refreshments are served, admission is free, and the public is invited to attend.

Titusville was named for Col. Henry Titus.
Brevard County Historical Commission

New Haven Avenue, Melbourne

New Haven Avenue in historic downtown Melbourne draws talent from down the street and around the world. The dynamic environment has been home to some artists for many years, while others are new to the area.

Imago Fine Art & Fine Wine

321-728-3938
701 E. New Haven Ave., Melbourne 32901
Open: Tues.–Sat. 11–10, Sun. noon–6

Is this an art gallery with wine or a wine bar with art? Curator and owner Mark Baker has transformed a second-floor space with floor-to-ceiling windows into a showcase for large and colorful fine art. Works by well-known and little-known artists are featured, and you're invited to grab a stool and sip a glass of wine or beer while enjoying the view.

Joyce Schumacher's Studio and Gallery

321-951-7797
909 E. New Haven Ave., Melbourne 32901
Open: Tue. and Wed. 8:30–4, Thurs. and Fri. 11–4, Sat. 10–4

Color and light connect the past and present. For almost 30 years Joyce Schumacher has created impressionistic oil washes set in the 19th and early 20th centuries. The same style carries over into commissioned portraits inspired by her children and grandchildren. Her fine art ranges from $500 to $3,000. The "student gallery" is a collection of wonderful original works at more affordable prices. When traveling, Schumacher discovered the small and colorful raku pottery from South Africa and now sells pieces in her gallery.

LoPressionism Gallery

321-722-6000
www.lopressionism.com
1010B E. New Haven Ave., Melbourne 32901
Open: Mon.–Sat. 11–7, Sun. noon–5

Angela St. Amant has created a sophisticated gallery that is a little off the beaten path but well worth the detour. Music and outdoor paintings lead upstairs into what feels like a metropolitan living room decorated with contemporary fine art from around the world. Talented artists working in all mediums are featured in the regular collection and in rotating shows, such as *Ten Women in Art*, which focuses on diversity in the style and dreams influencing women's art.

Historic Places

Although the area's Native American roots reach back centuries, most local historic sites date from settlements beginning about 150 years ago. A tour of historic places, still existing or captured in memory, provides a close look at the challenges and adventures inherent in taming this small stretch of Florida wilderness.

Cape Canaveral & Cocoa Beach

The footprints of ancient Indians who fished in these ocean waters and gazed out toward the same endless horizon have long since washed away. Only a frayed Spanish map from 1565, now in a museum archive, attests that Canaveral is the oldest, continuous place name in the continental United States. Nature swept away the remnants of a community of freed slaves who settled south of the geographical cape at the start of the 20th century, then moved inland to escape a hurricane. Perhaps the history of a place planted so softly in the sea is meant to be elusive. So with apologies to the Beatles—a magical history tour is waiting to take you away, take you away.

The trip begins at **Jetty Park,** where a monument just across from the playground identifies the Canaveral coast as the site of the last naval battle of the American Revolution, occurring on March 10, 1783. The *Duc de Lauzun,* heavy with gold and silver, was about a mile offshore on its way from Havana to Philadelphia. The treasure was to be used by Congress to fund the new country's first bank and reduce the war debt. Three British ships spotted the vessel and gave chase. Capt. John Barry, commander of the Continental Navy's *Alliance,* came to the defense and fired on the British ships, which then turned and fled. The precious cargo was saved, and the rest, as we know, is history.

In the distance, to the northeast, stands the **Cape Canaveral Lighthouse.** The original brick tower was built in 1848 and replaced in 1868. Launch pads are near the tower, and from a distance the lighthouse is often mistaken for a rocket. The story has been told that Dr. Wernher von Braun, renowned scientist and a leader of the U.S. space program, climbed up to the railed balcony at the top to watch the early launches. The lighthouse is located on Canaveral Air Force Base property and not accessible to the public.

In the heyday of the space program, more than two thousand members of the media descended on the area to watch a rocket launch. Walter Cronkite was often among them, and he might have been talking about the **Mousetrap** when he dubbed Cocoa Beach "sin city." The restaurant and bar was a favorite with astronauts and space workers unwinding at the end of a long and stressful day. The building remains but is reincarnated now as Durango Steakhouse at 5602 N. Atlantic Avenue in Cocoa Beach. Many of the original furnishings are there, including the top of the grand piano, which is now mounted on the wall. Imagine everyone gathered around for a late-night songfest: "Fly me to the moon, and let me play among the stars . . ."

The entrance to the south lot of Lori Wilson Park at 1500 N. Atlantic Avenue has been designated **I Dream of Jeannie Lane** to honor the virtual heritage of Cocoa Beach captured in the 1960s television show. Thank former Cocoa Beach mayor Joe Morgan for creating a great photo opportunity.

Our magical tour ends with an authentic historic landmark, the **Cocoa Beach Community Church,** at 350 S. Orlando Avenue. In 1927, mayor Gus Edwards built the small wooden structure at the request of his mother. A large cast-iron bell, once on top of the building and now housed inside, was dedicated to her. Eighty years later, in a twist that real estate developer Edwards would appreciate, the privately owned building is available for rent.

The Cocoa Beach Community Church was the first church in Cocoa Beach

Central Brevard

Cocoa Village began as a small riverside community and trading center for steamboat travelers. Just south of Cocoa, the town of Rockledge opened resort hotels and developed into a popular stop for visitors arriving by water and later by railroad. The river used to be much wider at Cocoa. About 40 years ago the city deepened the channel, and a dredge was used to expand the shoreline and add Riverfront Park.

The **S. F. Travis Building** at 300 Delannoy Avenue in Cocoa was built in 1907 for Col. Samuel Travis. Conveniently located next to the town wharf, Travis Hardware remains as the oldest existing business in Cocoa. Inside you'll find the original tin ceilings, wood shelving, and hardwood floors.

The **Porcher House** at 434 Delannoy was the home of prosperous citrus farmer Edward Porcher. This prestigious estate, originally on the banks of the Indian River, was built in 1916 using local coquina shell rock. Its turn-of-the-20th-century Classical Revival style, location, and grandeur make it a popular location for weddings. The bride enters from the upstairs balcony and floats down the wide central staircase.

St. Mark's Episcopal Church, 4 N. Church Street, reflects unique touches by the local shipbuilder who designed the building. The first Cocoa Village community service held in the completed church was a Thanksgiving service in November 1887. Originally christened as St. Michael's, the church's name was changed in 1890 in recognition of help received from St. Mark's parish in New Jersey. A coat of stucco was added atop the wooden frame in 1925.

Porcher House

At 401 Delannoy, the **Taylor Bank Building** was home to the first bank of Cocoa, opened by Albert Taylor in 1892. Today it's the Point Bar, but BANK is still visible, etched in brick just below the middle window of the flat-front Masonry Vernacular structure popular at this time. A picture of Delannoy Street on cattle day hangs inside. When a wooden bridge was built across the Indian River in 1917, it opened up a new market for cow hunters in Merritt Island. Cattle were herded across the bridge, down dirt-covered Delannoy, and loaded on boats headed to northern markets.

Looking a little out of place, the ornate marble building at 114 Harrison Street was built in 1925 by the newly arrived **Brevard County Bank & Trust Company.** Inside are the original vaults and chandeliers. The building outlasted the bank, which closed in the crash of 1928.

In 1925, **Trafford and Field Real Estate Firm** remodeled an old garage at 316 Brevard Avenue, turning it into a Mediterranean Revival–style office building. Their mark, T&F, still stands above the entry of what is now the Ossorio bakery and sandwich shop. The unusual and distinctive pecky cypress ceiling is original.

The **Aviles Building,** directly across the street at 310 Brevard, is another example of the Mediterranean Revival style of 1925. Currently occupied by Bailey's Jewelry, the building was the home of Campbell's Drug Store in the 1950s. Imagine grabbing a stool at the lunch counter, enjoying a burger and a Coca-Cola, and catching up on local news.

Cocoa Village Playhouse at 300 Brevard is a magnificent four-story Italian Renaissance building that originally opened as the Aladdin Theatre in 1924, hosting live performances. Motion pictures moved in during the 1940s. For more than a decade, this performing-arts center has been home to *Broadway on Brevard* and other theatrical productions. The building is on the National Register of Historic Places.

Next door, the cream walls of the **Bellaire Arcade** encircle an outdoor courtyard filled with potted plants and tables. Bellaire is French for "beautiful air," and the arcade was originally built in 1925 with stores on the ground floor and offices upstairs.

Rockledge Drive is a scenic byway and a National Historic District. Cocoa and Rockledge have long been considered sister cities, and Cocoa's downtown served both in the early years. Drive, bike, or walk from Cocoa Village via Riverside Drive at the end of Church Street. In just a few blocks the name of the road changes, and a sign marks the transition to the City of Rockledge. A mile down the road, pillars on the right lead into **Valencia Historic District,** a community of homes built during the land boom and designed by local architect Richard W. Rummell. Travel 2 blocks west, turn left on Osceola Drive, and come back east on Orange Avenue. When Henry Flagler brought the railroad to town, he built a spur line to transport visitors to the doors of nearby riverside resorts. The Hotel Indian River, on Rockledge Drive between Orange and Barton, once hosted President Grover Cleveland. The once-grand property disappeared in the 1950s to make room for condos, but the river view, framed by stately live oaks draped in hanging moss, remains. The original City Hall near the corner of Orange and Rockledge Drive is being converted into a Museum of Rockledge History. The **Barton Avenue Residential Historic District,** immediately south on Rockledge between Orange and Barton Avenue, features stately Queen Anne and Victorian homes from the turn of the 20th century. Most are privately owned, but Lawndale, the home of early citizen Hiram Williams, is being renovated and will soon be open to the public.

North Brevard

The roots of the Brevard County family tree are planted in the rich soils and marshes of north Brevard. In 1837, during the Seminole Wars, the U.S. government built Fort Ann to guard the strategic strip between Mosquito Lagoon and the Indian River, and a small center of trading developed nearby. Growth really took off in 1885 when Titusville became a transportation hub, with a railroad spur line connecting inland travelers to steamboats for a scenic excursion down the Indian River. Passengers lining up at the city wharf could not have imagined that less than a century later that sandy spot would be a front-row seat for history in the making—a trip to the moon.

The starting point for a walk through **historic downtown Titusville** is the intersection of Washington Avenue and Broad Street. The first rail service came east down Broad Street and linked to steamboat traffic at the river wharf. By the turn of the 20th century, the East Coast Railway depot was built 2 blocks south on Julia Street. This was the center of commerce. Most of the buildings on Washington date from around 1910 to 1920 and are a simple masonry design constructed following a fire that destroyed earlier wood structures. Stores, banks, and businesses lined the east side; hotels and boardinghouses were across the street. The **Washington Hotel** was on the corner, and you can still see balconies, once shaded with bright awnings. Kloiber's Cobbler Eatery at 337 S. Washington, once **Denham's** dry goods and clothing store, has been restored inside and out to bring back much of the original design features. The **Emma Parrish Theater** on the corner of Julia and S. Hopkins Avenue opened as a venue for silent movies in 1912 and quickly became the community's cultural center. Today it is commonly known as the Titusville Playhouse. Many of the furnishings are original.

St. Gabriel's Episcopal Church, at the corner of Pine Street and Palm Avenue, was built in 1887 with old stand longleaf pine, native to the area. This renovated and expanded neo-Gothic-style church maintains its original character. Names below the stained-glass windows tell the story of the area's early families. Across the street is the **Brevard County Courthouse,** built in 1913 to replace a small wood structure erected in 1882 when Titusville was designated as the county seat. Four large classical columns are at the entrance; the jail was on the third floor. On the opposite corner is the **oldest government building** still standing in the county, a brick and concrete facility built in 1903 for the Clerk of the Court. The 1891 **Pritchard House,** at the corner of Washington and Pine, was home to Capt. James Pritchard and his wife, leading citizens in the growing town. The stately two-story residence built with heart pine is an example of Queen Anne architecture popular in Florida during this period. The upstairs porch on the southeast corner of the second floor would have provided a magnificent view of the Indian River, just a block away at that time. Pritchard family members lived in the home until 2005. It now belongs to the county and is being renovated as a house museum, with original period furnishings throughout.

The historic **LaGrange Church** is just a short drive north to the intersection of Dairy Road and Old Dixie Highway. Built in 1869, it is the oldest Protestant church south of St. Augustine and is restored to its original condition, except for the addition of electricity. Colonel Titus, and civil rights activists Harry and Harriette Moore, are among those buried in the older front section of the shaded church cemetery. An open house is held 10–noon on the third Saturday of each month; the public is welcome.

South Brevard

Development of southern Brevard centered around two inlets, the **Eau Gallie River** bordering the town of Eau Gallie, and **Crane Creek,** the Melbourne harbor area. Eau Gallie is the older settlement, dating from 1859. The name Eau Gallie means "rocky water," referring to the coquina rocks that line the riverbank. By 1885 a boatyard and basin had been built, and the inlet had a reputation as one of the safest deep-water harbors on the east coast. Melbourne settlement began around 1870 when three black men, freed slaves, set up homesteads near Crane Creek. By 1880 the town had a small number of families, who gathered together and voted for the name of Melbourne, after the city in Australia that was once home to the English postmaster.

EAU GALLIE LANDMARKS

The **James Wadsworth Rossetter House,** 1320 Highland Avenue in Eau Gallie, was built in the 1860s and purchased by Rossetter in 1902. His daughters, Caroline and Ella, lived in the home until they donated it to the Florida Historical Society in 1992. The back section of the house was one of the original buildings when there was a pineapple and sugar plantation on the land. Rossetter purchased the front section from a family who lived downriver and rebuilt it in Eau Gallie. Tours of the period home, furnishings, and botanical gardens are conducted daily.

Directly across the street, the **Roesch House** was the home of William R. Roesch, the town's first mayor. The house, a turn-of-the-20th-century Frame Vernacular design common to early Florida, has been restored by the Florida Historical Society and serves as a museum for period pieces of furniture, household goods, and photographs.

The **Winchester Symphony House** is a Florida Cracker frame home built with a wide front porch typical of Eau Gallie homes in the 1890s. It may have originally been a winter residence. Today the offices of the Brevard Symphony Orchestra are located here.

MELBOURNE LANDMARKS

Front Street, the site of the original town of Melbourne business district, runs along a small peninsula between the Indian River and Crane Creek. A fire destroyed most structures in 1919, and the downtown was resurrected along nearby New Haven Avenue. Spared from the flames was the **John and Nannie Lee House** at the corner of Strawbridge and New Haven. Claude Beaujean, a talented carpenter and ferryboat operator, built the home in 1905.

At the intersection of New Haven and US 1, the **Melbourne Hotel,** also known as the 1900 Building, had businesses on the ground floor, such as shops and a barbershop, and rooms on the upper floors to serve northern visitors arriving mostly by train. The "strictly fireproof" building was erected in 1924 as downtown was developing west of the railroad tracks. **Campbell Park,** at New Haven and Melbourne Court, is named for C. J. F. Campbell, the town's first mayor, and was an early gathering spot for community activities.

The Melbourne Hotel Courtesy Brevard County Historical Commission

The nearby and recognizable **Flat Iron Building** is typical of most buildings on New Haven Avenue. The structures were all built in the 1920s, and most still have at least some original exterior designs and interior features. **Kempfer's Grocery,** still operating today at 916 New Haven, was the first local business to install an air conditioner.

The main building of the **Henegar School Complex,** at 625 New Haven Avenue, was built from 1919 to 1921 along what was then a dirt road. The high school was added in 1926. Today the facility is a well-used community performing-arts center.

Return east to Grant Place and walk a block south to Melbourne Avenue. Stately homes such as the Crane Creek Inn built in 1925 are still private residences. **Holmes Park** is across the street, and then the road goes under the wooden railroad track bridge constructed in 1921. Stop and relax at the **Crane Creek Promenade Manatee Observation Area.**

LIBRARIES

Learn more about Brevard County and Florida, or enrich your life with a workshop or lecture, at several libraries with a wealth of resources. Public libraries offer free access to the Internet and WiFi hookup. For a complete list of Brevard County Public Libraries visit their website at www.brev.org.

Cape Canaveral & Cocoa Beach

Cape Canaveral Public Library

321-868-1101
www.brev.org/locations/cape_canaveral/index.htm
201 Polk Ave., Cape Canaveral 32920
Open: Mon., Wed., Fri., and Sat. 9–5; Tues. and Thurs. 9–8; closed Sun

This cozy library located just off A1A offers a really great assortment of movies on tape and DVD, including choices for children and families. Visitors can get a temporary library card by showing a driver's license and copy of a local rental agreement. Two adjoining parks are perfect for outdoor relaxation or reading. Veteran's Memorial Park has picnic tables, benches, and a yard full of mature live oak trees that even adults may be tempted to climb. Xeriscape Park on Taylor Avenue models ideas for conserving water through the use of natural vegetation for landscaping.

Cocoa Beach Public Library

321-868-1104
www.brev.org/locations/cocoa_beach/index.htm
550 N. Brevard Ave., Cocoa Beach 32931
Open: Mon.–Wed. 9–9, Thurs. 9–6, Fri. and Sat. 9–5, Sun. 1–5

Centrally located, the Cocoa Beach library is ideal for visitors and residents looking for a quiet reading room. A newsletter located just inside the front door provides a calendar of presentations, classes, and group meetings covering just about every interest. Speakers almost always attract a crowd, and seating is limited, so arrive early. There's an extensive collection of aerospace books. Stop by the reference desk for guidance in learning more about the local environment and history.

Brevard County

Brevard County Historical Commission

321-433-4415
www.brevardcounty.us/history.
801 Dixon Blvd., Suite 1110, Cocoa 32922

Explore the rich and colorful past of Brevard County online or by stopping by this historical archive. Historians and families with ties to the area can delve into video clips, newspapers, and maps that tell the life stories of Spanish explorers, early settlers, and builders of the space program. A three-volume *History of Brevard County* is available for review or purchase at their office. Hours may vary, so call ahead to arrange a visit.

Central Brevard Library and Reference Center
321-633-1792
www.brev.org/locations/central_brevard/index.htm
308 Forrest Ave., Cocoa 32922
Open: Mon.–Thurs. 9–9, Fri. 9–6, Sat. 9–5, Sun. 1–5

Located just a few blocks from historic Cocoa Village, this is the largest library in the
Brevard County system and a great resource for studying the past. Michael Boonstra, certified genealogist and historian, oversees an extensive collection of Brevard County records,
including newspaper archives; marriage, real estate, and probate records; maps; and some
city directories. Records from around the world are also available, as well as online access
to the more popular family-history search engines.

Florida Historical Society Library of Florida History
321-690-1971
www.florida-historical-soc.org
435 Brevard Ave., Cocoa 32922
Open: Tues.–Sat. 10–4:30

This statewide society has been collecting, preserving, and publishing Florida history for
more than 150 years and now occupies the site of the first Cocoa post office in historic
Cocoa Village. An extensive collection of manuscripts, papers, maps, and other materials
are available for on-site research. The Print Shoppe offers books about Florida or by
Florida writers, including a large selection for children. Join the Saturday Lecture Series,
with talks by local historians and authors, at 2 PM. Events are scheduled on two Saturdays
each month. Call ahead for more information.

Indian River Lagoon House
321-725-7775
www.mrcirl.org
3275 Dixie Highway NE, Palm Bay 32905
Open: Mon.–Sat. 9–5

The Marine Resources Council operates this resource center, which overlooks the Indian
River Lagoon. Exhibits, photographs, and artifacts depict the development of Brevard
County, and a large model provides a three-dimensional look at the lagoon. The council
library contains extensive data and information about the history of the lagoon and the
natural resources of Brevard County. To get there, take US 1 southbound (Dixie Highway
NE) to Stephen Drive, 1.8 miles past US 192 in Melbourne.

Mosquito Beaters
www.mosquitobeaters.org
435 Brevard Ave., Cocoa 32922

Speedy Harrell is the founder and record keeper for this group of longtime Brevard County
residents, who are dedicated to researching and recording the history of the area once called
Mosquito County. Photographs, books, maps, and recorded stories are available to researchers
by visiting Speedy's desk in the Florida Historical Society Library of Florida History.

MOVIES

Cape Canaveral & Cocoa Beach

Merritt Square 16
321-459-3737
www.cobbtheatres.com/merritt.htm
Merritt Square Mall
777 E. Merritt Island Cswy., Merritt Island 32952
Directions: Merritt Square Mall is located on the north side of FL 520, 4.7 miles west of A1A.

Central Brevard

Satellite Beach Cinemas
321-777-3778
www.dtmovies.com
Atlantic Shopping Center Plaza
1024 A1A, Satellite Beach 32937
Directions: Atlantic Shopping Center Plaza is located on the west side of A1A, 12 miles south of FL 520.

Rave Motion Pictures Avenue 16
321-775-1210
www.ravemotionpictures.com
The Avenue Viera
2241 Town Center Ave., Viera 32940
Directions: Take FL 520 westbound to I-95; go south on I-95 to exit 195. Turn right onto Wickham Road and then right onto Town Center Avenue.

MUSEUMS

Brevard County's cultural landscape is preserved in several entertaining, informative, and reasonably priced museums. As in most areas, government or foundation funding usually subsidizes the operations, and the budgets don't allow for much marketing. Several museums have plugged into a cooperative venture, the MOB (Museums of Brevard) Tour. Pick up a brochure from any participant, and you'll get a 10 percent discount on all museum admissions. There are also special promotions periodically, so check their Web site at www.museumsofbrevard.org.

Cape Canaveral & Cocoa Beach

East Coast Surfing Hall of Fame Museum
321-799-8840
www.ecsurfinghallandmuseum.org
4275 N. Atlantic Ave., Cocoa Beach 32920
Open: Daily 8–8 Admission: Free; $2 donation requested

Surfing has been the cornerstone of Cocoa Beach culture for more than 50 years. Inside this museum, the history of the sport is told through art, exhibits, photographs, music, and surfboards. One display features Waikiki native Duke Kahanamoku, the most famous beach boy of his time—an Olympic swimmer and "the father of modern surfing." Hall of Fame members are recognized in plaques and pictures, including the infamous Jack "Murph the Surf" Murphy, who is credited with introducing surfing to the East Coast. The Tiki Theater features surfing movies. Recent exhibits focus on the Waterman's challenge and next generation of competitive surfers, including world champion Kelly Slater, who grew up and learned the craft on the shores of Cocoa Beach. The atmosphere is casual, the karma is good, and the waves are rolling.

East Coast Surfing Hall of Fame Museum

Central Brevard

Brevard Museum of History and Natural Science
321-632-1830
www.brevardmuseum.org
2201 Michigan Ave., Cocoa 32926
Open: Mon.–Sat. 10–4
Admission: Adults $6, seniors and military $5.50, ages 5–16 $4.50

Every community has a few hidden gems, and this museum, with a goal of making history come alive, is such a find in Brevard County. Everyone in the family will enjoy the interpretive exhibits, historic artifacts, and scientific specimens that guide you through the natural and social evolution of the area. An Ais Indian village display provides a look at how Brevard's earliest settlers lived. A Cracker house and furnishings re-create a time when cowboys carried and cracked long, leather whips to herd cattle, kill rattlesnakes, and communicate danger with a Morse Code–like pattern. Step to the edge of the dock and walk into a display about the diverse Indian River Lagoon habitat. Outside, learn about native plants and wildlife while strolling through 22 acres of nature trails. To get to the museum, take FL 520 to US 1, head north 2.6 miles to Michigan Avenue, and then turn left 1.1 miles to the museum.

North Brevard

American Police Hall of Fame and Museum
321-264-0911
www.aphf.org
6350 Horizon Dr., Titusville 32780 (west of the entrance to the Kennedy Space Center Visitor Complex)
Open: Daily 10–6; closed Christmas and Thanksgiving
Admission: Adults $12; seniors, military, and children $8

Law enforcement officers and family members of those killed on duty are admitted free to this museum, which pays homage to America's police force. A memorial to officers killed in the line of duty since 1960 includes a dedicated exhibit to personnel who perished on September 11, 2001. Entertaining exhibits trace the history of law enforcement, crime, and punishment from the days when bad behavior was punished with a visit to the guillotine. Reality and mythology mix with displays about the mobsters of the 1920s next to cars and memorabilia from television and the movies. Learn how a crime lab works or hop on a police motorcycle. The entire facility is kid-friendly, and in the Discovery Zone youngsters practice dialing 911, hear tips for staying safe, and make their own police officer badge to take home. The $40 Big Ticket covers museum admission, instruction and ammo on the gun range, and a 150-mile-per-hour helicopter ride. For just a helicopter ride, contact Katabi Helicopter Tour at 321-231-0802.

Harry T. & Harriette V. Moore Cultural Center
321-264-6595
www.brevardparks.com/htm/intro_htm.htm
2180 Freedom Ave., Mims 32754
Open: Mon.–Fri. 9–7, Sat. noon–4
Admission: Free

The story of civil rights pioneers Harry T. and Harriette V. Moore is the centerpiece of this center. A narrative and timeline of photographs place their experience in the context of African-American and civil rights history, and knowledgeable staffers are available to answer questions. This young nonprofit organization is just beginning to build a collection of documents, memorabilia, and artifacts. Performing-arts programs and classes are offered at the facility, and a picket fence surrounds the site of the Moores's home, adjacent to the museum. To get there, follow US 1 for 2.6 miles north of Main Street in downtown Titusville. Turn left on Parker Street. Freedom Road is 0.4 mile farther on the left.

North Brevard Historical Museum
321-269-3658
301 S. Washington Ave., Titusville 32796
Open: Tues.–Sat. 10–3
Admission: Free; donations appreciated

Try the stockade at the American Police Hall of Fame and Museum.

The rooms of this cozy facility, located in the center of historic Titusville, are chock-full of books, artifacts, and photographs telling the stories of north Brevard. One room focuses on tools and technologies used by early farmers and craftsmen; another includes household furnishings and decor. Visitors will enjoy a visual trip through the late 19th and early 20th centuries. Residents or others with roots in this area may find pictures of themselves or ancestors in school yearbooks and records of local organizations. The museum also displays uniforms representing every service branch.

South Brevard

Brevard Art Museum

321-242-0737
www.brevardartmuseum.org
1463 Highland Ave., Melbourne 32935
Open: Tues.–Sat. 10–5, Sun. 1–5
Admission: Adults $5, seniors $3, children and students with ID $2, free on Thurs.

Brevard's premier fine-arts museum is located in the heart of old Eau Gallie. Throughout five galleries, works from permanent holdings are blended with outstanding traveling exhibits to present a constantly shifting landscape of visual arts. The museum collection is an eclectic mix of contemporary and traditional, playful and dignified, and represents a myriad of cultures through artifacts such as Chinese porcelain, Egyptian statuettes, and Tibetan costumes. Frequent special exhibits feature regional and international artists working in a variety of media. Take a leisurely self-guided tour or join a docent-led group. Call ahead for information on special events such as receptions and lectures. The first Friday of every month is Jazz Friday, with evening performances from 5:30 to 7:30. Admission is $10. The museum and most events are free to museum members. To get there, take A1A to FL 518 and turn right on Highland Avenue.

Children's Hands-On Center

Brevard Art Museum
321-242-0737
www.brevardartmuseum.org.
1463 Highland Ave., Melbourne 32935
Open: Tues.–Sat. 10–5, Sun. 1–5
Admission: Included in admission to the museum

Young patrons will enjoy this hands-on corner of the museum, designed to feed the spirit and expand the imagination. Through exhibits, experiments, and interactive media, children explore space, the earth, weather, physics, and technology. Every Wednesday afternoon from at 4, art activities mix with fun and laughter for Art in the Park, a free program held at Pineapple Park, just across the street from the museum.

MUSIC AND NIGHTLIFE

"And they danced by the light of the moon, the moon. They danced by the light of the moon," said the owl to the pussycat in the poem by Edward Lear. Soft lights, bright lights, and moonlight mix with music throughout Brevard County, especially at the beach, where you'll find almost every musical genre. At many restaurants, live entertainment accompanies dinner, but at several locations music is the main course. Some areas have evolved into centers for dancing; club-hopping; imbibing, if you like; and savoring a feast for the ears. Web sites often post upcoming talents and events. Unless otherwise noted, smoking is permitted, and there is no cover charge.

Cocoa Beach & Cape Canaveral

Groucho's Comedy Club (900 N. Atlantic Ave., Cocoa Beach; 321-799-2557) opens its doors every Thursday night for live comedy performances. The chemistry changes each week with a different mix of comedians and audience. Bring an open mind and sense of humor, and you'll have a great time. The topics and language are for adults only in this no-smoking facility. Shows start at 9:00. Reservations are suggested, but in the off-season tickets are usually available at the door.

The Cove at Port Canaveral is a waterside entertainment center blending melodies and sea breezes until the wee hours of the morning. Convenient and affordable taxi service is available between beach hotels and the port clubs. Locals and visitors meet and mingle at the outdoor **Tiki Bar at Grills** (505 Glen Cheek Dr.), where bands perform Friday night, Saturday afternoon and evening, and Sunday afternoon. Dress is casual, the mood is fun, and classic rock music keeps the dance floor hopping. Relax on the upper deck at **Fishlips Waterfront Bar & Grill** (610 Glen Cheek Dr.), a gathering spot for young and old. Dance to live entertainment on Friday and Saturday, or a DJ on Wednesday. Join in on the karaoke on Thursday. Sports fans can catch the game on one of the big-screen TVs. Open the door to live music, gourmet appetizers, and a martini for every taste at the upscale **Redhead Martini and Cigar Bar** (626 Glen Cheek Dr.). Indoor and outdoor seating are available, and owners Thomas and Ninette (the redhead) Mamczur guarantee a good time. Come as you are and enjoy live entertainment on Friday, Saturday, and Sunday on the outside deck at **Rusty's Seafood & Oyster Bar** (628 Glen Cheek Dr.). Boaters returning from excursions and fishing trips mix with landlubbers cooling off after a day at the beach.

Bars dot A1A in Cocoa Beach like seashells scattered along the shoreline. Ocean waves fill in the backbeat for live music at the **Cocoa Beach Pier** (401 Meade; 783-7549). Stop by the open-air **Oh Shucks Seafood Bar** for Sing-Out-Loud Karaoke on Tuesday or Cool Runnin' Reggae on Wednesday. On the weekends, music blends with the sound of surf on the **Boardwalk**, where local house band Birks & Dugan has perfected the art of beach entertainment. For a change of pace, stop down the road at **Paddy Cassidy's Irish Pub** (2009 N. Atlantic Ave.). Guinness and 20 other beers are on tap. Expect some Gaelic tunes and an occasional Irish jig as part of the live entertainment every Wednesday through Saturday. A wee bit of outdoor seating is a breath of fresh air for nonsmokers.

The **Beach Shack Blues Bar** (1 Minutemen Cswy.), located where the road meets the sand at the end of Minutemen Causeway, is the premier spot for blues in central Florida. Each week six bands from all over the world stage shows: inside on Thursday, Friday, Saturday, and Sunday nights; on the beachfront deck on Saturday and Sunday afternoons. Manager Bill, who hails from Detroit, has created a juke-joint atmosphere that attracts blues lovers of every age. Directly across the street, join the party at the **Coconuts on the Beach** deck (2 Minutemen Cswy). Cover bands entertain after-dinner and late-night partiers and dancers from Tuesday through Sunday. During spring break and summer, expect a young, hip, and sometimes rowdy crowd.

Heidi's Jazz Club (7 N. Orlando Ave., 321-783-4559; www.heidisjazzclub.com) has been a cozy retreat for jazz lovers on the Space Coast since the 1990s. The club is open Tuesday through Sunday from 5 PM to 1 AM and features world-class live entertainment. Sunday night is an open-mike jam session. The dress code, atmosphere, drinks, and prices are a little more upscale than the typical beach bar, but this is a first-class showroom decorated in warm reds and soft lights, and dotted with small tables covered with white linen cloths. Food may be ordered off the lighter bar menu or from the full dinner menu of the adjoining Heidelberg's restaurant. Smoking is allowed at the bar, but the size of the room and extensive ventilation keep the rest of the club relatively smoke-free. Special shows require a ticket purchase, and reservations are recommended. Across the street, **Big Licks Cigar Lounge** is a quiet gathering spot open until 2 am. Enjoy a full liquor bar, walk-in humidor, and local musicians on the weekends.

Central Brevard

Cocoa Village is taking baby steps to attract and keep crowds into the evening hours. **The Point** (401 Delannoy Ave.) is a stylish bar and dance club. Upstairs, **Zen Bar** has a more relaxed atmosphere and quieter music. Both locations are 21-and-older and feature live entertainment. Suggested attire is casual but nice. Open Monday through Thursday 4–midnight, Friday and Saturday 4–2 AM; closed Sunday. The **Dog 'n' Bone** (9 Stone St.) is just what you'd expect an English pub to be. Smoky rooms are crowded with twentysomethings enjoying conversation, darts, and music. Upstairs, a DJ spins Top 40 dance music; downstairs live musicians play rock or reggae from Thursday through Saturday. Patrons must be 21 years old, and the bar is open until 2 AM Wednesday through Saturday.

South Brevard

On Friday and Saturday nights, historic downtown Melbourne is transformed into a trendy, urban gathering spot. **Mainstreet Pub** (705 E. New Haven Ave.) is a bright two-story outdoor bar catering to young professionals. Smooth piano or acoustic guitar music is the backdrop at **Moonstruck Wine Company** (836 E. New Haven Ave.), a comfortable indoor and outdoor spot offering fine wines, appetizers, tempting desserts, and coffees and espressos—a nice complement to dinner at one of the nearby restaurants. The **Executive Cigar Shop & Lounge** (832 E. New Haven Ave.) has an old-world feel. Cigar buffs will enjoy the walk-in humidor. Relax and kick back at **Foo Bar & Lotus Gallery** (816 E. New Haven Ave.)—a relaxing indoor patio bar serving light snacks and cocktails. **Club 702** (702 E. New Haven Ave.) pulses with a Latin beat. The dance club DJ spins Mexican and Central American music on Friday, the Caribbean sound on Saturday.

Lou's Blues Upstairs (3191 N. A1A, Indialantic; 779-2299) is a two-story waterfront bar just south of A1A and FL 518. The view from the upstairs deck is one of the best on the beach. Live music plays every night at this good-time tavern and dance hall—mostly blues, but also rock classics, jam bands, and karaoke. Occasionally, special performances or fund-raisers will require a separate event ticket. A full menu is available. As you might guess, a popular choice is the "bluesburger," a burger with blue cheese.

PERFORMING ARTS

In Brevard County, the King Center for the Performing Arts in Melbourne is the star of professional productions, featuring the Brevard Symphony Orchestra and Space Coast

Ballet, as well as an array of world-renowned musicals, plays, and headliners. A talented and entertaining supporting cast includes several community theaters with deep roots and a reputation for excellence, and other local groups that appear in smaller venues.

Cape Canaveral & Cocoa Beach

Surfside Playhouse

321-783-3127
www.surfsideplayers.com
300 Ramp Rd., Cocoa Beach 32931
For more than 25 years, the Surfside Players have staged high-quality theatrical productions in Brevard's only beachside venue, the Surfside Playhouse. Every seat in the house is
a good one in this small, comfortable facility that features traditional works, like *Our Town*
or *A Chorus Line*, as well as shows targeted to families and children. Productions appealing
to more contemporary audiences are presented under the Second Stage brand. Summer
programs provide theatrical arts education and experience to young people.

Central Brevard

Brevard Theatrical Ensemble

321-676-0697
www.brevardensemble.com
Lady Gail B. Ryan leads this troupe of storytellers, who blend medieval tales with
Renaissance music and theater. Performances are held in venues throughout the area.
Reserve ahead for recurring shows that sell out, including *Celtic Tales* in March, *Canterbury
Tales* during the summer, and *Isitsoornot,* a favorite during the Halloween season. An
evening of *Dickens of a Christmas* adds a twisted candy cane of fun to holiday plans.

Historic Cocoa Village Playhouse

321-636-5050
www.cocoavillage.com/playhouse
300 Brevard Ave., Cocoa 32922

This beautiful performing-arts venue has had many reincarnations since opening in 1924.
Today the restored five-hundred-seat facility features Brevard Community College's
Broadway on Brevard Series, bringing entertaining, top-quality musical productions to the
local community. Showings of *A Christmas Carol* have become an annual tradition for many
area families.

Melbourne Chamber Music Society

321-956-8775
www.melbournechambermusicsociety.com
P.O. Box 033403, Indialantic 32903

Fine musicians from around the world perform classical music at St. Marks United
Methodist Church in Indialantic, 18 miles south of FL 520 and A1A. Tickets are $30; $10
for students.

A scene from The Seven Year Itch, *performed by the Surfside Players*

North Brevard

Titusville Playhouse at Emma Parrish Theater
321-268-1125
www.titusvilleplayhouse.com
301 Julia St., Titusville 32796

This lovely and well-designed venue is steeped in nearly a century of tradition. Enjoy favorites like *Cabaret, On Golden Pond,* and *The Glass Menagerie* in the main auditorium, with floor and balcony seating, and great acoustics. Upstairs in Emma's Attic, edgier works offer an alternative theater experience. The facility is a popular spot for presentations by local musicians and other community groups.

South Brevard

Brevard Symphony Orchestra
Orchestra in Residence at King Center for the Performing Arts
321-242-2024
www.brevardsymphony.com
1500 Highland Ave., Melbourne 32936

More than 50 years ago, a group of Brevard musicians joined forces to accompany a presentation of *The Mikado.* Today, the Brevard Symphony Orchestra is one of the finest in the country. Maestro Christopher Confessore conducts talented musicians in an extensive repertoire of performances. The group offers a "teaching concert" for fifth-grade students each year, as well as a free family concert as part of their fall season. The orchestra's offices are housed in the historic Winchester Symphony House, built in 1886.

Brevard Symphony Youth Orchestra
Most concerts at King Center for the Performing Arts
321-254-9583
www.bsyo.org

With the belief that music can excite the human spirit and stimulate the imagination, founders of this organization bring together two hundred of the most talented young musicians in Brevard County. Orchestra members, from elementary level to high school, commit to a weekly schedule of rehearsals and performances. Professional and seasoned conductors lead a symphony orchestra, concert orchestra, and string ensemble.

Henegar Center for the Arts
321-723-8698
www.henegar.org
625 E. New Haven Ave., Melbourne 32901

This facility opened in 1919 as the Melbourne School. The building is named for Ruth Henegar, a teacher and principal, and is a learning center for creative workshops as well as a center for performing arts. The five-hundred-seat theater is a perfect setting for intimate and eclectic presentations.

Maxwell C. King Center for the Performing Arts

321-242-2219
www.kingcenter.com
3865 N. Wickham, Melbourne 32935

Concerts, Broadway musicals, dramas, and presentations for children ensure this facility is busy almost every week. The main stage features world-renowned performers in touring shows, concerts, and comedy performances. The cozier Studio Theatre offers offbeat productions, with an invitation to join the artists at a Tuesday opening-night reception following the show. The King Center is also the resident venue for many of Brevard County's most talented artistic groups.

Melbourne Civic Theatre

321-723-6935
www.mymct.org
817 E. Strawbridge Ave., Melbourne 32901

Brevard County's oldest community theater group stages several plays each season, some from early Broadway and others more contemporary productions. Most are funny, and all are entertaining. The space is small, so this is a very intimate theater experience. Dinner theater is sometimes offered, but not on a consistent schedule. Acting classes are available.

Space Coast Ballet

Most performances at King Center for the Performing Arts
321-253-0544
www.spacecoastballet.com.

Former Kirov dancers Boris Chepelev and Janna Kirova direct the Space Coast's only professional ballet company. The troupe dances classical ballets, like their annual performance of *The Nutcracker,* as well as modern works developed by today's most talented choreographers. Each summer they introduce the medium of ballet to children and novices with their presentation of *The Making of a Ballet.*

Seasonal Events

Seasonal changes are subtle in Florida. Soft, translucent spring leaves grow bold in the summer and deepen to a rich forest green in winter. Whatever the time of year, fun and festive events are planned. Because the weather is so nice, many events are outdoors and near the water. A few of the most popular and unique to the area are the Grant Seafood Festival and South Brevard Strawberry Festival, both held in the spring, and the Space Coast Art Festival and Cocoa Beach Christmas Boat Parade during the holiday season. Dates and times vary each year, so check details before heading out. The Brevard Cultural Alliance maintains an events calendar; call 321-690-6819 or log on to www.artsbrevard.org.

Monthly

Cocoa Village Friday Fest (Cocoa Riverfront Park, Delannoy St.). On the fourth Friday night of each month, step into an old-fashioned family festival set alongside the banks of the picturesque Indian River. Music is staged in the amphitheater; vendors offer everything from hot dogs to temporary tattoos. Historic Cocoa Village borders the park, and galleries, restaurants, and shops remain open for the evening.

Downtown Melbourne's Friday Fest (New Haven Ave. near US 1, Melbourne). Join the street party beginning at 6 PM on the second Friday of each month, except December. Fun spills into the streets when New Haven Avenue is closed to traffic, bands set up on the sidewalks, and shops and restaurants open their doors.

Eau Gallie First Friday (Highland Ave., downtown Eau Gallie). Galleries and restaurants roll out the red carpet on the first Friday of each month. The Brevard Art Museum presents Jazz Friday, an evening ticketed event that includes a concert and access to the museum. Gallery schedules show openings and receptions.

Historic Titusville Art Walk (Washington Ave. and Broad St., Titusville). Browse through galleries offering an evening of art discovery. Many of the works reflect the dual influences of nature and space travel. Get a brochure stamped at each participating gallery to enter a drawing for a chance to win an impressive basket of gifts. The event kicks off at on the third Friday evening of each month.

Downtown Melbourne's Friday Fest

January

Cape Canaveral Fine Arts Show (321-636-3673; www.brevardart.org; Cape Canaveral Library, 201 Polk Ave., Cape Canaveral 32920). The Central Brevard Arts Association kicks off their year with an amazing showcase of member talent at this small community show. The organization, committed to promoting the visual arts in this area, holds several other exhibits throughout the year. The event is held in late January.

Sebastian Inlet Pro Surfing Competition (Sebastian Inlet). See the Beaches and Surfing chapter for information.

Space Coast Birding & Wildlife Festival (www.nbbd.com/fly; Brevard Community College Campus, 1311 N. US 1, Titusville 32796). For more than a decade, birders and environmentalists from around the world have gathered in north Brevard for a week dedicated to showcasing how science and technology benefit wildlife. Rated as the nation's top birding and wildlife event, the SCBWF is held in January, when the bird population is at its peak and rare species are in the area. Renowned experts offer classes and demonstrations covering every aspect of the hobby, and guided field trips begin at daybreak. Mingle with other birders at an opening reception, or pick up new ideas and information at the exhibit center.

February

Grant Seafood Festival (www.grantseafoodfestival.com). Nearly 40 years ago, the town of Grant, located 12 miles south of Melbourne off US 1, held a fish fry to raise money for the community center. Today, the still-small town of 2,400 sponsors this all-volunteer event, which has become the Southeast's largest and longest-running seafood festival—attracting nearly 50,000 people over two days. Expect live entertainment, handmade crafts, and special exhibits, but the main attraction is the seafood: clams, crab, scallops, shrimp, oysters, conch fritters, and all the fixin's! The festival held the last weekend in February; admission and parking are free.

Greek Festival (321-254-1045; St. Katherine's Greek Orthodox Church, 5965 N. Wickham Rd., Melbourne 32940). For more than 35 years, St. Katherine's has sponsored a two-day celebration of Greek culture. Enjoy authentic foods, dance, music, and, of course, ouzo. Fantastiko!

Indiafest (1-877-724-0101; www.indiafestbrevard.org; Wickham Park Pavilion, Melbourne). Sample the amazingly diverse foods and fashions of India, a country where more than a billion people speak a dozen languages. This weekend-long festival includes music and dance programs, yoga demonstrations, palm readings, and even advice on how to wear a sari. Organizers use the event to raise money for local and international charities.

Space Coast Mardi Gras (321-639-3500; www.spacecoastmardigras.com; Cocoa Village and Riverfront Park, Cocoa). The City of Cocoa sponsors this family carnival, and gates to the ticketed midway of rides, games, and concessions open at 5 PM on Thursday and Friday and noon on Saturday and Sunday. Lots of activities are free, including concerts at the River Park Amphitheatre. A boisterous and spirited crowd fills the street for the Saturday-night masquerade party and parade starting at 9 pm. Sunday festivities begin with a church service at 10; free admission to the midway begins at noon with Paws in the Park, presented by the Central Brevard Humane Society.

March

Calema Midwinters Windsurfing Festival (321-422-5362; www.calema.com; Kelly Park, Merritt Island). World Cup professionals, Olympic-class competitors, and amateurs of all ages compete for four days. Races are held in the Banana River off Kelly Park. Participants and spectators enjoy this premier event, which is also a stunning display of color.

Cocoa Beach Jazz Fest (Heidi Deleuil, 321-783-4559; www.cocoabeachjazzfest.com). Every spring, jazz artists from around the world gather in Cocoa Beach for a three-day musical extravaganza. One admission price for each day opens the door to multiple shows featuring legendary musicians, as well as talented newcomers.

St. Patrick's Day Parade (321-724-1741; www.downtownmelbourne.com; downtown Melbourne). Irish and the Irish at heart wear the green proudly at this daylong party in downtown Melbourne. The streets are closed to traffic, the Ancient Order of the Hibernians puts on an afternoon parade, and Meg O'Malley's Restaurant and Irish Pub delivers traditional music, food, and drink. 'Tis said that God needed laughter in the world, so he made the Irish. Enjoy the party!

South Brevard Strawberry Festival (321-255-5800; www.brevardhabitat.com; Wickham Park Pavilion, Melbourne). Bring family, friends, and a big appetite to this festive get-together sponsored by Brevard Habitat for Humanity. Musical entertainment, craft exhibits, and a classic car show are window dressing for the main event—fresh-picked, red, ripe strawberries piled high over shortcake, spooned over rich vanilla ice cream, or dipped in chocolate. The fun starts with a pancake breakfast at 7 and continues until 5. The event is held the first Saturday in March.

TICO Warbird Airshow (321-268-1941; www.vacwarbirds.org; Space Coast Regional Airport, US 1 and FL 405, Titusville). For three days in March, the skies over Titusville come alive with aircraft. The lineup changes each year, but expect everything from vintage planes to powerful fighter jets. The closing show on Sunday is always the Missing Man Formation. Purchase a ticket for each day or a pass for the entire event.

April

Art on the River (321-267-3036; www.titusville.org; Sand Point Park, Titusville). Spring is the ideal season for this two-day fine art and crafts show at Sand Point Park by the Indian River. The juried event, sponsored jointly by the Titusville Area Chamber of Commerce and downtown merchants, brings together accomplished artists and talented crafters. Enjoy live music, food, and children's activities.

Easter sunrise services (various locations). Greet Easter morning at one of many services held along the beaches. Contact your denomination of choice to get information on the spot you might prefer, or just head to the beach and join one of the services held between Jetty Park and the Minutemen Causeway. Most begin about a half hour before sunrise to get the full effect of the golden glow sneaking over the horizon. Dolphins often make an appearance when the ocean is calm. Bring a chair or beach towel, dress comfortably, and celebrate a new day. Parking is a challenge. Use one of the public parking lots, or consider walking from your hotel.

Images in Art (321-868-1320; Manatee Sanctuary Park, Cape Canaveral). Beautiful Manatee Sanctuary Park, along the banks of the Banana River, is the perfect backdrop for this showing of fine art. Held the first Saturday and Sunday in April, the event is hosted by the City of Cape Canaveral and the Central Brevard Arts Association.

Indian River Festival (321-267-3036; www.nbbd.com/festivals/IRF; Sand Point Park, Titusville). Sand Point Park comes alive with rides, games, concerts, an arts and crafts show, and tasty treats. This is one of Brevard County's longest-running events, kicking off on a Thursday in late April and running through Sunday.

Melbourne Art Festival (321-722-1964; www.melbournearts.org; downtown Melbourne). Art lovers will enjoy this juried art show, featuring more than 250 participants and ranked among the top 25 art shows in the country. The streets of historic downtown Melbourne are filled with exhibits and workshops. An entire section is dedicated to hands-on activities and free stage performances just for kids. Top this all off with an abundance of food and entertainment. Because of the crowds, this event does not allow pets (except service animals), roller blades, skateboards, or coolers.

Ron Jon Easter Surfing Festival (Cocoa Beach Pier and Shepard's Park, Cocoa Beach). See the Beaches and Surfing chapter for information.

May

Beachfest at Cocoa Beach Pier (Cocoa Beach). See the Beaches and Surfing chapter for information.

June

Teen Fest (321-455-1380; www.spacecoastteens.com; Kiwanis Island, off FL 520 on Merritt Island, just west of the Cocoa Beach Cswy). This annual musical event, held by and for teens, rocks. Continuous performances on two stages beginning at 4 PM feature local bands and artists, and a freestyle rap competition. Preregister to participate in extreme sports. Event ends at 9 PM.

Wildlife Profile: Roseate Spoonbill

If the local wildlife community had a red-carpet night, the roseate spoonbill would garner all the attention. The wading bird stands about 3 feet high and has bright red eyes, long pink legs, and a white back, neck, and chest. A feather shawl, in hues of rosy pink fringed in coral, wraps around the lower back, wings, and belly. The roseate spoonbill is named for its unique feature, a flat bill that is narrow at the top and spoon-shaped at the end.

Its beauty was nearly the downfall of the glamorous bird. Turn-of-the-20th-century travelers shot the roseate spoonbill to use the sought-after colorful plumage for hats and fans. Today the population has recovered. Bird lovers capture photographic images of these majestic flyers as they travel in a row with their legs and long necks extended straight out, wings stretching to a span of 4 feet.

Roseate spoonbill (Ajaia ajaja) |Jim Angy

The sociable creatures thrive in coastal flats and often live in large colonies with herons, egrets, and other roseate spoonbills. They forage by sweeping their bill from side to side. When prey is detected by touch, the bill snaps shut on a crustacean, snail, small fish, or marine insect. In the spring, a male and female will mate and roost in the mangroves. They stay together to build a nest and care for the eggs and young. Eggs incubate for about 22 days, and the babies develop and learn to fly five or six weeks later. Immature roseate spoonbills are all white with a slight pink color on the tip of their wings. They are adults by about three years of age.

Space Coast Sightings: Black Point Wildlife Drive at the Merritt Island National Wildlife Refuge, Wild Florida exhibit at Brevard Zoo.

Waterman's Challenge Surf Contest Weekend (Holiday Inn Cocoa Beach–Oceanfront, Cocoa Beach). See the Beaches and Surfing chapter for information.

July

Fourth of July on the Beach (Cocoa Beach). Bring a blanket, a picnic basket, and some patriotic tunes on a boom box for a spectacular fireworks show staged from a barge in the water off Cocoa Beach. The show begins just after sunset.

  Herbert L. Shulman Memorial Fourth of July Concert (321-242-2024; www.brevardsymphony.com; Riverfront Park, Cocoa). The park turns red, white, and blue at this free all-day celebration sponsored for the community by the Brevard Symphony Orchestra. The concert of patriotic and Pops classics begins at 8 PM. The day ends with fireworks over the river.

August

Let's Celebrate Greece (321-433-7355; www.brevardcc.edu/moorecenter; Moore Multicultural Center, Brevard Community College–Cocoa, 1519 Clearlake Rd., Cocoa 32922). Enjoy traditional Greek music, folk dancing, art, and food at this evening event.

September

National Kidney Foundation of Florida Pro-Am Surf Festival (Lori Wilson Park, Cocoa Beach). See the Beaches and Surfing chapter for information.

  Family Salsa Festival (Wickham Park, Melbourne). Follow the sounds of rhythmic salsa music, and the savory aroma of island seasonings, to the Wickham Park pavilion. This one-day event features live music, culinary treats, children's activities, and a Miss Puerto Rico contest. United Third Bridge, an organization dedicated to Hispanic education and culture, sponsors the festival.

October

Meg-O-Ween (www.downtownmelbourne.com; New Haven Ave., downtown Melbourne). On the Saturday closest to Halloween, crowds of young and not-so-young adults spill onto New Haven Avenue for an outrageous and over-the-top good time. Families with children may want to head home as evening activities begin. The highlight is a risqué costume contest. The event is sponsored by Meg O'Malley's and has become a Space Coast tradition.

  Polish American Festival (321-633-3099; www.nbbd.com/festivals/polish; Fox Lake Park, Titusville). Grab your partner and get ready to polka. This ticketed event, held the first Sunday in October, is an afternoon celebration of the Polish culture. Traditional foods are available for purchase.

  Space Coast Oktoberfest (321-633-4028; www.space-coast.com; Wickham Park Pavilion, Melbourne). In 1810 a celebration was held in Munich, Germany, to commemorate a royal marriage. Now mid-October is a traditional time to enjoy German music, dance, food, and beer. The party begins on Friday night and continues through the weekend.

November

ArtWorks of Eau Gallie Fine Art Festival (www.artworksofeaugallie.org; Highland Ave., Eau Gallie). For two days in mid-November, Highland Avenue is transformed into an outdoor working art studio. More than one hundred local artists display their works while creating new works and demonstrating their technique at the same time. Community musicians and food vendors add to this hometown event.

Festival of Trees (www.kingcenter.com; King Center for the Performing Arts, 3865 N. Wickham, Melbourne 32935). A stroll through this forest of creative and themed Christmas trees marks the unofficial start of the holiday season in Brevard County. The Junior League of South Brevard sponsors this event, which benefits local organizations. Bid on a fully decorated tree, or just enjoy refreshments, crafts, and a visit with Santa.

Melbourne Independent Filmmakers Festival (www.3boysproductions.com; Melbourne). This weekend of movie screenings, workshops, and activities promotes local filmmakers and a general interest in film. Buy a weekend pass or tickets to individual events, including a VIP reception and courtyard party for adults and children. All proceeds support a local nonprofit organization.

Native American Heritage Celebration (321-433-7355; www.brevardcc.edu/moorecenter; Moore Multicultural Center, Brevard Community College–Cocoa, 1519 Clearlake Rd., Cocoa 32922). A month of activities centers around a day in mid-November, when dancers, musicians, and storytellers invite people of all nations to share the diverse heritage and customs of Native Americans. Members of many tribes, including the Florida Seminoles, bring the past to life with costumes and artifacts. Sample traditional foods such as venison stew and fry bread.

Space Coast Art Festival (www.spacecoastartfestival.com; intersection of A1A and Minutemen Cswy., Cocoa Beach). Thanksgiving weekend, the streets of downtown Cocoa Beach are closed to traffic and the sidewalks opened to display the works of nearly 250 juried artists, most from Florida and many from Brevard County. The official start of the weekend is a 5K Turkey Trot early Thursday morning, with the art show on Friday and Saturday. Enjoy the exhibits, shop for a one-of-a-kind souvenir, and visit the Student Art Show. Let children try a hands-on craft booth. Eat, drink, and have a very merry time.

Space Coast State Fair (321-639-3976; www.cocoaexpo.com/fair; Cocoa Expo Sports Center, 500 Friday Rd., Cocoa 32926). For 10 days, old-fashioned family fun runs rampant at the Cocoa Expo Center. One daily admission price covers name-talent concerts, thrill rides and midway, monster truck and extreme motorcross contests, and rodeo acts. 4H groups participate in food, agriculture, arts and crafts, and farm exhibits.

December

Cocoa Beach Christmas Boat Parade (321-783-1207; 321-302-0544 [Debbie Sheridan, organizer], Cocoa Beach). Santa Claus is escorted into this island town by a flotilla of large and small boats decorated for the season. At sunset, boats embark from the southwestern shore of the Banana River at FL 520, parallel the causeway as they cross the river, then hug the shore heading south to the Cocoa Beach Country Club. Two favorite viewing spots are Bicentennial Park, midway along the Cocoa Beach Causeway, and Sunset Grill restaurant, at the eastern point where the boats begin their turn south. Good viewing spots fill up early for this very popular event. Check the newspaper schedule for seasonal boat parades held in other venues throughout the county.

Chef prepares breakfast to order at the Omelet Station

5

RESTAURANTS AND FOOD PURVEYORS

Catch of the Day

Dining on Florida's Space Coast is a culinary mix of simple and gourmet dishes. Seafood is often the specialty, but there are lots of choices for landlubbers. Savor ethnic flavors from around the world, or sample a uniquely Florida dish such as fried gator or Key lime pie. The atmosphere is almost always casual, but a summer dress or sport coat may be appropriate for fine-dining restaurants. The community is a haven for musical talent, and many places feature live entertainment on the weekends. Dinner seating is usually available with a short wait or none at all, unless it is a holiday or special-event weekend, but it never hurts to make a reservation if you're going at a prime time. Most restaurants recommend you call ahead when you have a group of six or more so they can prepare the table.

The best eateries for everything from a quick sandwich to a leisurely dinner have been summarized and reviewed in this chapter to help you navigate through the vast sea of choices. The list is weighted toward locations in the beach communities and favors local establishments rather than chain operations. Restaurants are listed alphabetically within each geographical area, and they are recapped in the Appendix by price and cuisine. Price codes are based on an appetizer, dinner entrée (or lunch if dinner is not served), and dessert, but they do not include tax, tip, or beverages. Florida's reputation for early-bird specials is well earned, so inquire about reduced rates for early seating. Restaurants are open daily unless otherwise noted. Smoking is banned inside all Florida food establishments.

Prices are broken down into the following categories:

Inexpensive	Up to $15
Moderate	$15 to $25
Expensive	$25 to $35
Very Expensive	$35 or more

The following abbreviations are used for credit card information, and to identify what meals are served:

AE:	American Express
D:	Discover Card
DC:	Diner's Club
MC:	Master Card
V:	Visa

B: breakfast
L: lunch
D: dinner
SB: Sunday brunch

RESTAURANTS

Cape Canaveral & Cocoa Beach

Anacapri Pizzeria
321-868-2266
605 N. Atlantic Ave., Cocoa Beach 32931
Price: Moderate
Cuisine: Italian
Meals Served: L, D
Credit Cards: D, MC, V
Wheelchair Access: Yes

The aroma of fresh bread greets you as you walk inside. Crispy thin-crust pizza is baked to perfection and loaded with cheese. Select from a list of 24 choices, and pair with white or red sauce. A very generous antipasto makes a satisfying lunch. For heartier appetites, try the flavorful eggplant Parmesan or stuffed shells served smothered in marinara sauce, both topped with melted cheese. Many entrées include pasta on the side and yeast rolls dripping in butter.

Atlantic Ocean Grille
321-783-7549
401 Meade Ave., Cocoa Beach 32931
Price: Moderate–Expensive
Cuisine: Seafood
Meals Served: B, D, SB
Credit Cards: AE, D, MC, V
Wheelchair Access: Yes.

Enjoy fine dining at the pier. Tiered tables and glass walls ensure an unobstructed view of the Atlantic Ocean in a comfortable air-conditioned environment. Dinner service begins at 5 each evening, and seafood is the star. Appetizers include coconut beer shrimp and scallops wrapped in bacon. Pasta dishes feature mussels marinara and seafood scampi. For the entrée choose from seafood, chicken, or steak. The Venetian chicken and shrimp combines two choices with Italian herbs and spices, or try a grilled filet mignon with golden-fried shrimp.

Atlantis Bar and Grill
321-799-0003
1550 N. Atlantic Ave., Cocoa Beach 32931
Price: Moderate–Expensive
Cuisine: Seafood and steak
Meals Served: B, L, D
Credit Cards: AE, D, DC, MC, V
Wheelchair Access: Yes

The setting and the food are both exceptional at this oceanfront restaurant, located within the Hilton hotel. Dine inside, where many seats have an ocean view, or choose a table on the large outside deck and enjoy sea breezes and music with your meal. Chef Andrew Wintz is passionate about combining fresh local ingredients to create simple and elegant dishes. Chicken Florentine and Jack Daniel's beef tenderloin are two dinner favorites. Grouper and mahimahi sandwiches are excellent choices for lunch. A full bar is available, and the blender is always churning out tropical fruit drinks. Reservations are recommended for groups.

Azteca Two
321-784-1188
1600 N. Atlantic Ave., Cocoa Beach 32931
Price: Moderate
Cuisine: Mexican
Meals Served: L, D
Credit Cards: AE, D, MC, V
Wheelchair Access: Yes

You don't have to be staying at the Cocoa Beach Resort to enjoy eating at their on-site Mexican restaurant, with indoor and outdoor seating. The lunch menu includes tacos and burritos, sandwiches, and the Azteca Salad, a blend of chicken, avocadoes, cheeses, and vegetables with a special house dressing. For dinner consider a 12-ounce steak grilled with onions and green chiles and served with a cheese enchilada, rice and beans, or the enchilada Del Mar, stuffed with crab and shrimp. The huge circular bar stocks Mexican beers and 70 varieties of tequila. Authentic Mexican decor and music add spicy flavor to a fun evening. Reservations are recommended.

Barrier Jack's

321-784-8590
410 N. Atlantic Ave., Cocoa Beach 32931
Price: Inexpensive
Cuisine: Eclectic
Meals Served: B, L, D
Credit Cards: AE, D, MC, V
Wheelchair Access: Yes.

Grab a table in the dining room or under the shaded breezeway of this small, casual eatery, perfect after a morning or afternoon on the beach. Before coming to Cocoa Beach, Chef Jack spent time floundering off the California coast, then wandered east to the Smoky Mountains, and finally headed south. The service is friendly, and the food is an all-American mix of hot Tex-Mex, barbecue, seafood, and steak. For lunch try salad, soup, and a hot or cold sandwich, such as a fresh-baked hoagie topped with oysters, scallops, shrimp, fish, or catfish. Youngsters can try the Pirates Planks. Closed Monday; reservations are recommended for groups.

The Boardwalk

321-783-7549
401 Meade Ave., Cocoa Beach 32931
Price: Inexpensive–Moderate
Cuisine: Seafood, burgers
Meals Served: L, D
Credit Cards: AE, D, MC, V
Wheelchair Access: Yes

Grab some lunch, take a break from the sun, and enjoy a great view. Adults and children will feel comfortable in their bathing suits at this open-air eatery and bar at the center of the Cocoa Beach Pier. Most weekends and some evenings, house band Birks & Dugan covers all the favorite sit-back-and-relax tunes.

Dress is off-the-beach casual at the Boardwalk at Cocoa Beach Pier. Eileen Callan

Boston Beef and Seafood

321-784-4000
6910 N. Atlantic Ave., Cocoa Beach 32931
Price: Inexpensive
Cuisine: Seafood, New England
Meals Served: L, D
Credit Cards: MC, V
Wheelchair Access: Yes

Red Sox fans will be right at home amid home-team memorabilia. Boston seafood is flown in daily fresh—never frozen. Specialties are New England favorites from the sea, such as Ipswich clams and rich, creamy chowder thick with tender clams. Friday's special is lobster rolls. Burgers, roast beef, and chicken complete the menu. Closed Sunday.

Bunky's Raw Bar and Seafood Grille

321-799-4677
315 W. Cocoa Beach Cswy., Cocoa Beach 32931
Price: Moderate
Cuisine: Seafood

Meals Served: L, D
Credit Cards: AE, D, MC, V
Wheelchair Access: Yes.

Bunky's has been urging local diners to "get shucked" for more than 25 years. The seafood choices at this tropical and spacious restaurant and bar are nearly endless: gumbo, fish dip, calamari, clams, and shrimp. Hand-shucked oysters are served from bars scattered throughout the large dining room. This fun and casual spot offers fresh seafood, prompt friendly service, fair prices, and a wide choice of spirits. Closed Monday for lunch.

Cactus Flower

321-452-6606
1891 E. Merritt Island Cswy., Merritt Island 32952
Price: Moderate
Cuisine: Mexican
Meals Served: L, D
Credit Cards: AE, MC, V
Wheelchair Access: Yes.

Cactus Flower's riverside deck

The *bella vista*—beautiful view—of the Banana River is the setting for this festive Mexican eatery. Dine amid the relaxing south-of-the-border interior decor or on the waterside deck. Julieta Colxani grew up in Acapulco and uses family recipes to prepare traditional Mexican fare such as *carni-* *tas de puerco*, tender roasted pork, or *bistec a la Mexicana*, steak sautéed with jalapeños, tomatoes, and onions. Tex-Mex favorites include enchiladas, burritos, and tamales, as well as beef, chicken, and *pescado* (fish) tacos. Servers are friendly and knowledgeable. Choose from several imported beers or cool, fruity sangria by the glass or pitcher. Closed Monday; reservations are recommended for groups.

The Cape Codder

321-868-2500
2690 S. Atlantic Ave., Cocoa Beach 32931
Price: Inexpensive–Moderate
Cuisine: Seafood, New England
Meals Served: L, D
Credit Cards: MC, V
Wheelchair Access: Yes

Once upon a time, a transplanted Boston businessman grew very hungry for fresh seafood from home, so he opened a restaurant. Enjoy fresh, imported Ipswich clams; full-bellied steamers, oysters, shrimp, and chowder; and Maine "lobstah" in rolls or salad. They also serve pasta dishes. There are Nathan's New England hot dogs for the landlubbers. Closed Monday.

Captain J's Ocean Deck Restaurant

321-783-1717
211 E. Cocoa Beach Cswy., Cocoa Beach 32931
Price: Moderate
Cuisine: Seafood and steak
Meals Served: L, D
Credit Cards: AE, D, MC, V
Wheelchair Access: No

The ambience, breeze, and view are a magic combination on this upper deck at the corner of Shepard's Park and the Atlantic Ocean. Blue and white cushioned chairs pull up to umbrella-shaded tables, where you can enjoy a fruity drink while deciding on your order. For an appetizer, try oysters on the half shell or peel-and-eat shrimp.

Pair homemade crabcakes or blackened mahimahi with fries for a lunchtime sandwich, or add a salad and vegetables and enjoy as a dinner entrée. Meat lovers can select grilled steak, barbecued ribs, pasta, or chicken. After dark, head inside, where a cascading fountain, plantation-style furniture, and ceiling fans continue the tropical effect. On the weekends, there is live music outside on the deck.

Captains Grill

321-392-1693
1300 N. Atlantic Ave., Cocoa Beach 32931
Price: Moderate
Cuisine: American
Meals Served: B, L, D
Credit Cards: AE, D, MC, V
Wheelchair Access: Yes

Sun streams in through the wide windows surrounding this bright and cheerful dining room, which overlooks the pool at the Holiday Inn. Tropical green plantings landscape the deck; tables shaded by the overhang are perfect for outdoor dining. Enjoy a full breakfast buffet until 11 AM. Favorites for lunch are blackened grouper, Buccaneer burger, and barbecue chicken salad with a marvelous vinaigrette dressing. For dinner try the mango mahimahi, sweet and sour pork, or homestyle meat loaf. Check for daily dinner specials.

Coconuts on the Beach

321-784-1422
2 Minutemen Cswy., Cocoa Beach 32931
Price: Moderate–Expensive
Cuisine: American
Meals Served: L, D
Credit Cards: D, DC, MC, V
Wheelchair Access: Yes

Locals continually select Coconuts as the best beach waterfront restaurant in Brevard County. The view is phenomenal, and the service and food are terrific. Just step in from the beach, rinse your feet under the outdoor shower, and head to a table right on the deck. The lunch menu has lots of sandwiches, including a Coconut's original—blue crab on an English muffin topped with melted cheese and Hollandaise sauce. For dinner, start with peel-and-eat shrimp, then an entrée like coconut-crusted mahimahi with a pineapple and orange sauce, or the fresh catch of the day, caught by their own local fishing fleet and then grilled, blackened, or jerked, and flavored with Key lime mustard sauce or mango salsa. Much of the time this is a great family restaurant where the kids enjoy the comfortable atmosphere and watching all the beach activity. During spring break and summer weekends, however, the music cranks up, and a young party crowd gathers to meet, greet, and sample the daily drink special.

The weekend crowd at Coconuts on the Beach
Eileen Callan

DiLorenzo's

321-784-5662
8125 Canaveral Blvd., Cape Canaveral 32920
Price: Inexpensive–Moderate
Cuisine: Italian
Meals Served: L, D
Credit Cards: AE, D, MC, V
Wheelchair Access: Not in restrooms

For 25 years Luigi DiLorenzo has been the

owner-chef of this friendly, affordable restaurant, the oldest in Cape Canaveral. He learned to cook at home in Italy and then traveled around Europe before coming to America. Decorative murals reflect his native country. A large menu covers the familiar Italian dishes, tempting seafood, great pizza, fresh pasta, and wonderful salads suitable as entrées. The wine list includes domestic California varieties and some from Sicily and Australia. Closed Sunday.

Durango's Steak House

321-783-9988
5602 N. Atlantic Ave., Cocoa Beach 32931
Price: Moderate–Expensive
Cuisine: Steak
Meals Served: L, D
Credit Cards: AE, D, DC, MC, V
Wheelchair Access: Yes

Named for an old mining town in Colorado, this Florida-based chain made a claim on the local dining market when it settled in a spacious, rustic facility that was the Wild West of Cocoa Beach during the space-age gold rush. Many of the interior furnishings, including the long, mahogany bar, remain from the days when astronauts, engineers, and reporters shared stories over steaks and cocktails, and photos depicting scenes from Cocoa Beach's history adorn the walls. Today, a pleasant aroma from an oak-fire grill reminds you you're hungry, and this is the right place for a hearty meal. Entrées include chicken, fish, pork chops and steaks in a variety of cuts and sizes. If you dare, try the 20-ounce Jesse James Porterhouse. The children's menu offers a small and affordable sirloin. The specialty of the full-service bar is a homemade mix that is the base for 28 different flavored margaritas. The service is exceptionally friendly; the steaks are tender and prepared just as you request. During busy times there may be a wait. Reservations are recommended for groups.

Eagle's Nest Sports Bar and Grill

321-868-8264
20 N. Brevard Ave., Cocoa Beach 32931
Price: Inexpensive
Cuisine: American, New England
Meals Served: L, D
Credit Cards: AE, MC, V
Wheelchair Access: Yes

Welcome to Philadelphia on the beach at this neighborhood tavern, which has an extensive display of memorabilia from all the city's teams. Amoroso rolls are flown in to make authentic Philly cheesesteaks. They also serve burgers, subs, hot dogs, and fish sandwiches. For dessert, take a trip back in time with a Tastykake. Brews include Pennsylvania favorites like Yuengling and Rolling Rock by the bottle or bucket. Come early on game day for a front row seat to one of the eight televisions or the large plasma screen set on the patio.

Fishlips Waterfront Bar & Grill

321-784-4533
610 Glen Cheek Dr., Port Canaveral 32920
Price: Expensive
Cuisine: Seafood
Meals Served: L, D, SB
Credit Cards: AE, D, MC, V
Wheelchair Access: Yes

Whether you dine downstairs or on the upper deck, inside or out, you can be sure of a great seat to view a parade of birds, boats, and cruise ships at Port Canaveral Cove. Beef, chicken, pork, and vegetarian dishes are available, but the house specialty is seafood, prepared as simply as you like or presented in gourmet treats such as lobster ravioli, fettuccine Alfredo with fire crusted mahimahi, or sesame tuna teriyaki. A special menu for kids has all the traditional choices, as well as a basket of fried shrimp. Desserts are tasty and big, especially the Brownie Overboard, which you might want to order with extra spoons to share. Stop by from 10 to 2 on Sunday for the Mimosa

Brunch, which features crabcakes Benedict, an island twist on a traditional favorite. Sometimes there is live entertainment on the deck. Reservations are recommended for groups.

Flamingos at the Radisson Hotel
321-868-6571
8701 Astronaut Blvd., Cape Canaveral 32920
Price: Expensive
Cuisine: American, Florida
Meals Served: B, L, D, SB
Credit Cards: AE, D, MC, V
Wheelchair Access: Yes

The Radisson is home to an upscale restaurant that vies for the best fine-dining experience in the area. Fresh flowers on every table and windows overlooking the pool and a garden of tropical greenery create an idyllic setting. Start dinner with Florida State Soup, a blend of rock shrimp, crabmeat, and alligator dumpling. The menu offers several à la carte choices, along with specialties such as veal cutlet with sage butter and asparagus, or portobello mushroom and shallots in an Asiago cream sauce. The extensive wine list includes domestic and imported labels. There is a gala seafood buffet every Saturday evening and a champagne brunch on Sunday. Reservations are recommended.

Florida's Seafood Bar & Grill
321-784-0892
480 W. Cocoa Beach Cswy., Cocoa Beach 32931
Price: Moderate–Expensive
Cuisine: Seafood, Florida
Meals Served: L, D
Credit Cards: AE, D, MC, V
Wheelchair Access: Yes

Crowds line up for this popular restaurant known for seasonal rock shrimp, broiled or fried, and an ocean of seafood cooked in a variety of ways. Clam chowder served in a crusty bread bowl is a meal in itself. The fish sandwich is made with a flaky whitefish and fills up the plate; the fried oyster sandwich is tasty and unusual. For dinner start with conch fritters, and then select an entrée such as the Canaveral combo, with rock shrimp, fish, scallops, medium shrimp, and a crabcake. This family-friendly restaurant offers little mates lots of seafood choices, along with fries and ice cream. Grown-ups can finish with a slice of Key lime pie. Reservations are recommended for groups.

Gregory's
321-799-2557
900 N. Atlantic Ave., Cocoa Beach 32931
Price: Very Expensive
Cuisine: Steak
Meals Served: D
Credit Cards: AE, D, MC, V
Wheelchair Access: Not in restrooms

This upscale dining room, which shares part of the ground floor with Ocean Landings Resort, is the setting for an elegant evening. Chicken and seafood are available, but steak is the star. Gregory's serves only certified, high-quality Angus beef, hand cut and grilled to your specifications. Most of the starters are culinary twists on seafood, such as bite-sized portions of Maine lobster wrapped in bacon and topped with teriyaki sauce. For the entrée, select your favorite cut of beef—sirloin, New York strip, porterhouse, or filet mignon, or prime rib served with au jus and horseradish sauce. Pair dessert with a Gregory's coffee flavored with Kahlúa, Baileys, or Grand Marnier and topped with whipped cream and a cherry.

Grills Seafood Deck
321-868-2226
505 Glen Cheek Dr., Port Canaveral 32920
Price: Moderate–Expensive
Cuisine: Seafood, steak, and chicken

Meals Served: B, L, D
Credit Cards: D, MC, V
Wheelchair Access: Yes

Locals and visitors mingle at this indoor/outdoor diner anchoring the restaurants at Port Canaveral Cove. Start your evening watching the cruise ships leave port or the fishing fleets returning home. True to the diner's name, fresh fish is marinated and grilled (never fried) for a delicious and healthy meal. The fresh fish of the day is served with Tahiti taters, wild rice, or steamed vegetables, or dressed up in a tasty creation like shrimp, fish, and scallops in an Alfredo sauce atop of bed of linguine. Sandwiches and burgers, including vegetarian versions, are available. Breakfast is served daily starting at 7. In addition to the standard fare, try a seafood omelet or lemon-seared tilapia. On weekends, there are live music and dancing on the deck. Reservations are recommended for groups.

Relaxing at Grills Seafood Deck at Port Canaveral

Heidelberg Restaurant

321-783-6806
7 N. Orlando Ave., Cocoa Beach 32931
Price: Expensive–Very Expensive
Cuisine: European
Meals Served: L, D
Credit Cards: AE, MC, V
Wheelchair Access: Yes

More than 20 years ago, Heidi and Eddie arrived from Europe and opened a restaurant featuring classical continental dishes, including old-world favorites from Austria. This may be the only place in Brevard County where you'll find Beluga caviar, escargots bourguignon, Wiener schnitzel, and sauerbraten on the same menu. They specialize in quality, seasoned beef fillets, served as a full-portion dinner entrée or a smaller cut in a sandwich for lunch. Breads and pastries are made from scratch each day. Chef Eddie's fresh, flaky apple strudel is topped with homemade vanilla ice cream. Lunch is casual and comfortable, but it's not suitable for bathing-suit attire. Dinner is served in a setting of crisp white linens, fine china, and an accompaniment of American musical standards like "All of Me" on the piano. This award-winning restaurant is tops in food and service. Heidi's Jazz Club, adjacent to the restaurant, has live entertainment Tuesday through Sunday. Reservations are recommended for dinner.

Experience fine dining at Heidelberg Restaurant.
Eileen Callan

Italian Courtyard

321-783-0413
350 W. Cocoa Beach Cswy., Cocoa Beach 32931
Price: Moderate
Cuisine: Italian
Meals Served: L, D

Credit Cards: AE, D, MC, V
Wheelchair Access: Not in restrooms

La vita e bella. Life is good at this spacious pastaria, lavishly designed to transport you to an Italian village for the evening. For two decades Francesca and Domenick have prepared traditional dishes flavored with a robust blend of herbs and garlic. Families are easily accommodated, and there's a special Bambini menu with favorites like spaghetti and lasagna. For dessert try the spumoni: gelato in vanilla, strawberry, and pistachio layers. Pizza is also available, and they have a full bar. Dine indoors or on the covered outdoor patio. There is live music on the patio Friday and Saturday evenings. Reservations are recommended for groups. *Buono appetitto!*

Kelsey's Pizzeria

321-783-9191
8699 Astronaut Blvd., Cape Canaveral 32920
Price: Moderate
Cuisine: Italian, Pizza
Meals Served: L, D
Credit Cards: AE, MC, V
Wheelchair Access: Yes

A tantalizing aroma of fresh ingredients seeped in garlic and Italian spices fills the dining room. The full menu offers soups, salads, pizzas, calzones, and a variety of pastas. The Tuscan bean soup is a hearty and robust starter. Penne Gorgonzola has sautéed mushrooms, Roma tomatoes, grilled chicken strips, garlic, and penne pasta tossed in a creamy Gorgonzola sauce. Portions are generous; share a pizza and Greek salad. Families with small children will enjoy the casual environment, affordable food, and friendly service. Reservations are recommended for groups.

La Fiesta

321-783-7755
7802 N. Atlantic Ave., Cape Canaveral 32920
Price: Inexpensive–Moderate
Cuisine: Mexican
Meals Served: L, D
Credit Cards: AE, D, MC, V
Wheelchair Access: Yes

If buildings could talk, this landmark restaurant would tell tales of astronauts and engineers lingering over a morning cup of coffee, sketching out rocket telemetry on the back of a napkin. Nearly 50 years later, shuttles have replaced rockets, and the all American Moon Hut has been transformed into a popular and affordable Mexican eatery with enchilada, taco, and burrito combo plates, or sizzling steak, chicken, vegetable, or shrimp fajitas served with rice and refried beans. The memories remain, captured in photos and mission badges adorning the walls.

Lobster Shanty & Wharfside

321-783-1350
2200 S. Orlando Ave., Cocoa Beach 32931
Price: Moderate
Cuisine: Seafood
Meals Served: L, D
Credit Cards: AE, D, MC, V
Wheelchair Access: Yes

This restaurant is one of the few on the eastern shore of the Banana River, and patrons enjoy a great sunset view along with excellent seafood, good prices, and efficient service. Kids of all ages enjoy feeding the fish at the entrance pond or off the dock. Dine inside or by the river. Every table gets piping hot, crispy hush puppies dusted with powdered sugar. Daily seafood specials always include several seasonal fish entrées cooked almost any way you like—grilled, barbecued, blackened, or Jamaican jerked. The long, impressive salad bar can be the main course or accompany your meal. Save room for dessert; maybe the turtle cheesecake. Reservations are recommended.

The Mango Tree

321-799-0513
118 N. Atlantic Ave., Cocoa Beach 32931
Price: Very Expensive
Cuisine: Continental
Meals Served: D
Credit Cards: AE, MC, V
Wheelchair Access: Yes

For an evening of romance or to celebrate a special occasion, make reservations at the Mango Tree. A tropical garden brimming with hanging orchids, piano entertainment, and candlelight set the mood for a leisurely and magical evening. The staff will see to your every need, and award-winning chefs create exceptional dishes presented with style and flair. Begin with smoked Norwegian salmon, or artichoke hearts and cucumber in herb vinaigrette dressing and sprinkled with blue cheese. For your entrée consider the roast Long Island duckling with mango salsa, fruit, and macadamia nuts, or sea scallops in a puff pastry shell. Seared tuna is available as an appetizer or main course. Every meal is served with a salad and fresh vegetables, and a selection from the fully stocked bar or wine cellar can complement the meal. If dinner is out of your price range, splurge with dessert and coffee on the garden patio. Closed Monday; reservations are recommended.

Mangroves

321-783-4548
6615 N. Atlantic Ave., Cape Canaveral 32920
Price: Expensive
Cuisine: American, Florida
Meals Served: B, L, D
Credit Cards: AE, D, MC, V
Wheelchair Access: Yes

Palm trees, waterfalls, murals of tropical gardens, and wicker furniture create the illusion of a relaxing meal on a southern veranda, with fresh ingredients spiced with sunshine and the flavors of Florida. For lunch choose a soup, a salad, or a sandwich such as the portobello mushroom burger. Dinner appetizers range from the popular crab-stuffed mushrooms to the unusual bourbon-glazed Brie. Many of the entrées have a citrus touch—coconut shrimp with an orange sauce and pistachio grouper with grilled pineapple and island butter. Vegetarians will find lots of tasty choices. Live entertainment is presented on the weekends. Closed Monday; reservations are recommended for groups.

Marlins Good Times Bar and Grill

321-783-4050
401 Meade Ave., Cocoa Beach 32931
Price: Moderate—Expensive
Cuisine: American, pub fare
Meals Served: L, D
Credit Cards: AE, D, MC, V
Wheelchair Access: Yes

Located about halfway down the Cocoa Beach Pier, this authentic sports bar and restaurant has a surfing theme, as well as a view of the surfer action captured in the panoramic ocean view. Enjoy the casual setting and a relaxed meal featuring sandwiches, home-made soups, and desserts. Lower-priced entrées such as fried flounder or clam strips are served with seasoned fries. Main Sail dinners include grilled salmon and Venetian chicken and come with a salad, rice, and rolls. Burgers are a popular choice any time of day. Children can select from the Minnow's Menu. For a unique sweet treat, try the Pier Pleasure bread pudding, topped with a buttery rum sauce and whipped cream. A full bar can serve up a beer or a frozen and fruity beach drink.

Oh Shucks Seafood Bar

321-783-7549
401 Meade Ave., Cocoa Beach 32931
Price: Inexpensive—Moderate
Cuisine: Seafood
Meals Served: L, D

Credit Cards: AE, D, MC, V
Wheelchair Access: Yes

Relax in this open-air, bathing-suit-casual restaurant and bar situated right at sea and sand level at the Cocoa Beach Pier. Grab a stool and order your favorite beach drink, maybe a tropical breeze blend of banana, strawberry, and Midori, or gather the family at a table and choose from a full menu of sandwiches and seafood. The specialty of the house is oysters on the half shell. Kids will enjoy the outdoor atmosphere during the day, but their menu choices are limited. Bands perform on the weekends, with karaoke on Tuesday night and reggae on Wednesday.

The Omelet Station

321-783-1038
www.theomeletstation.com
5590 N. Atlantic Ave., Cocoa Beach 32931
Price: Inexpensive—Moderate
Cuisine: American
Meals Served: B, L
Credit Cards: AE, D, DC, MC, V
Wheelchair Access: Yes

Order from the menu, or select from a smorgasbord of ingredients like meats, sun-dried tomatoes, roasted peppers, and cheese, and the chef will create an omelet just for you. All the traditional breakfast entrées are offered. Try the I Dream of Jeannie waffle covered in cinnamon apples, strawberries, or blueberries—and take it à la mode with a topping of ice cream and whipped cream. Sandwiches, salads, burgers, and wraps are also on the menu.

Pita Garden

321-799-9933
269 W. Cocoa Beach Cswy., Cocoa Beach 32931
Price: Moderate
Cuisine: Middle Eastern, Shawarma
Meals Served: L, D
Credit Cards: AE, D, MC, V
Wheelchair Access: Yes

Fresh ingredients blend with a myriad of flavors to create amazingly tasty, authentic Lebanese dishes, served by Sue and Eddy Raouda as though you're a guest in their home. Everything is prepared daily using family recipes and fresh ingredients. The heart-healthy Mediterranean cuisine is spiced with generous touches of garlic, lemon, olive oil, and herbs. Vegetarians will love the emphasis on produce and hummus. Lightly seasoned, grilled kabobs come in beef, chicken, or lamb. Wine and beer are available. Dessert is a shortbread cookie filled with dates, walnuts, or pistachios, accompanied by a cup of Arabic coffee spiced with nutty, sweet cardamom. The decor at this cozy diner is simple, the prices are reasonable, the atmosphere is friendly, and the food is outstanding. Reservations are recommended for groups.

Chef Eddy oversees dinner preparations at Pita Garden.

Roberto's Little Havana

321-784-1868
26 N. Orlando Ave., Cocoa Beach 32931
Price: Moderate
Cuisine: Cuban
Meals Served: B, L, D
Credit Cards: AE, MC, V
Wheelchair Access: Yes

When Cuban native Roberto came to Cocoa Beach more than a decade ago, he brought the taste of the island with him. All his recipes are original and prepared using traditional methods. A large painting of the beautiful Havana harbor, the Malacon, hangs in the dining room, and copies of a local Spanish paper, *La Voz Latina en la Florida,* are available in a stand near the front door. Breakfast favorites, along with eggs, include the *plantanos muduros* (sweet plantains) and chorizo (Cuban sausage). Lunch patrons like *sandwiche de ropa vieja,* loosely translated as "old clothes" but actually spicy shredded beef on Cuban bread. The dinner menu offers *camarones enchilados,* shrimp Creole seasoned with garlic, onions, green peppers, and spices. Other dishes feature *pollo, carnes,* and *pescados y mariscos* (chicken, beef, and seafood). Locals agree with *The New York Times,* which cited Roberto's as one of Florida's best local spots. Closed Monday.

Ron Jon Surf Grill

321-328-2830
1000 Shorewood Dr., Cape Canaveral 32920
Price: Expensive
Cuisine: Seafood, steak
Meals Served: L, D
Credit Cards: AE, D, MC, V
Wheelchair Access: Yes

Rattan chairs with warm coral-striped cushions make for an inviting setting at this new, tropical restaurant inside the lively Ron Jon Caribe Resort. Dine inside or out on the pool deck, landscaped with lush greenery and overlooking the water park, where music is often playing. Menu selections are limited but varied. A bowl of the exceptional Atlantic Coast seafood chowder is a good start, followed by a large salad with chicken or shrimp, a pizza and house salad, or "The Burger," 8 ounces of sirloin topped with just about everything and served with fries or onion rings, slaw or salad. Dinner entrées include pasta dishes

such as vanilla-seared shrimp capellini, filet mignon, fresh grouper, and baby back ribs smoked in a special cola barbecue sauce. This is a family resort, and there are several choices on the children's menu, although most are the usual fare. Adventurous youngsters might prefer splitting an adult entrée. A large indoor bar is a great spot to chat or watch a game while waiting for others in your party. No bathing suits, please. Reservations are recommended.

Rusty's Seafood & Oyster Bar

321-783-2033
628 Glen Cheek Dr., Port Canaveral 32920
Price: Moderate
Cuisine: Seafood, steak
Meals Served: L, D
Credit Cards: AE, D, MC, V
Wheelchair Access: Yes

Rusty's is a pleasantly crowded favorite gathering spot at Port Canaveral Cove. Every chair has a great view of the water, whether it's a stool at the oyster-bar table, a table in the dining room, or outside on the spacious deck. Fishing captains and crew stop here, so you might hear some authentic fish tales. The menu offers plenty of options for landlubbers, but the main course is seafood. From the oyster bar, get clams, mussels, or oysters by the bucket (raw or steamed). Baskets come with a generous portion of fish, shrimp, clam strips, fried oysters, or chicken tenders, along with sides of fries and slaw. Pair an appetizer of Gorgonzola bread with a salad that includes shrimp, scallops, grouper, or tuna. Finish the meal with Mississippi Mud Pie. Music is usually playing, and the drinks are always cold and refreshing after a hot day on the boat or at the beach. Reservations are recommended for groups.

Shark Pit Bar and Grill

321-868-8952
4001 N. Atlantic Ave., Cocoa Beach 32931

Price: Moderate–Expensive
Cuisine: American, brick-oven pizza
Meals Served: B, L, D
Credit Cards: AE, D, MC, V
Wheelchair Access: Yes

The aquarium at Shark Pit is a great place to pose for a photo.

Join local surfers for the dawn patrol breakfast specials served from 6:30 to 9 in this dining spot, located in the lobby of the Sheraton Four Points. A wall of water frames the centerpiece 5,600-gallon aquarium stocked with tropical fish and small sharks. The restaurant name comes from a rumored secret wave break along the east coast—popular with surfers and sharks. The menu offers a variety of tasty and well-prepared items. Crusty and flavorful pizza is cooked in the open brick oven in the corner. Salads, sandwiches, burgers, and entrées such as bourbon-glazed pork chops and baby back ribs complete the choices. Serving sizes are large, and the staff easily accommodates patrons who choose to share an entrée. The

junior surfer menu has all the usual options; vegetarians will enjoy the grilled vegetable salad with a balsamic glaze dressing. While you're finishing a slice of Key lime pie or mocha cheesecake, check out the daily surf report on your cell at 321-868-8967. Reservations are recommended for groups.

Siam Orchid

321-783-4545
1275 N. Atlantic Ave., Cocoa Beach 32931
Price: Moderate
Cuisine: Thai, Japanese
Meals Served: L, D
Credit Cards: AE, D, MC, V
Wheelchair Access: Yes

Siam Orchid is the restaurant that locals recommend for great Thai food in a relaxing setting. The six-page menu offers everything from sushi to temaki (cone-shaped hand roll) stuffed with crab, salmon, shrimp, eel, and octopus. The pad lo mein, stir-fried egg noodles mixed with chicken, features a tasty blend of spices. Try the sushi and sashimi combo or the makimono sushi rolls. You may find a new adventure waiting for you. The staff is happy to answer questions and help you make a good choice. Closed Sunday for lunch.

Silvestro's

321-783-4853
2039 N. Atlantic Ave., Cocoa Beach 32931
Price: Very Expensive
Cuisine: Italian
Meals Served: D
Credit Cards: AE, D, DC, MC,V
Wheelchair Access: Yes

A native of Rome, chef Silvestro Antonioli learned the joy of cooking from his mother, and later he developed his craft at the legendary Il Pasticcio in Savannah, Georgia. The elegant, simple dining room is set with fresh linens, sparkling glassware, and gleaming silverware. The appetizers are tempting, and the *insalata caprese* exceeds expectations. The rack of lamb, veal tenderloin, and risotto are near perfection. *Florida Today* gave this authentic Italian restaurant its highest rating. Their location in the Banana River Square strip center is unimpressive, but the gourmet creations and exceptional service make this a good choice for an extra-special occasion. Reservations are recommended.

Simply Delicious Café and Bakery

321-783-2012
125 N. Orlando Ave., Cocoa Beach 32931
Price: Inexpensive
Cuisine: American
Meals Served: B, L, SB
Credit Cards: AE, D, MC, V
Wheelchair Access: Yes

Diners savor waffles topped with fruit and whipped cream at Simply Delicious.

In 2001, Chie and Larry Walh converted a cozy Cocoa Beach cottage into a whimsical gathering spot with citrus-colored walls and glass bottles on a mantle atop a blue and white fireplace. Chie, originally from Japan, greets the guests; Larry is an experienced chef. For breakfast try thick slabs of French toast topped with strawberries, bananas, chocolate chips, or a pecan-apple glaze. Quiche and soup are standard menu items, but the selections change each day. Either goes well with a raspberry or peach iced tea. Light eaters can mix a flavorful soup, salad, or half sandwich stuffed with fresh fixings piled high on fresh-baked bread. An abundant assortment of pastries from the front display make for a difficult dessert decision. Consider having one on the spot and taking another home for later. Children are welcome, but because the tables are close together, they might disturb other diners if they get restless. Closed Monday; reservations are recommended for groups.

Slow and Low Barbeque Bar & Grill

321-783-6199
306 N. Orlando Ave., Cocoa Beach 32931
Price: Moderate
Cuisine: Barbecue
Meals Served: L, D
Credit Cards: AE, D, MC, V
Wheelchair Access: Yes

Dine indoors or outside on the covered patio while you enjoy slow-cooked, hickory-smoked pork, chicken, beef, and turkey. Ribs cooked St. Louis style nearly fall off the bone. The specialty sandwiches are affordable, delicious, and messy, especially the Low Down and Dirty, with pork, onions, and green peppers drenched in a sweet sauce. Select from a list of sides, the best of which may be the sweet potato fries. Take note of a small plaque near the front door: This building was the site of the first doctor's office in Cocoa Beach. Reservations are recommended for groups.

Sonny's Real Pit Bar-B-Q

321-868-1000
2005 N. Atlantic Ave., Cocoa Beach 32931

Price: Inexpensive—Moderate
Cuisine: Barbecue
Meals Served: L, D
Credit Cards: AE, D, MC, V
Wheelchair Access: Yes

This chain began more than 40 years ago in a small shack just a few blocks from the University of Florida campus in Gainesville. As alumni have spread throughout the state, Sonny's has followed, and the smoked, slow-cooked taste defines Florida barbecue. Cocoa Beach has a location in Banana River Square and serves ribs, pork, beef, and chicken with a great selection of sides. The atmosphere is casual and family-friendly.

Sunrise Cafe

321-783-5647
365 W. Cocoa Beach Cswy., Cocoa Beach 32931
Price: Inexpensive
Cuisine: American, Greek
Meals Served: B, L, D
Credit Cards: AE, D, MC, V
Wheelchair Access: Not in restrooms

This landmark diner, previously called the Ranch House, has been hosting local guests since the 1970s. Slip into a 1950s-style vinyl-upholstered booth or onto a counter bar stool and sip a cup of coffee while you check out the menu. The decor is minimal, and the food, served from sunrise to sunset daily, is simple and hearty. The dinner menu features seven Greek entrées, salads, Italian dishes, and seafood. This popular local spot endures with good cooking, fast service, and fair prices.

Sunset Café Waterfront Bar & Grill

321-783-8485
500 W. Cocoa Beach Cswy., Cocoa Beach 32931
Price: Moderate
Cuisine: American
Meals Served: L, D

Credit Cards: AE, D, DC, MC, V
Wheelchair Access: Yes

This aptly named eatery is right at the Cocoa Beach side of the Banana River at the start of the Cocoa Beach Causeway. From the spacious waterside deck, diners can watch boaters and dolphins pass through the channel. Pelicans dive for dinner as you savor yours, delivered right to your table. Crowds gather at this ideal spot to share a drink and watch the sun go down and enjoy musical entertainment. For dinner, try a cornucopia of seafood, including Florida grouper, mahimahi, shrimp, scallops, flounder, or snow crab legs. Chicken and beef are other menu choices.

The Surf Bar and Grill

321-783-2401
2 S. Atlantic Ave., Cocoa Beach 32931
Price: Expensive
Cuisine: Seafood and beef
Meals Served: L, D, SB
Credit Cards: AE, D, DC, MC, V
Wheelchair Access: Yes

Pull open the large oak door and step into a time capsule of Cocoa Beach history. Since 1948, the Surf Bar and Grill (formerly Bernard's Surf) has been a favorite spot for locals—the fine-dining place recommended to visitors. In the heyday of the 1960s, astronauts, media, and visiting celebrities gathered here to savor steaks that were large and rare, and linger over brandy and a cigar. Favorites still include appetizers such as shrimp cocktail and oysters on the half shell. Caesar salad is prepared with great flourish right at your table. Fresh seafood and tender cuts of meat are presented in entrées that include bleu-cheese-encrusted filet mignon, Chateaubriand for two, or a live Maine lobster. Complement your meal with a selection from the extensive wine list. Save room for Bananas Foster Flambé, a specialty of the house. For more casual dining, order oysters, sandwiches, and salads. The large mahogany bar in the lounge has a history all its own: Before there was a bank in town, space workers stopped here to cash their paychecks. That's no longer the case, but one tradition remains. ANYONE HAVING A DRINK IN THE LOUNGE DURING THE TIME OF A LAUNCH FROM THE CAPE WILL RECEIVE A FREE DRINK, promises the now-fading sign on the wall. Reservations are recommended for dinner.

Taco City
321-784-1475
2955 S. Atlantic Ave., Cocoa Beach 32931
Price: Inexpensive
Cuisine: Tex-Mex
Meals Served: L, D
Credit Cards: MC, V
Wheelchair Access: Not in restrooms

This roadside diner south of Cocoa Beach has been a fixture for more than 25 years. Locals like the casual, simple western decor and self-serve informality. Order at the counter, and they'll hand you your drink and a basket of tortilla chips to munch on while waiting for your meal. The food, mostly a variety of enchiladas, tostadas, and quesadillas, is fresh and cooked with just a touch of spice for the timid, or extra hot for the bold. Wine and beer are available. Ask about the daily specials. Closed Sunday; reservations are recommended for groups.

Taste of Goa
321-799-8600
8501 Astronaut Blvd., Cape Canaveral 32920
Price: Moderate
Cuisine: Indian
Meals Served: L, D
Credit Cards: AE, D, MC, V
Wheelchair Access: Yes

The European sailors who originally landed in Florida may have intended to sail west to India in search of exotic spices, but today the aroma of foods basted in curry, corian-

der, and cumin are right here in Cape Canaveral. Lunch is an all-you-can-eat buffet. The signature dish at dinner is chicken vindaloo, a boneless breast sautéed with spices and flavored with a tangy hot-and-sour sauce. Owner Tudor Mazarelo, who is from Goa, a vacation spot on the west coast of India, also recommends the kingfish cooked in spicy masala sauce and paired with jasmine rice. Closed Monday; reservations are recommended for groups.

Thai Japanese
321-868-0066
24 N. Orlando Ave., Cocoa Beach 32931
Price: Moderate
Cuisine: Thai, Japanese
Meals Served: L, D
Credit Cards: MC, V
Wheelchair Access: No

Chef Eddie Hill, a newcomer from Miami, operates this family restaurant, featuring friendly, quick service and an extensive menu of traditional dishes, including rice noodles and a sushi bar. Domestic and imported beers (such as Sapporo and Kirin Ichiban) are served, as well as plum wine. It's an easy walk from the beach at the Minutemen Causeway. Eat in, take out, or call for delivery. Reservations are recommended for groups.

Three Wishes
321-783-9222
2080 N. Atlantic Ave., Cocoa Beach 32931
Price: Expensive–Very Expensive
Cuisine: American
Meals Served: B, L, D
Credit Cards: AE, D, MC, V
Wheelchair Access: Yes

Enjoy a skillet breakfast such as the garden frittata, a light salad or sandwich for lunch, and fine dining in the evening at this beachside restaurant at the Doubletree Hotel. It has a panoramic view of the Atlantic whitecaps just beyond the dunes.

Start dinner with toasted ravioli and fried calamari, and then choose from among gourmet seafood entrées or the daily market catch, broiled, blackened, or grilled. For a meat selection, consider the Caribbean glazed pork chops or sautéed chicken with spiced rum and a tropical fruit salsa. They have an extensive wine list and an assortment of themed beach drinks, including the infamous Florida Hurricane. A trademark dessert is bananas Foster, served in a chocolate-chip cookie bowl. A breakfast buffet is served on the weekend. Reservations are recommended.

Yen-Yen
321-783-9512
2 N. Atlantic Ave., Cocoa Beach 32931
Price: Moderate–Expensive
Cuisine: Chinese, sushi bar
Meals Served: L, D
Credit Cards: MC, V
Wheelchair Access: Yes

Original Asian artwork surrounds tables draped in crisp white linens at this upscale Chinese restaurant, famous for snow white prawns and sushi. Hot and sour soup is a good starter, as are the crispy egg rolls stuffed with tasty meat and vegetables. Moo goo gai pan and chicken with broccoli or cashews are popular selections. Service is sometimes a little slow, but each order is handled with care. A well-stocked bar can handle your drink order. Closed Monday; reservations are recommended for dinner.

Zachary's Family Restaurant
321-784-9007
8799 Astronaut Blvd., Cape Canaveral 32920
Price: Moderate
Cuisine: Greek, American
Meals Served: B, L, D
Credit Cards: MC, V
Wheelchair Access: Yes

A picture of the Acropolis on the cover of the menu sets the tone for the Greek recipes. Breakfast, served until 3 in the afternoon for late risers, features traditional dishes, as well as a feta cheese, spinach, and tomato omelet. For lunch, try the sampler, with a mouthwatering stuffed mushroom cap, spinach pie, cheese pie, stuffed grape leaves, gyro meat, and pita bread. Dinner entrées include leg of lamb or thin slices of lamb and beef seasoned with Greek spices and served on pita bread topped with tomato and tzatziki (cucumber sauce). The beer and wine list includes Greek varieties when available.

Central Brevard

Black Tulip
321-631-1133
207 Brevard Ave., Cocoa 32922
Price: Expensive–Very Expensive
Cuisine: Continental
Meals Served: L, D
Credit Cards: AE, D, MC, V
Wheelchair Access: Yes

For more than two decades the Black Tulip has earned a reputation as the best of fine dining in Brevard County. Chef Peter Yates creates delicious and insprired recipes. The lunch menu has a light offering of soups, sandwiches, and salads such as the Avocado Ritz Platter, a shrimp salad–stuffed avocado served with fruit and vegetables. Their signature dish for dinner is roast duckling covered with a sweet sauce of apples, cashews, and red wine. Familiar gourmet offerings such as chicken Cordon Bleu and grouper in puff pastry are available, and the restaurant has a full bar. Dine on the shady patio or in the elegant, warmly decorated dining room. Closed Sunday and Monday; reservations are recommended.

Café Flamant
321-631-0505
313 Delannoy Ave., Cocoa 32922
Price: Inexpensive

Cuisine: Continental
Meals Served: L; D Sun. and Mon.
Credit Cards: AE, D, MC, V
Wheelchair Access: Yes

Decorated in retro-European style, with an array of humorous "bad" bird paintings by artist John Kalinowski, this cozy café is a great stop for a pleasant lunch or light dinner. The menu features sandwiches, soups, salads, and quiche, along with a variety of coffee drinks, beer, and wine. On Sunday and Monday nights, chef Huie Martin Sr. serves fancier dishes. Jazz musicians, playing on Sunday, Monday, and Thursday evenings, promise jam sessions that sizzle. Closed Tuesday.

Café Margaux
321-639-8343
220 Brevard Ave., Cocoa 32922
Price: Very Expensive
Cuisine: Continental, French
Meals Served: L, D
Credit Cards: AE, D, DC, MC, V
Wheelchair Access: Yes

This jewel of a place, tucked away in a corner of a courtyard, has won several dining awards and was selected by Zagat as one of the most popular restaurants on the Atlantic coast. French cuisine fuses with Mediterranean and Asian influences, reflecting the international training of chef Erol Tugrul. Romantic dining rooms are decorated with elegant drapes and sparkling dinnerware. Waiters provide attentive service. Exotic hors d'oeuvres include baked Brie coated in macadamias with citrus cassis sauce, and fine duck liver and peppercorn pâté. For lunch enjoy blackened red snapper sandwich on warm French bread served outside in the courtyard. Dinner entrées include pastas, seafood, and meat dishes, including some adventurous choices like seared ostrich tenderloin and sesame-seared ahi tuna with a caramelized ginger-mango sauce.

Several dishes will appeal to vegetarians, and there is a separate menu for young adults. Cocktails, beer, and premium wines are available by the bottle or glass. Closed Sunday and Tuesday; reservations are recommended for dinner.

Diners enjoy an outdoor lunch at Café Margaux.
Eileen Callan

Cara Mia Riverside Grill
321-639-3388
11 Riverside Dr., Cocoa 32922
Price: Moderate–Expensive
Cuisine: Italian
Meals Served: L, D
Credit Cards: AE, D, MC, V
Wheelchair Access: Yes

After an afternoon in the shops and galleries of historic Cocoa Village, stroll down to the river and drop in at this pleasant, casual eatery, with a romantic view of the wide Indian River. Service and satisfaction are high priorities for this family-run business, which serves northern and southern Italian dishes. Chefs prepare the food in an open kitchen. Start with an antipasto such as mussels Cara Mia, the New England variety served in a white wine or marinara sauce. Chicken, veal, and seafood are cooked to order or combined with fresh pasta, seasonings, and a myriad of sauces and vegetables to create delicious entrées.

The wine list includes Italian and Californian varieties; house wines are available by the glass. Reservations are recommended for dinner.

Da Kine Diego's Insane Burritos

321-779-8226
1360 FL A1A, Satellite Beach 32937
Price: Inexpensive
Cuisine: Mexican
Meals Served: L, D
Credit Cards: MC, V
Wheelchair Access: Not in restrooms

On the surf highway, this small outdoor roadside diner, recently featured on the Food Network, is the exit for a cultural adventure. After working up an appetite on the waves, surfers stop to take on the challenge of the Insane Burrito, a mammoth mix of meat, beans, and rice wrapped in a tasty tortilla. A variety of smaller but equally delicious options are available. Come casual and grab a seat at one of the tables, and then add your name to the signatures left by famous and not-so-famous patrons over the years. Pack your board and head south about 12 miles from Cocoa Beach.

Lone Cabbage Fish Camp

321-632-4199
FL 520 at St. Johns River, Cocoa 32922
Price: Inexpensive
Cuisine: Casual fare
Meals Served: L, D
Credit Cards: AE, D, MC, V
Wheelchair Access: Not in restrooms

A meal at this rustic camp is about as close as you'll come to catching your own fish and frying it up in the pan. Try catfish, a house favorite, or something more adventurous, such as gator tail, frog's legs, or turtle. Everything is served in a basket with fries, hush puppies, slaw, or baked beans. Sit on a picnic bench on the deck outside overlooking the beautiful St. Johns River. The best time to visit is on the weekends, when you can enjoy an afternoon of bluegrass or country tunes, always held on Sunday and sometimes Saturday, too. Dessert is simple: Just pick your favorite from the Good Humor wagon. Beer, wine, and soft drinks are available, or go with a real Southern treat—sweet tea poured over a tall glass of ice. Airboat rides take off about every 30 minutes. Families, bikers, young, and old gather here for a good time and a taste of old Florida.

Bikers stop for Sunday-afternoon bluegrass at Lone Cabbage Fish Camp.

Wildlife Profile: Pelican

The big, bulky brown pelican is an odd-looking bird, with dull gray-brown feathers and a white head. A long, flat bill scoops up water, and an expandable black pouch holds the catch. On land, the pelican waddles on short legs and wide-webbed feet.

Everything changes when this amusing creature takes flight. Often flocks of pelicans form a V and glide and flap in unison like synchronized swimmers dancing in the blue waters of the sky. A single bird may coast for a long distance, just skimming the water's surface. In its most daring move, a pelican soars up to 60 feet high, suddenly diving headfirst into the water to grab a fish.

A more attractive cousin, the American white pelican, with white, black-tipped wings, arrives annually from the north to winter along Florida's shallow, fish-filled coastal lagoons.

Continued on next page

In spring both species of pelicans roost in colonies in the mangroves of the Indian River Lagoon, where eggs can be protected from predators and food is more readily accessible. Immature birds are distinguishable from adults by a brown head that turns white at three or four years of age.

Brown pelican (Pelecanus occidentalis) Jim Angy

The brown pelican is one of the most entertaining birds in the area. The adult eats 4 pounds of fish daily and is busy and visible even during the hottest hours. Pelicans track fishermen as well as fish. When boats return to the docks at Port Canaveral in late afternoon, the birds patiently queue up like theme-park visitors in line for the next attraction. Once the catch of the day is unloaded, pelicans sift the water for remnants of the day's catch. Remember that pelicans are wild and should not be directly fed.

Space Coast Sightings: Brown pelicans are always near the water—at the beach and in inland waterways. Spot them up close on fishing piers and docks. The best places to see white pelicans (November to March) are Merritt Island National Wildlife Refuge, Cocoa Beach Thousand Island, and the Port Canaveral locks.

Madison's Café

321-433-0234
630 Brevard Ave., Cocoa 32922
Price: Inexpensive
Cuisine: American
Meals Served: B, L
Credit Cards: AE, MC, V
Wheelchair Access: Yes

At the south end of Cocoa Village, this charming spot offers eclectic dining in a casual setting. Homemade soups and specialty salads are on the menu, along with 10 different kinds of gourmet chicken salads. Locals have given Monica, the owner, an informal award for the best grits in the area. Paintings by Fabian Marquez, Monica's father, decorate the warm, cocoa brown walls. Closed Sunday.

The Melting Pot

321-433-3040
2230 Town Center Ave., Viera 32940
Price: Very Expensive
Cuisine: American (fondue)
Meals Served: D
Credit Cards: AE, D, MC, V
Wheelchair Access: Yes

Gather around the fondue pot and dip in for fun, filling, and delicious food. Select your favorites from four courses. Start with a cheddar or Swiss cheese dip and a signature salad such as mushrooms and greens with a Parmesan Italian dressing. For the entrée, chunks of seasoned chicken, sirloin or filet mignon, seafood, and vegetables are gently lowered into hot oil or a vegetable bouillon base. For dessert, fruit, pound cake, and marshmallows are coated in milk or dark chocolate, which can be flavored with a liqueur such as like amaretto or Baileys. To accompany your meal, choose from a full bar and extensive wine list. This is a leisurely dining experience equally perfect for an intimate evening for two or a festive group outing. The restaurant opens at four each afternoon; reservations are recommended.

Murdock's Bistro and Char Bar

321-633-0600
600 Brevard Ave., Cocoa 32922
Price: Moderate–Expensive
Cuisine: Eclectic, Southern
Meals Served: L, D, SB
Credit Cards: AE, D, MC, V
Wheelchair Access: Yes

A grocery store back in 1940, this building has been renovated into a bright and airy restaurant with historical remnants from throughout Cocoa Village—windows from the old Hotel Brevard, rustic doors reclaimed for the bar top, and stained-glass windows on the ceiling. Dine inside, on the back porch, or at umbrella-covered side-walk tables. Live music is played Thursday through Saturday evenings. The fried olives and pickles are an unusual and tasty appetizer, and hamburgers come in five different combinations. They also have soups, salads, and sandwiches. The dinner menu includes old-fashioned dishes, including chicken fried steak, pork chops, and meat loaf, served with Southern sides such as fried okra, black-eyed peas, and grits. A full bar can handle any wine, beer, or cocktail request. Reservations are recommended for groups.

Murdock's Bistro and Char Bar in picturesque Cocoa Village

Ossorio

321-639-2423
316 Brevard Ave., Cocoa 32922
Price: Inexpensive–Moderate
Cuisine: American
Meals Served: B, L, D
Credit Cards: AE, MC, V
Wheelchair Access: Yes

Windows and bright colors transform this 1925 building in the center of historic Cocoa Village into an ideal spot for a break from shopping or to linger over a late lunch with friends. Behind the serving counter you'll find an array of delicious offerings, including French pastries, flat-bread pizza, sandwiches and salads, and an assortment of homemade, creamy ice creams. Seating spills onto the sidewalk, with an outside serving window and umbrella-covered tables. The coffee shop uses fresh-roasted beans to brew tempting lattes and cappuccinos. Wine and beer are available.

Pizza Gallery & Grill

321-259-7598
2250 Town Center Ave., Viera 32940
Price: Moderate
Cuisine: American, pizza
Meals Served: L, D, SB
Credit Cards: D, MC, V
Wheelchair Access: Yes

Food becomes art at this roomy, colorful, and casual restaurant located at the Avenue Viera. The walls are lined with local artwork that's available for sale, and your meal is served on an artist's paint palette. Pizza is the main attraction, and they carry the largest gourmet pizza menu in Brevard. Combine any of the 82 toppings in a style just your own, or pick one of the chef's masterpieces. Other food choices include the Warhol, a ground-chuck triple cheeseburger with onions, bacon, and cheddar and mozzarella cheeses, topped with lettuce, tomato, ketchup, and mustard. Seafood, chicken, and pasta entrées are also available, and they have a full bar and out-door patio. Sunday brunch includes complimentary mimosas and a sweet breakfast pizza with fruit, cinnamon cream sauce, powdered sugar, and a honey butter glaze. Reservations are recommended for groups.

Ulysses Prime Steakhouse

321-639-3922
234 Brevard Ave., Cocoa 32922
Price: Very Expensive
Cuisine: Steak
Meals Served: D
Credit Cards: AE, D, DC, V, MC
Wheelchair Access: Yes

This relative newcomer to Brevard County has taken fine dining up a notch and already has built a reputation as one of the best restaurants in central Florida. It's a true gourmet steakhouse with a nod to the Greek heritage of owners Alex and Pamela Litras. *Florida Today* restaurant critic Gene Cate dubbed it "the area's fine dining mecca." Culinary skill, artistic presentation, and impeccable service weave together for a truly exquisite and unforgettable evening. The Avgolemono soup, a traditional Greek chicken soup blended with egg, lemon, and orzo pasta, makes a great starter. Most entrées are beef, prepared to melt-in-your-mouth perfection. A tender filet mignon is filled with roasted plum tomatoes, spinach, kalamata olives, and feta. End the evening with the macadamia-pecan baklava, a sweet, flaky treat flavored with Mt. Rainer fireweed honey and a tangerine glaze. Fine wines and cocktails complement your meal. Be prepared for sticker shock: Most entrées are about $40. Closed Sunday; reservations are recommended.

North Brevard

Caffe Chocolat

321-267-1713
304 S. Washington Ave., Titusville 32796
Price: Inexpensive–Moderate
Cuisine: Sandwiches, salads, soups, and pizza
Meals Served: B, L, D
Credit Cards: AE, D, MC, V
Wheelchair Access: Yes

Tickle your taste buds in this European-style café, decorated in comfortable cream and espresso tones. The menu choices are what you'd expect—muffins, scones, and eggs for breakfast; sandwiches, soups, pizza, and salads for lunch and dinner; hot and cold coffee drinks; and chocolate desserts. The difference is the cornucopia of flavors that proprietors Joe and Huey Huberta add to the mix: Partner a pineapple muffin with a butter toffee latte. Drizzle feta cheese and Aegean dressing over a salad, and top pita chips with sesame, garlic, and lemon-seasoned hummus. Finish with an elaborate chocolate dessert or one exquisite piece fused with hazelnut, or cappuccino. The prices are reasonable and the servings are plentiful, with lots of choices for vegetarians. Wine and beer are available. Chocolate concoctions are available to take home, and the adjoining gallery sells wine and themed gifts. Closed Sunday; reservations are recommended for groups.

Dixie Crossroads

321-268-5000
1475 Garden St., Titusville 32796
Price: Moderate
Cuisine: Seafood, rock shrimp
Meals Served: L, D
Credit Cards: AE, D, MC, V
Wheelchair Access: Yes

Situated at the intersection of Garden Street and the path of the original Old Dixie Highway, this local landmark's signature is ocean-grown seafood served with a side of Southern hospitality. Their specialty is melt-in-your-mouth rock shrimp. Other shrimp varieties, such as red, pink, and Canaveral white, are available in season. Every meal starts with a basket of warm corn fritters sprinkled with powered sugar. The menu is simple, with seafood, chicken, and steak cooked to order, and a list of side dishes that includes fries, fresh vegetables, and a cinnamon-topped baked sweet potato. Shrimp are sold by the dozen, so you know just what to expect on your plate. The kid's menu has fish, shrimp, and clams, as well as the usual hamburger and chicken nuggets. Prices are reasonable, and most entrées are available in a small, medium, or large portion. This popular, don't-miss family restaurant often has a wait during peak times, so order a drink at the gazebo, enjoy the murals depicting native birds and animals, or feed the fish in the outdoor pond. Call ahead for priority seating.

Dixie Crossroads has great food in a casual setting.
Roger Scruggs

Fishing—and Dining—Run in the Family

Fishing has always been good on Florida's Space Coast. Capt. Rodney Thompson, whose father operated the Titusville fishing pier, made his living from the fruits of the sea. He was already a master shipbuilder when he decided to try his luck catching shrimp in the coastal waters. The biggest hauls came from rock shrimp, known locally as poor man's lobster. The tiny, hard-shelled crustaceans were nearly impossible to sell because they were so difficult to open and prepare. Thompson and his daughter Captain Laurilee teamed up to develop a machine to split the shells and then butter and broil the tender, tasty meat that is now a regional specialty. Seafood is still the family business: Thompson's daughter Sherri operates Wild Ocean Seafood market at Port Canaveral, and Laurilee serves boatloads of rock shrimp to guests at Dixie Crossroads, a Titusville landmark.

Kloiber's Cobbler Eatery

321-383-0689
337 S. Washington Ave., Titusville 32796
Price: Inexpensive
Cuisine: American
Meals Served: L, D
Credit Cards: D, MC, V
Wheelchair Access: Yes

In the heart of historic downtown Titusville, the building that now houses this diner was originally Denham Department Store, built in the 1890s. Exposed brick and broad wooden beams retain the rustic feel. The menu includes salads, quiche, sandwiches, and their specialty, fruit cobbler, served warm and topped with a scoop of rich, creamy vanilla ice cream. There is a small art gallery on the upper level. Closed Sunday.

Paul's Smokehouse

321-267-3663
3665 S. Washington Ave., Titusville 32796
Price: Moderate–Expensive
Cuisine: American, barbecue
Meals Served: D
Credit Cards: AE, D, MC, V
Wheelchair Access: Yes

Over the last quarter century, owner and Kentuckian Paul Salisbury's original riverside barbecue shack has grown into a three-story restaurant with a hybrid menu of home cooking and fine dining. Three dining rooms and a screened-in porch offer a stunning view of the Indian River and the towering Kennedy Space Center vehicle assembly building. Fresh seafood and beef are the specialties. Try steak or prime rib served along with an exceptionally soft and creamy baked potato, or enjoy a tender, tasty barbecue sandwich. Oysters are served raw, steamed, or fried. Two talented chefs enjoy preparing simple dishes, including grilled steak and shrimp scampi, as well as more unusual offerings such as mahimahi covered with avocado salsa. Finish your meal with a juicy slice of pie. Salisbury, an avid flyer, is associated with Angel Flights, a group that transports patients to distant medical centers. Closed Monday; reservations are recommended for groups.

South Brevard

Bella's

321-723-5001
1904 Municipal Ln., Melbourne 32901
Price: Moderate–Expensive
Cuisine: Italian
Meals Served: L, D
Credit Cards: AE, D, MC, V
Wheelchair Access: Yes

Step into the quiet and calm atmosphere of an old-world dining room. The bustling waiters and the aroma of garlic and fresh yeast breads will soon have your mouth watering. The menu is extensive; it's an almost overwhelming chore to read, but the food is all very good. Salads, soups, specialty pizzas, and hot subs made on Bella's Italian bread represent many of the casual dining choices. For a heartier dinner, try lasagna with three imported cheeses, spinach, and marinara sauce, or shrimp scampi peppered with Romano cheese and served over a bed of spaghetti. The food and atmosphere both feel like authentic Italian, with generous portions and gregarious hospitality. The restaurant is near the Henegar Center, making it a natural choice for dinner before the theater. Closed Sunday.

Chart House Restaurant

321-729-6558
2250 Front St., Melbourne 32901
Price: Expensive
Cuisine: Seafood, prime rib, steak
Meals Served: D
Credit Cards: AE, D, MC, V
Wheelchair Access: Yes

This upscale chain steak and seafood restaurant is located on a small peninsula in Melbourne Harbor that separates the Indian River and Crane Creek. The waterfront view is breathtaking and makes it a wonderful spot for a special occasion or romantic evening. Exceptional service begins with valet parking. A raw bar, impressive salad assortment, and appetizers such as calamari and crab-stuffed mushrooms are great starters. In addition to signature entrées such as Snapper Hemmingway—a sautéed snapper encrusted in a Parmesan and cracker mix and topped with jumbo lump crab—expect to find local favorites unique to the Melbourne location. Dessert lovers will drool over the hot chocolate lava cake. Reservations are recommended.

Continental Flambé

321-768-2445
936 E. New Haven Ave., Melbourne 32901
Price: Moderate
Cuisine: European
Meals Served: L, D
Credit Cards: AE, D, MC, V
Wheelchair Access: Yes

This stately establishment offers a relaxing and satisfying dining experience at an affordable price. The prix fixe menu includes an appetizer, salad, entrée, and dessert. Start with baked Brie, escargots with garlic and hazelnut butter wrapped in puff pastry, lobster crêpes, or chicken breast with shrimp in a pistachio basil cream sauce. Entrées include pasta, seafood, chicken, and beef dishes. Flaming desserts such as crêpes suzette and cherries jubilee are prepared at your table and end a pleasant evening with a dash of flair. More than four thousand wines are available from their cellar. Dine inside or at outdoor tables. Closed Sunday; reservations are recommended.

Island Pasta Company

321-723-1584
903 E. New Haven Ave., Melbourne 32901
Price: Moderate
Cuisine: Caribbean
Meals Served: L, D
Credit Cards: AE, D, MC, V
Wheelchair Access: Yes

The bright, colorful decor and fresh, healthy dishes here merge for a quick island getaway. Try shrimp-and-crab cakes with a Key lime and pineapple tartar sauce or the Blue Lagoon salad, with greens, candied walnuts, blue cheese, red onion, and grapes. Hawaiian pork is served with a spicy pineapple barbecue sauce. A delectable assortment of desserts is made on the premises. This casual spot has a full bar and is perfect for a leisurely lunch or dinner. Reservations are recommended for groups.

Meg O'Malley's

321-952-5510
812 E. New Haven Ave., Melbourne 32901
Price: Moderate
Cuisine: Irish, American
Meals Served: L, D
Credit Cards: AE, D, MC, V
Wheelchair Access: Yes

From lovely beginnings to happy endings, the leprechauns promise a good time at this friendly and popular restaurant and Irish pub. The food is first-rate. With a bow to tradition, a cup of the flavorful Irish Parliament soup is priced at 18 cents. Corned beef and cabbage with spicy grain mustard is served with colcannon, an Irish cabbage and potato dish, or boiled red bliss potatoes. The blackened prime rib sandwich is tender, juicy, and seasoned to perfection, topped with grilled onions and

farmhouse cheddar, and served on a kaiser roll with lettuce and tomato. End with Bushmill's bread pudding, made fresh daily from an old Irish recipe. Guinness on tap is just one of many domestic and imported beers, along with a full bar. Live entertainment lasts into the wee hours, with local music on Wednesday and Thursday, Irish music on Friday and Saturday. Reservations are recommended for groups.

Nosh & Ganache

321-254-1451
1540 Highland Ave., Melbourne 32935
Price: Moderate
Cuisine: French, American
Meals Served: L
Credit Cards: AE, D, MC, V
Wheelchair Access: Yes

Enjoy a casual lunch in the delightful garden patio at this cozy restaurant, located in the heart of Eau Gallie. The menu features soups, sandwiches, and salads. Inside is a wonderful assortment of hand-dipped chocolates, so it's not surprising that their signature dish is a puff pastry topped with soft Asiago, candied walnuts, and juicy cocoa-dusted Bosc pears. Closed Sunday.

Yellow Dog Café

321-956-3334
905 US 1, Malabar 32950
Price: Very Expensive
Cuisine: Gourmet
Meals Served: L, D
Credit Cards: AE, MC, V
Wheelchair Access: Yes

The Yellow Dog Café is an exercise in contrasts: fine dining served in a wooden shack; comfort food with gourmet touches. The restaurant is located along US 1 next to the Indian River, and every table has a front seat for a parade of boats and birds. Owners Stuart and Nancy Barton oversee this award-winning fine-dining restaurant. One tasty appetizer could be called "not your grandmother's potato pancakes." The crunchy patties are topped with sour cream, smoked salmon, and a spoonful of caviar. Stuart's favorite entrée is onion-crusted chicken with a caramel citrus glaze. Vegetarians have several choices, including a grilled portobello mushroom sandwich paired with roasted red peppers, artichoke hearts, spinach, and havarti cheese. Meat lovers will enjoy the well-seasoned mixed grill with the chef's combination of meats, such as duck, chicken, sausage, and lamb. Complement your meal with a choice from their extensive wine list. For dessert, bite into a chewy brownie shaped like a dog bone and topped with vanilla ice cream and fudge sauce. The service is phenomenal, and selections are presented with flair. There are four dining areas; one is the library, with floor-to-ceiling books and intimate tables, and another is a back porch deck. Dress is Florida casual, or a little dressier for dinner. Bring a framed photo of your favorite pooch to add to their collection. Closed Monday; reservations are recommended.

Food Purveyors

While dining is a fun part of the vacation experience, sometimes you want something quick and easy. Many fast food chains have locations along A1A, but there are also several local alternatives for coffee and a light breakfast, sandwiches to go, or easy meals to fix at the hotel while the little ones wind down from a day in the sun and surf. In addition to the sites listed here, most restaurants are happy to pack your order for take-out.

Coffee Shops and Bakeries

Cape Canaveral & Cocoa Beach

The Art of Coffee (321-783-0626; 2053 N. Atlantic Ave., Banana River Square Plaza, Cocoa Beach 32931). Paintings and pottery from local artists provide a colorful canvas for this welcome corner café. Sip a cappuccino or espresso, along with light breakfast or lunch. The doors may close early on weekends if the surf's up.

Carrie Lee's Coffee and Tea Co. (321-783-2230; 3550 N. Atlantic Ave., Cocoa Beach 32931). Open just briefly from 7–11 each morning, this quiet oasis inside the Wakulla Suites hotel, located just south of FL 520, offers coffee and tea drinks, along with freshly made muffins and rolls.

Starbucks (321-868-8950; 4001 N. Atlantic Ave., Cocoa Beach 32931). Feed your passion for your favorite flavored latte—skinny, no whip; you know the drill, and so do the baristas, who will have you quickly on your way, coffee in hand. It's part of the Four Points by Sheraton and is open daily from 6 AM to late evening. You can use short-term parking at the rear and enter through the lobby, or walk in via the separate front door.

Wahoo Coffee Co. (321-799-2464; 5675 N. Atlantic Ave., Cornerstone Plaza, Cocoa Beach 32931). Twenty-two different blends of fair-trade, organic coffees are freshly ground and roasted, ready for your favorite blend. Bagels, pastries, and homemade biscotti are the perfect accompaniment. Stop by for quiche on Sunday mornings.

Brevard County

Le Bon Cafe (321-725-2600; 802 E. New Haven Ave., Melbourne 32901). The aroma of fresh-brewed coffee—including more than 75 flavors, such as chocolate hazelnut and pumpkin spice—spills onto the sidewalk and draws you into this tiny diner. Enjoy Melbourne moonshine, a blend of cinnamon, Kahlúa, rum, and egg nog. Bagels and wraps are available.

Oleander Village Bakery and Fine Food (321-504-4301; 10 Oleander St., Cocoa Village 32922). A tempting assortment of salads, canapés, and baked goods are available at this tiny shop, reminiscent of a European patisserie. Try smoked salmon on a breakfast bagel, with a salad, or in a sandwich made from fresh-baked bread. Homemade desserts such as almond croissants and carrot cake are as pretty as they are delicious. Open for breakfast and lunch.

Sunrise Bread Company (321-268-1009; 315 S. Hopkins Ave., Titusville 32796). By the time this bright and welcoming shop opens its doors at 6 AM, the bakers have spent several hours milling whole-grain flour and baking it into all-natural breads, scones, bagels, and muffins, most without any preservatives, fats, or oils. Locals arrive early to be sure and get their favorite, like cranberry orange walnut, rosemary garlic, or nine grain. Baked goods are supplemented with a rainbow of coffees, teas, and smoothies. Two stories provide plenty of seating, so relax a while, or grab and go.

Village Cappuccino (321-632-5695; 407 Brevard Ave., Cocoa Village 32922). In the heart of historic Cocoa Village, this small Victorian parlor with a hint of old Florida serves guests coffee drinks and teas in porcelain cups, along with pastries and light sandwiches.

Enjoy a latte and a newspaper at the Art of Coffee.

Ice Cream and Candy

CAPE CANAVERAL & COCOA BEACH

Dairy Queen (321-784-8787; 3690 N. Atlantic Ave., Cocoa Beach 32931). Smooth, cold soft ice cream is just the thing on a hot beach day. Walk over to this longtime favorite for a cone or shake, a specialty such as the Peanut Buster Parfait, or a banana split.

Ricky's Ice Cream Treats (321-868-2990; 3690 N. Atlantic Ave., Cocoa Beach 32931). Ricky's offers a cool break for the warm sun, right across from the Cocoa Beach Pier. Pizza and sandwiches are available, but the specialty is ice cream. Try the Red & White, strawberry and vanilla ice cream with strawberry syrup, covered with whipped marshmallow, sprinkled with chopped walnuts, and topped off with a maraschino cherry.

Scoops of Cocoa Beach (321-783-9446; 7 S. Atlantic Ave. and Minutemen Cswy., Cocoa Beach 32931). This shop is so close to the beach at Shepard's Park, your ice cream won't have a chance to melt before you're back on the sand. They also offer cold drinks, fruit smoothies, and gourmet gelatos.

BREVARD COUNTY

Grimaldi Candies (321-724-0535; 815 E. Strawbridge Ave., Melbourne 32901). Visitors from other parts of Florida make side trips to this small shop to pick up a box or two of the legendary Florida-made Grimaldi candies. The most popular choice is probably the Chips 'N Chocolate, a deliciously delicate blend of sweet and salty.

Kilwin's of Melbourne (321-723-1141; 906 E. New Haven Ave., Melbourne 32901). If you've forgotten what it feels like to be a kid in a candy store, come visit this bright, charming shop in historic downtown Melbourne. Rich, creamy chocolates are made daily using the same recipes that have made Kilwin's a favorite with chocoholics for more than 60 years.

Tin Roof Popcorn Company (321-723-0200; 924 E. New Haven Ave., Melbourne 32901). Pick your favorite from more than 30 different flavors, such as savory and spicy honey mustard, sweet red cherry, or cheddar cheese. Seasonal choices include gingerbread and candy cane in the winter, and for spring a mix of blue raspberry, strawberry, and banana.

The Village Ice Cream and Sandwich Shop (321-632-2311; 120 Harrison St., Cocoa 32922). Pick up a quick lunch to go from the menu board of sandwiches and combine it with an old-fashioned grape or orange crush. Finish up with a cone from one of 35 flavors.

The Village Scoop (321-837-1050; 2001 Vernon Pl., Melbourne 32901). Pop into this old-time ice cream parlor for your favorite flavor of ice cream or a special candy treat.

Pizzerias and Cafés

CAPE CANAVERAL & COCOA BEACH

Calzoni's Pizza (321-783-1112; 6290 N. Atlantic Ave., Cape Canaveral 32920). Choose from pizza, 23 subs on fresh-baked bread, or their specialty—a Calzoni, a baked pizza sandwich that is part calzone and part stromboli.

The Italian Way Pizza and Cheese Steaks (321-783-5315; 5675 N. Atlantic Ave., Cornerstone Plaza, Cocoa Beach 32931). Eat in or take out hoagies, wings, calzones, salads, and pizza.

Juice and Java (321-784-4044; 20 N. Orlando Ave., Cocoa Beach 32931). Drop in at this neighborhood meeting place for fresh-ground coffee, teas, or healthful smoothies. Grilled sandwiches and deli wraps are made to order. Fresh bagels are served with cream cheese and salmon, or egg and cheese, plus meats, peppers, and onion. Wednesday evening is set aside for wine tasting and mingling.

Kim Bo (321-868-0188; 5675 N. Atlantic Ave., Cornerstone Plaza, Cocoa Beach 32931). Wide selection of Chinese foods are prepared at this small eatery, geared mostly for take-out. No MSG.

Mio's Pizzeria (321-784-4774; 9 S. Atlantic Ave., Cocoa Beach 32931). Right at the end of the Minutemen Causeway and close to Shepard's Park, this very casual eatery serves economy-priced pizza, pasta, sandwiches, calzones, and wings.

Mr. Cubana (321-799-2200; 6550 N. Atlantic Ave., Cape Canaveral 32920). Enjoy authentic dishes such as Cuban sandwiches and frita burgers—ground beef and chorizo sausage on a toasted bun, topped with cheese, diced onions, and shoestring potato chips. There is a small gallery of Cuban artifacts. Open for breakfast and lunch.

New China (321-868-7588; 2035 N. Atlantic Ave., Cocoa Beach 32931). Select from a menu of Cantonese-, Szechuan-, and Hunan-style choices.

The New Habit (321-784 6646; 3 N. Atlantic Ave., Cocoa Beach 32931). Before healthy eating was so popular, Connie, the owner, was mixing natural ingredients into salads, sandwiches, smoothies, and specialties such as spinach pie or a black bean enchilada. Fat-free and sugar-free frozen yogurt is blended with fruit and other flavors for a tasty, refreshing, low-calorie treat. This small shop is just steps from the beach ramp at the end of the Minutemen Causeway.

Indulge in a tasty and healthy frozen yogurt at New Habit.

Oceanside Cafe (321-868-0088; 6710 N. Atlantic Ave., Cape Canaveral 32920). This casual diner is a perfect stop for a quick meal. They open at 7 for breakfast and carry one of the best assortments of bagels on the beach. Lunch includes sandwiches and salads; dinner features traditional meals such as meat loaf and potatoes.

Papa Vito's (321-784-0050; 6200 N. Atlantic Ave., Cocoa Beach 32931). This small restaurant, located in an A1A strip mall, is known for its New York–style pizza. Two dining rooms are nicely decorated to create a relaxed setting.

Smokehouse Foods (321-784-9300; 525 Glen Cheek Dr., Port Canaveral 32920). For more than a decade, locals have enjoyed Smokehouse's smoked meats and seafood in sandwiches, salads, or packaged to go in six kinds of fish dip.

Thai Basil Takeout Cuisine (321-868-8262; 675 N. Atlantic Ave., Cocoa Beach 32931). Appetizers, soups, salads, curry, noodles, fried rice, and dinner entrées are all available for take-out.

3 Locos (321-868-3880; 4295 N. Atlantic Ave., Cocoa Beach 32931). This shop, on the corner of A1A and FL 520, serves creative combinations of panini sandwiches, including several for vegetarians. Smoothies are a welcome treat on a warm afternoon.

Uncle Al's New York Style Hot Dogs (321-799-9734; 5675 Atlantic Ave., Cornerstone Plaza, Cocoa Beach 32931). Take your pick from 13 different styles of grilled hot dogs, plain or piled high with chili, cheese, onions, and other toppings. Match it up with fries or crunchy onion rings. Burgers and sandwiches are also on the menu.

BREVARD COUNTY

Depot Café (321-722-9050; 1929 Depot Rd., Melbourne 32901). Located at the edge of downtown Melbourne, right along the railroad tracks, this is a great choice for breakfast or lunch. Favorites are burgers and homemade soup.

enJoy Café (321-956-8414; 820 E. New Haven Ave., Melbourne 32901). After a morning of shopping, enjoy a few minutes of relaxation and a salad, sandwich, or burrito at this open-air eatery in the Le Gallerie courtyard.

905 Café (321-952-1672; 905 E. New Haven Ave., Melbourne 32901). This quaint and cozy spot is perfect for meeting friends or grabbing a quick bite while shopping. Choose from the many flavors of coffee, or try an iced mocha with the popular Brie, apple, and walnut sandwich.

Ryan's Village Pizza (321-634-5555; 405 Delannoy Ave., Cocoa 32922). There's a new Irish lad in town, and he makes a perfect pizza with a crispy thin crust, a sweet tomato sauce, and piles of mozzarella cheese. The dough and sauce are freshly made every day. Stromboli, calzones, and submarine sandwiches are also on the menu. Add wine and beer, a tropical fruit slushie, or an iced mocha blend of espresso and chocolate.

The Sun Shoppe Cafe (321-676-1438; 540 E. New Haven Ave., Melbourne 32901). This friendly local hangout serves breakfast, lunch, and dinner. Enjoy soups, salads, and sandwiches, mostly homemade. Outside diners are welcome to bring their dogs.

Specialty Markets

CAPE CANAVERAL & COCOA BEACH

Canaveral Meats and Deli (321-799-2875; 8109 Canaveral Blvd., Cape Canaveral 32920). This small store off N. Atlantic Avenue is a one-stop shop for prepared salads, soups, and sandwiches; cold cuts and cheeses; and a sampling of grocery and produce products. The location is ideal for visitors staying in a Cape Canaveral vacation rental.

Deli at Publix Supermarket (321-783-1014, 5645 N. Atlantic Ave., Cornerstone Plaza, Cocoa Beach 32931; 321-784-0667, 2067 N. Atlantic Ave., Banana River Square, Cocoa Beach 32931). This Florida-based chain has two convenient area locations—one north of FL 520 and the other a few miles south. The deli features Boar's Head meats and cheeses, sandwiches made to order, and roasted and fried chicken with sides. In the produce section you'll find prepared salads and fruit bowls.

Harvey's Indian River Groves (321-783-8640; 3811 N. Atlantic Ave., Cocoa Beach 32931). The Indian River Lagoon area has produced world-famous citrus for more than 150 years. Take some fresh oranges, grapefruits, or other selections home during the season. Open late October–late April/early May.

Seafood Atlantic (321-784-0333; 520 Glen Cheek Dr., Port Canaveral 32920). Order fresh fish by the fillet, or pick from crabs, mussels, clams, scallops, and shrimp. Some choices, such as the crabcakes, are ready to pop in the oven.

Sunseed Food Co-op (321-784-0930; 6615 N. Atlantic Ave., Cape Canaveral 32920). For more than 30 years, Sunseed has carried a complete supply of natural foods, including bread and dairy products, produce, cereals, frozen meals, and baby food.

Wild Ocean Seafood Market (321-783-2300; 710 Scallop Dr., Port Canaveral 32920). Ocean-grown seafood is the specialty of this portside market. Purchase shrimp with or without the shell, whole lobsters or lobster tails, crab legs, and fish in season. Seasonings and sauces are extra; cooking advice is on the house.

BREVARD COUNTY

The Green Turtle (321-773-2001; 855 E. Eau Gallie Blvd., Indian Harbour Beach 32937). Grab a basket at the door of this gourmet to-go market, because you're going to find lots of goodies. Unique fruit and vegetable salads are prepared fresh each day. Soups and sandwiches are available, or an entrée such as stuffed chicken breasts, ready for the oven. You'll find bakery goods, snacks, candies, and other tempting treats, as well as more than eight hundred wines. The market is located on FL 518, just a short distance from A1A.

Hop N' Johns (321-639-6770; 200 Willard St., Cocoa 32922). In addition to shelves of packaged foods, this Southern-style gourmet grocery and deli carries an assortment of meats, cheeses, and freshly prepared salads. Browse through a wide selection of wines and create a personalized six-pack from an eclectic, international assortment of microbrewery beers.

Wild Ocean Seafood Market (321-269-1116; 688 S. Park Ave., Titusville 32796). Take home Florida's wild-caught seafood and ship gifts to family and friends anywhere in the continental United States.

Famous Indian River citrus is sold fresh in season at Harvey's. Eileen Callan

World Champion and Brevard County favorite son Kelly Slater masters the waves at Cocoa Beach   Roger Scruggs

6

Beaches and Surfing

Make a Splash

Morning arrives as a small golden bud swiftly blossoms into a vibrant sunflower against the backdrop of the velvety blue horizon. White-tipped waves crash against the sand in rhythmic tones. Early birds arrive with bold-colored towels, canvas chairs, coolers, and toys. Music and conversation mingles with seagull laughter. Surfers tug their boards against the tide, and then stand and entertain onlookers as they catch a wave and ride it to shore. Before the sun sets, beachgoers will broaden their horizons, go with the flow, and watch time slip away like sand through the hourglass.

Welcome to the beach!

Wide honey-colored beaches stretch out along the eastern coast of Brevard County like a endless Southern veranda. Settle in your chair and sip a cool drink while the sun warms your back and a soft breeze massages your skin. This is *the* original oceanfront property.

To find the beach, just head east on almost any street veering off A1A. In Florida the state constitution holds life, liberty, the pursuit of happiness, *and* access to the beach as self-evident rights. All land below the high-water mark is public property. Florida Supreme Court rulings have upheld the tradition. "The lure of the ocean is universal; to battle with its refreshing breakers a delight . . . the people of Florida—a State blessed with probably the finest bathing beaches in the world—are no exception to the rule . . . we, and our visitors too, enjoy bathing in their refreshing waters."

Today is your day to make a splash.

ATLAS OF BEACH PARKS

Access to Brevard County's 76-mile coastline is always just a few blocks away. The challenge is finding a location close to parking, restrooms, and other amenities. There are beach parks in every community, lining the shore like a string of pearls—each similar when seen from a distance, but distinctive in color and texture upon closer inspection. Every park is a jewel, but some might be more to your taste than others. This sampling covers beaches from Port Canaveral south to Patrick Air Force Base. Information is also provided for the undeveloped beaches of Canaveral National Seashore and Sebastian Inlet, which anchor the north and south ends of the county.

Cape Canaveral & Cocoa Beach

Cherie Down

321-455-1380
8492 Ridgewood Ave., Cape Canaveral 32920
Directions: From A1A, turn left on Jackson Ave. Turn left again on Ridgewood Ave. and travel for 5 blocks.
Open: Daylight hours
Parking: Free, in a small lot; tickets are issued for parking on the grass
Lifeguards: May–Sept., 10–7

Etchings of whimsical sea life lead to a ramped 200-foot boardwalk over the sand dunes and down to the beach. This small neighborhood beach park has been designed with children in mind. The clean, quiet beach is convenient if you're driving over from the Orlando area to spend a few hours by the surf. At low tide, the wide expanse of hard, flat sand is ideal for playing and building sand castles. The park has restrooms, outdoor showers, drinking fountains, picnic pavilions, and grills. Call ahead to book a picnic shelter.

Cocoa Beach Pier

321-783-7549
www.cocoabeachpier.com
401 Meade Ave., Cocoa Beach 32931
Directions: The pier is about 12 blocks north of FL 520
Open: 7–2 AM

The Cocoa Beach Pier: 800 feet of adventure

Parking: $7 per car per day; higher for special events
Lifeguards: May–Sept., 10–7

Built in 1962, the 800-foot Cocoa Beach Pier is a historic landmark and something-for-everybody beach recreational area. Waves break around the pilings, making the surrounding beaches popular with surfers and great for boogie boards and wave jumping. The pier has a ramp, shops, restaurants, and bars. To fish or just enjoy the view, pay the $2 fee to access the back section of the pier. Rent a rod and reel to fish; no license is necessary. Amenities include beach chair and umbrella rentals, arcade games, surf machine, volleyball nets and equipment, and a photo booth. Check out the live surf cam on the Web site for a great preview of the area.

Whimsical illustration of Cocoa Beach Pier Steve Harris

Jetty Park
321-783-7111
400 E. Jetty Rd., Port Canaveral 32920
Directions: Exit port entrance B and follow George King Blvd. to the end
Open: Daylight hours; fishing pier open 24 hours
Parking: $5 per car to park for the day; $10 for resident's annual pass
Lifeguards: Year-round

The Jetty Park beach is wide and long, the sand light and silky. In 2006 the Clean Beaches Council included Jetty Park among just 50 beaches in the country to receive their Blue Wave certification for quality and cleanliness. Parking space is plentiful unless it's an especially busy time, like a shuttle launch day or holiday weekend. The name comes from the jetty—a long stretch of rock piled high to separate the beach from the sea inlet. Walk to the end of the 1,200-foot Malcolm E. McLouth Fishing Pier for a great view of the continuous boat traffic. Amenities include nearby picnic pavilions, grills, and a playground; and restrooms, changing rooms, and showers. Inquire at the nearby campground office for use of volleyball and horseshoe equipment, and beach-accessible wheelchairs. A ramp extends from the parking lot to the boardwalk, and the chairs have large pneumatic wheels that roll through the soft sand. Alcohol and pets are not permitted. A small bait and tackle shop sells basics such as sunscreen, hats, towels, and drinks. The snack bar offers burgers, hot dogs, fries, and other items, and features an inside air-conditioned dining room or a rooftop patio.

Sunshine and socializing at Jetty Park beach

Lori Wilson Park

321-455-1380
1500 N. Atlantic Ave., Cocoa Beach 32931
Directions: 1.4 miles south of FL 520 and A1A
Open: Daylight hours
Parking: Free; two large lots are located on the north and south sides of the park
Lifeguards: Weekends Easter–Labor Day; daily Memorial Day–early August

This is the beach that feels most like a park. Enjoy the playground, sand volleyball court, pavilions, picnic tables, and grills on the north side. More picnic tables and a recently opened dog park are near the south lot. Both sites have restrooms, outdoor showers, drinking fountains, and vending machines. Almost all facilities are wheelchair accessible. This stretch of beach is perfect for swimming or celebrating a special occasion or family gathering.

Parking is plentiful and free, and concessions are within walking distance. Have your picture taken next to the I Dream of Jeannie Lane street sign at the entrance to the south parking lot. If it seems a little high, it's because when it was lower it was often mysteriously missing.

Minutemen Causeway in Cocoa Beach
321-868-3289
East end of Minutemen Cswy., Cocoa Beach
Directions: 2.7 miles south of FL 520 and A1A
Open: Daylight hours
Parking: Private lots and metered street parking
Lifeguards: None

This popular beach spot has long been a giant magnet drawing carloads of day-trippers on weekends and hot summer days. Teens and young adults cruise to see and be seen in this retro beach town. This is the kind of beach where you lug a cooler full of food and cold beverages, spread out the blanket, and make yourself at home. Dueling bars at the end of the Minutemen Causeway ensure lots of laughter, music, and good times. (Both bars feature live music on the weekends and some weekday evenings.) Volleyball games are often in progress. Finding a parking place is a challenge, however; a few private lots offer paid spots. If you park at a meter, bring plenty of quarters and stay paid up, because patrols continuously monitor and issue tickets. There are no public amenities, but the nearby bars are easygoing about letting folks use the restrooms. A wide variety of restaurants and food choices is available, and the more casual ones are fine with bathing-suit attire at lunch.

Patrick Air Force Base Seashore
321-494-1110
A1A, south of Cocoa Beach
Directions: 7 miles south of FL 520
Open: Daylight hours
Parking: Free; two lots
Lifeguards: None

Since 1940, U.S. military forces have maintained a base of operations south of Cocoa Beach, on a narrow strip of land between the Banana River and the Atlantic Ocean, and kept 4 miles of gorgeous, undeveloped beachfront open to the public. The coast curves a little here, providing a panoramic view of blue sky and cresting, white-tipped waves. Experienced surfers flock to this beach due to its highly desirable wave action. Two parking lots are at spots known locally as First Light and Second Light. As you head south, ignore the blinking light that's been added since the monikers were given, and you can easily find them. Amenities are about 3 miles away in downtown Cocoa Beach.

Robert P. Murkshe Memorial Park
321-455-1380
1600 S. Atlantic Ave., Cocoa Beach 32931
Directions: 5 miles south of FL 520
Open: Daylight hours
Parking: Free; small lot
Lifeguards: None

Murkshe was mayor of Cocoa Beach from 1963 to 1972 and an avid surfer. The crowds are usually sparse on this wide, sandy beach. Active waves make it a great spot for intermediate surfers. Amenities include restrooms, an outdoor shower, and a picnic shelter. Parking and restrooms are ADA accessible.

Shepard Park

321-868-3258
East end of FL 520 at Ocean Beach Blvd.
Directions: 1 block east of FL 520 and A1A
Open: Daylight hours
Parking: $6 per car per day; gated lot for 320 cars
Lifeguards: Weekends Easter–Labor Day; daily Memorial Day–early August

Old-timers remember when this was a quiet beach at the end of FL 520, once the main road from the inland. Today this city park, named for astronaut Alan Shepard, is right in the middle of the action and a quick walk from shops, food outlets, and hotels. There are surf lessons and rentals for gear, and chairs and umbrellas are available on the beach or at nearby locations. The parking lot fills up by midday during busy times. Amenities include picnic tables and pavilions, indoor and outdoor showers, and restrooms. A wheelchair-accessible boardwalk leads to the beach.

Multitasking Eileen Callan

Sidney Fischer Park
321-868-3258
2200 N. Atlantic Ave., Cocoa Beach 32931
Directions: 1 mile south of FL 520 and A1A
Open: Daylight hours
Parking: $5 per car per day; gated lot for 120 cars
Lifeguards: Weekends Easter–Labor Day; daily Memorial Day–early August

Families love this less-hectic beach within walking distance of food outlets. Amenities at the park include picnic tables and pavilions, indoor and outdoor showers, restrooms, and vending machines with snacks and cold drinks. The parking lot fills up quickly. The gate is automatic, and $1 or $5 bills are necessary to get through.

Brevard County

Playalinda Beach at Canaveral National Seashore
321-267-1110
FL 402, Titusville
Directions: From US 1, head east on FL 406/402 to the coast
Open: Daylight hours; closed for space launches
Entrance fee: $7 per person
Lifeguards: May 1–Sept. 1 at Lot 2

Playalinda Beach remains much as it might have looked when European sailors landed here nearly five hundred years ago—4 miles of undeveloped, wild coast at the southern end of Canaveral National Seashore. The pristine dunes and beach are a sanctuary for birds and wildlife. There are no amenities other than restrooms at each of the parking areas. Lot 8 has wheelchair-accessible parking and a beach ramp. If nudity offends you, consider stopping before you get to Lot 13 (the farthest lot), which has become a popular spot for natural sunbathers. Pets are not permitted, but alcohol is allowed in nonglass containers. For more information see the Merritt Island National Wildlife Refuge listing in the Recreation chapter.

Sebastian Inlet State Park
321-984-4852
www.floridastateparks.org/sebastianinlet/
9700 S. A1A, Melbourne Beach 32951
Directions: From A1A and US 192, go south for 20 miles
Open: Daylight hours
Parking: $5 per car
Lifeguards: Memorial Day–Labor Day

The 3 miles of beautiful beaches at Sebastian Inlet are a great compromise between minimal development and modest concessions. Beachgoers will find conveniently located restrooms and eating facilities. Sebastian Inlet has one of the best surfing breaks in Florida and is popular with experienced amateurs and professional surfers. For information on other activities, refer to the Sebastian Inlet State Park listing in the Recreation chapter.

The fishing pier at Sebastian Inlet is a front-row seat for professional surfing competitions Roger Scruggs

BEACH ENVIRONMENT & SAFETY

The Brevard County coast is a compromise between development and habitat preservation, and the beaches and waters are ranked among the cleanest in the state. Waves and erosion are a constant natural strain on sandy shores, but the wide, flat beaches south of Port Canaveral are replenished with sand dredged from miles out to sea. The beach begins at the dunes, a protective, sandy stretch thick with greenery such as saw palmetto palms and bushy sea grapes. Sea oats, the tall, wispy grasses with deep roots that trap the sand, strengthen the dunes. Tread lightly, however. While these sturdy reeds resist wind, drought, and saltwater, they are often done in by the footsteps of beachgoers.

The ocean is alive with life. Many marine creatures, including sea turtles, sharks, and the northern right whales, migrate to the warm Atlantic waters off Brevard. Dolphins and small rays are present year-round. Less-popular sea residents are the jellyfish and Portuguese man-of-war. Stings are not common, but they happen. The usual reaction is a rash in the contact area. Get medical attention if it gets worse. These creatures sometimes wash up on shore as clear or blue-tinted bubbles. Curious children are attracted to them, but they should stay away because venom can still be released. Coastal birds such as gulls and pelicans are common at the beach. The tiny sanderling is a favorite with children, who love to watch them play catch-me-if-you-can with the waves. The gray and white birds dine on marine morsels left behind as the ocean ebbs and flows. Low fence posts sometimes mark off upper sections of the beach, protecting nests made during the night by giant sea turtles.

Wildlife Profile: Great Blue Heron

One of the most engaging members of the beach community is the great blue heron. The lanky blue-gray birds wade in the surf at dawn and dusk, waiting to snatch fish caught by a surf fishermen. Each heron works alone and usually has a specific territory where it shows up on a regular basis. The majestic

Great blue heron (Ardea herodias) Jim Angy

birds stand picture-perfect without much concern about the humans around them.

At a height of 4 feet, the great blue heron is the tallest and most common North American member of the long-necked, long-legged heron family, which includes numerous species of herons, egrets, and bitterns. The wading birds thrive in the shallows and marshes of the Indian River Lagoon and set up breeding colonies on the mangrove islands. There they find sturdy branches to support their nests, a barrier of water to dissuade predators, and prime fishing waters. The common names given to the birds generally relate to their color and size. Several types live in this habitat: great and small, snowy, blue, reddish, green, and even a tricolored, with a bright blue head, gray feathers, and a black-tipped beak.

Many great blue herons prefer the banks of the lagoon waters, where they will patiently and slowly walk in the shallow mud until they spot a fish, snake, or shrimp. Then they dip their long, pointed bills into the water with great speed and precision and seize the prey, which they swallow whole. Because of their size, they can fish in deeper water than other wading birds. Like any good angler, the great blue heron is an early bird—most active at dawn and again at dusk when the fish are biting, or ready to be bitten.

Space Coast Sightings: Cape Canaveral and Cocoa Beach beaches, Ramp Road Park, Kelly Park, Viera wetlands, Merritt Island National Wildlife Refuge, most piers and docks.

Wildlife has adapted to living in populated beach locales, but visitors not familiar with the hot Florida sun may not adapt so easily. Use sunscreen, drink plenty of water, and wear sunglasses with protective lenses. Alcohol is permitted on Brevard County beaches, but be aware that drinking and *diving* can be as disastrous as drinking and driving.

Respect the power of nature. Get indoors if there's even a hint of lightning. Swim with others and stay close to shore when the waves are strong. If you find yourself caught in a rip current, swim parallel to the coast until free from the outbound current. Lifeguards are present at most beach parks during the busy seasons; pay attention to their warnings about current conditions.

Fun & Games

Activities at the beach range from doing absolutely nothing to doing a great deal, and then following it up with doing absolutely nothing for dessert. You might have your own favorite distraction, but here are some suggestions.

Beachcombing. When the high tide recedes, it leaves behind seashells, sea beans, and other ocean remnants. Because of the strong wave action and the way the ocean floor breaks, Space Coast beaches are not ideal for collecting seashells, but there are some perfect finds. Go slowly and look closely. The best time is early morning or low tide. Several shops, including Ana Lia Gift Shop and Exotic Shells & Gifts by Eleanor, both near the Minutemen Causeway, sell an assortment of shells, along with books to help identify each type.

Games. Beach shops carry an assortment of games and equipment, such as Frisbees, kites, and Velcro Ping-Pong sets.

Photography. A photo at the beach is the picture postcard everyone wants. Family groupings are always fun, or take a series of pictures to tell a story. Use a landmark to distinguish the setting, maybe a departing cruise ship in the background or in front of the Cocoa Beach Pier.

Reading. Settle your beach chair just beyond the incoming surf. Grab a cold drink and a crunchy snack. Close your eyes and listen to the lapping waves, squawking sea birds, and laughing children. Now reach into your beach bag, pull out a book, and drift into the pages. (For a list of Florida-themed books, see the Information chapter.)

Children love a day at the beach.

Sand Art. With the simplest of equipment—a bucket, small shovel, and some plastic cups—the youngest member of your party will be designing sand castles held together by the grout of imagination. Seashells become giant pencils for sketching in the sand at low tide. Sculpt flowers, trees, or large fish.

Turtle Walks. From May to August, in the dark of night, giant sea turtles lumber onto the beaches of Brevard County and create a nest to deposit their eggs. The sight is overwhelming. The turtles are protected, but four local groups are authorized to escort small groups onto the beaches during June and July: Canaveral National Seashore (321-428-3384, ext. 18), Merritt Island National Wildlife Refuge (321-861-0667), the Sea Turtle Preservation Society (321-676-1701), and Sebastian Inlet State Park (321-984-4852). Walks begin with an information session and last for three or four hours. They are not recommended for disabled people or small children. Bring bug repellent. If you're visiting during turtle season, check booking dates and guidelines as early as possible. Sometimes there are cancellations, and last-minute spots may be available.

Volleyball. Joining a fast-paced game of volleyball is the beach version of pick-up basketball at the neighborhood court. Nets are always up and games frequently in process at Jetty Park, Cocoa Beach Pier, and the Minutemen Causeway. Bring your own ball, and chances are you'll find others ready to jump into the fun.

Beach volleyball games are popular with the young crowd. Eileen Callan

Walking. The long, uninterrupted stretch of sand along Cape Canaveral and Cocoa Beach makes it the perfect path for walking, running, or biking. At low tide, the hard sand close to the water is a smooth, easy surface. Go barefoot at your own risk and keep an eye cast downward to avoid broken shells. Find a landmark to track your starting point.

Water Sports. You don't have to be a world-class athlete to boogie board or bob in the waves on an inflatable dolphin or inner tube. Bring some water-ready gear with you and dive right in. The latest craze is skimming—jumping on a small thin board and coasting along the shallow water.

BEACH GEAR

Beach Rentals of Cocoa Beach
no phone
3650 N. Atlantic Ave., Cocoa Beach 32931
Owner Adrianne continues a business started by her grandfather John more than 50 years ago, when Cocoa Beach was just gaining in popularity and cars drove on the sand. Trailers at Shepard Park and 2 blocks south at the end of Marion Lane rent chairs, umbrellas, cabanas, and surf and body boards.

Beach Unlimited
321-784-3310
3650 N. Atlantic Ave., Cocoa Beach 32931

Choose from a wide assortment of reasonably priced beach towels, T-shirts and tanks, sand toys, and practical supplies.

Beach Wave
321-783-0180
5490 N. Atlantic Ave., Cocoa Beach 32931
321-783-3399
1275 N. Atlantic Ave., Cocoa Beach 32931
321-783-1848
185 W. Cocoa Beach Cswy., Cocoa Beach 32931

Three stores scattered along A1A supply affordable necessities for hitting the beach and catching some rays, including towels, chairs, umbrellas, mats, bathing suits, sunscreen, and more.

Cocoa Beach Surf Company
321-799-9930
4001 N. Atlantic Ave., Cocoa Beach 32931

Wander through a vast selection of surf, boogie, and skim boards; bikes; skateboards; wet suits; and sport accessories. The third floor is for hard-core players and features top-of-the-line, professional brands of surfboards and skateboards for sale and rent. For more information see the Shopping chapter.

Sign up for surfing lessons at the Cocoa Beach Surf Company tent.

Ron Jon Surf Shop

321-799-8888
www.ronjons.com
4151 N. Atlantic Ave., Cocoa Beach 32931

More than 40 years ago, Ron Jon Surf Shop opened as an outlet to sell surfboards. That's still their most important product—longboards, mini boards, fish boards with a notched tail at one end, and egg boards. Find them in every color and style. For variety, look for bodyboards, Indo boards, skateboards, and skimboards. They carry everything you need to hit the waves, including wax, protective pads, wet suits, and leashes. Look through a collection of DVDs and books for surfing entertainment and information. There may be numerous Ron Jon Surf Shops around the world

Ron Jon Surf Shop

today, but a visit to the 52,000-square-foot Cocoa Beach location is still a one-of-a-kind adventure. For more information see the Shopping chapter.

SURFING

Surf's up! The Space Coast beaches are perfect for weekend surfers and experts honing their skills. If surfing is something you've never experienced but always wanted to try, this is the perfect place to start. Coaches promise that with a small investment of time (one or two hours) and money, almost anyone at any age can ride a wave—a great photo for the mantle back home. The waters along the Cape Canaveral and Cocoa Beach coast are usually mild, and the ocean is rock-free. The beaches at Patrick Air Force Base and farther south are for more experienced surfers. Sebastian Inlet, with strong surf and challenging waves, is for experts. For reports on surf conditions and surf cam videos, go to www.surfguru.com.

Cocoa Beach Surf Company Surf School
321-868-8966
www.cocoabeachsurf.com.
4001 N. Atlantic Ave., Cocoa Beach 32931

Local surf legend Joe Twombly (left) invites Urban Meyer, University of Florida football coach, to give surfing a try. Courtesy Joe Twombly

Debbie and Jimmy Walker manage this operation under the umbrella of the Cocoa Beach Surf Company. Lessons begin in the store on a pop-up board, and then continue in the ocean down the street near Shepard's Park. Rent surfboards, bodyboards, and wet suits, as well as bikes, umbrellas, and chairs. Soft boards are available for beginners; high-performance boards for experienced riders. Take private lessons, or sign up with a group. A three-hour clinic starts every Saturday morning at 9. There's no need to register; just arrive a little early and sign up at their beach tent. Summer camps are conducted from May through August. Surfboard rental is $15–40 for a day; private lessons are $75 per hour.

Catch a Wave

Surfing was born in Hawaii, swept into California, flowed across America, and rolled up on the shores of Cocoa Beach. Like many teens, Joe Twombly moved here with his family during the buildup of the space program. These new kids in town hit the waves and never looked back. Twombly learned to surf when "hang 10" was a skill set, not a catch phrase—the art of balancing on a long and heavy wooden board with all 10 toes hooked around the front edge.

By the time Neal Armstrong stepped onto the lunar surface, Cocoa Beach was gaining recognition and respect from surfers around the world. Under the tutelage of professional surfer and coach Dick Catri, home-grown athletes such as Twombly and Gary Propper were competing and winning world championships. Sons and daughters of engineers were experimenting with foam, fiberglass, and resin to create boards that were shorter, lighter, and more flexible. Cocoa Beach became a center of excellence for the sport of surfing.

Today Cocoa Beach is undisputedly the East Coast surfing capital. The distinctive cape jutting into the ocean creates swells along the coastal curve, with smaller and shorter waves. Surfers have to develop maneuverability and finesse to have a great ride. A good analogy might be parallel parking in a tight space. After mastering that, pulling into a parking lot spot is much easier. At Sebastian, in the south, the ocean floor contour rises about a third of a mile from the beach, and often has monster waves that challenge the experienced surfer.

Kelly Slater, another surfer who grew up on the waves of Cocoa Beach, has won a record eight world titles during his professional career, which has spanned more than a decade. Twin brothers Damian and C. J. Hobgood are also winning competitors on the world surfing tour. Somewhere in Cocoa Beach, future champions dream of their turn in the sunshine. When word spreads that the waves are good, local teens grab their boards, paddle out toward the horizon, and wait to catch the wave.

Natural Art Surf Shop
321-783-0764
www.naturalart.com
2370 S. Atlantic Ave., Cocoa Beach 32931

Learn from the pros. Deb Dooley fell in love with surfing as a young teen, and when she graduated from high school, she packed up her car and headed for Cocoa Beach. Today, she and husband Pete are both members of the East Coast Surfing Hall of Fame and provide novices and experienced riders with tips and techniques for mastering the sport. Call 321-784-2400 for a daily surf report. Surfboard rental is $20 for a day; private lessons are $50 per hour.

Nex Generation Surf School
321-591-9577
www.nexgensurf.com
P.O. Box 218A, Indian Harbor Beach 32937

Brian Gale has been surfing since 1987 and competing since 1992. He and a team of experienced instructors offer private and group lessons, parties, and summer camps. Every session begins with a 15-minute ocean-water safety and marine-life awareness discussion. Participants range from as young as age four to well past retirement years. Competitive training sessions are available. Lessons are given at the Comfort Inn & Suites at 3901 N. Atlantic Avenue in Cocoa Beach. Three-hour surf clinics begin every Saturday morning at 9 AM. Private lessons are $60 per hour.

Ocean Sports World
321-783-4088, 1-800-777-2613
www.oceansportsworld.com
3220 S. Atlantic Ave., Cocoa Beach 32931

Surfer Roy Scafidi and his wife, Pam, run this outpost on the narrowest part of the island, near the beaches of Patrick Air Force Base. Rent surfboards, kayaks (with life jackets), paddleboards, wave skis, and kiteboards. Used equipment is for sale. Lessons are available by the hour or through one of the weekly camps, and they are held in the ocean or river near the shop. Surfboard rental is $30 for a day; private lessons are $50 per hour.

Quiet Flight Surf Shop

321-783-1530
www.quietflight.com
109 N. Orlando Ave., Cocoa Beach 32931

Rent boards by the day from this shop, conveniently located just a few blocks from downtown Cocoa Beach. Private lessons are available for groups of one to three surfers. Check their Web site for daily reports on wind, tide, and wave conditions. A credit card deposit is required for all rentals. Surfboard rental is $20 for a day; private lessons are $40 per hour.

Ron Jon Surf School by Craig Carroll

321-868-1980
www.ronjonsurfschool.com
150 E. Columbia Ln., Cocoa Beach 32931

Professional surfer Craig Carroll has been riding the waves of Cocoa Beach for 40 years and now runs this school for beginner and advanced students. Summer camps are held for students age eight and older. Private and group lessons are available. Safe, soft surfboards are used, and lessons include safety and marine-awareness instructions. Lessons begin at the school building and continue at nearby Shepard's Park. Private lessons are $60 per hour.

Ron Jon Watersports

321-799-8888
www.ronjons.com
4275 N. Atlantic Ave., Cocoa Beach 32931

Located just across the road from Ron Jon Surf Shop, this store has everything you need for an active day at the beach. Surfers can rent foam and fiberglass boards, beach bikes, kayaks, and wet suits. Renters must be 18 or older, and a credit card deposit is required. Surfboard rental is $10–20 for a day.

Space Coast Surfing Academy

321-783-0222
www.spacecoastsurfingacademy.com
8401 N. Atlantic Ave., Cocoa Beach

Competitive surfer and lifeguard Jeff Kennedy is on a mission to teach the joys of surfing in a safe, fun, and successful way—and even guarantees anyone can learn to surf. Private and group lessons and summer camps are usually held on the beaches off Lori Wilson Park, where the waves are usually a mild-to-medium intensity. A session on safety, marine-life awareness, and surfing etiquette is part of every class. Jeff recommends pupils be age seven or older. Private lessons are $50 per hour.

Surfet's Surf Shack

321-868-3021
www.surfet.com
165 N. Orlando Ave., Cocoa Beach 32931

Monica Dyer specializes in teaching girls and women to hit the waves with confidence in programs for individuals and groups, beginner and advanced. Take a private class, attend a weekend clinic, or register for a special program such as the mother/daughter weekend or Fiesta Party, perfect for groups of 10–20 celebrating a birthday or special occasion. Weekly summer day camps are held from late May through July. Rent boards for the day or half day. Surfboard rental is $20 for a day; private lessons are $40 per hour.

BEACH AND SURFING EVENTS

January

Sebastian Inlet Pro
Sebastian Inlet
The first World Qualifying Series surfing competition of the year is held in early January at Sebastian Inlet State Park. Ron Jon presents the event, which features the elite on the World Championship Tour. Four days of events are spread over a week, and the surfing schedule varies based on the tides, waves, and weather.

March

Ron Jon Easter Surfing Festival
Cocoa Beach Pier and Shepard's Park
In 1964 a Cocoa Beach community group held an Easter weekend surf festival to attract crowds, and the tradition continues. In 2007 more than a hundred thousand gathered to watch the best surfers in the world compete for top prizes in men's and women's championship shortboard and longboard events. The family-friendly festivities begin on Thursday and include concerts, beach games, exhibits, special events, an Easter egg hunt, and sunrise services on Easter morning. Everything is free; everything is fun.

May

Beachfest
Cocoa Beach Pier
Each Memorial Day weekend, beach culture blends with the military heritage of Florida's Space Coast for three days of food, fun, music, activities, and contests. More than five hundred military and law enforcement personnel, firefighters, and lifeguards compete in events such as an ocean relay race, a paddleboat race, and a volleyball tournament. Members of the armed forces hold exhibits and demonstrations, and on Monday they join together for a special tribute to the military. The event ends with a bugle rendition of taps.

June

Waterman's Challenge Surf Contest Weekend
Holiday Inn Cocoa Beach–Oceanfront Resort
Since 2001 the East Coast Surfing Hall of Fame has presented this summertime, family-friendly surfing competition. Held over two days, the event is designed to highlight the

history of surfing, encourage participation in the sport, and provide amateurs with a less-intense forum for competing. In keeping with the broad definition of a waterman (a term from the 1950s used to describe surfers, lifeguards, swimmers, and others who lived and played on the water), activities such as paddling may also be part of the weekend. The weekend is sponsored by Ron Jon Surf Shop and hosted by Holiday Inn Cocoa Beach–Oceanfront Resort.

September

Doctors, Lawyers, and Weekend Warriors
Sebastian Inlet
Surfing goes upscale each September when professionals and grown-up surfers from throughout the state join to spread a positive message about the sport, raise money for charity, and have a great time.

National Kidney Foundation of Florida Pro-Am Surf Festival
Lori Wilson Park
Presented by Cocoa Beach Surf Company, this surfing event, which started in 1985, is the largest event of its kind to benefit a charity. Professional surfer Richard Salick was at the peak of his career when his kidneys failed. His twin, and fellow pro surfer, Phil, was a tissue match and donated a kidney, and Richard was able to return to competition. Both brothers remain involved in this popular surfing competition and family festival, held over Labor Day weekend.

October

International Sea-Bean Symposium and Beachcomber's Festival
www.seabean.com
Cocoa Beach Public Library
550 N. Brevard Ave., Cocoa Beach 32931

Since 1995 this low-key two-day event has combined education and fun with activities, speakers, and displays to draw attention to the joy of collecting sea beans (also known as drift seeds, they fall from plants and trees into waterways and eventually reach the ocean) and the importance of ecological awareness. Saturday morning begins with a Bean-a-Thon beachcombing trek. When things wrap up on Sunday at 5, everyone present is invited to join the group for dinner at a nearby restaurant.

Sail down the Indian River with Indian River Cruises Courtesy Indian River Cruises

7

RECREATION

Nature's Theme Park

"A true conservationist is a man who knows that the world is not given by his fathers but borrowed from his children." John Audubon said this, and he would have liked Brevard County, where an abundance of green space and natural habitat are preserved as a safe, secure playground for birds and wildlife. Fortunately, this also creates a myriad of great recreational opportunities for two-legged creatures to enjoy. Take a nature tour, paddle a kayak, or rent a boat and explore the waterways. Head to the ocean on a fishing charter or cruise. Pick up some binoculars and do a bit of bird-watching. Grab the family for a day at the zoo or the springtime thrill of baseball. Golfers will discover that courses are often in harmony with natural habitats.

This natural "theme park" has thrills and surprises, such as playful dolphins scooting around a kayak, a magical snowy egret posing regally at river's edge, and stoic alligators lying in wait at Merritt Island National Wildlife Refuge. The natural cast of characters is unpredictable and spontaneous, and your adventure is sure to be memorable.

ATLAS OF NATURE PRESERVES & PARKS

The following are just a few of the brightest jewels on an exquisite chain of emerald green parcels dotting the Brevard County landscape. They are easily accessible to visitors and are popular sites for most recreational activities. Wildlife is present at all of these natural environments. For your protection and theirs, keep your distance. If the birds and animals become too accustomed to human intervention, they lose the ability to survive in the wild. Depending on the activity, consider whether you need to take along water, binoculars, bug repellent, comfortable shoes, a hat, and sunscreen.

Cape Canaveral & Cocoa Beach

Johnnie Johnson Nature Trail
321-868-1123
www.brevardparks.com/nature
1500 N. Atlantic Ave., Cocoa Beach 32931
Directions: At Lori Wilson Park, 1.5 miles south of FL 520
Open: 7 AM–dark

Admission: Free
Activities: Birding, wildlife

Located in the middle of Lori Wilson Park, this nature boardwalk offers a glimpse of one of the last undeveloped maritime hammocks at the beach. The short walk is ADA accessible, and signs identify plants and trees. Birds, butterflies, raccoons, snakes, and other small critters call the area home. Guided tours are available for groups.

The Johnnie Johnson Nature Trail at Lori Wilson Park is stroller- and wheelchair-friendly.

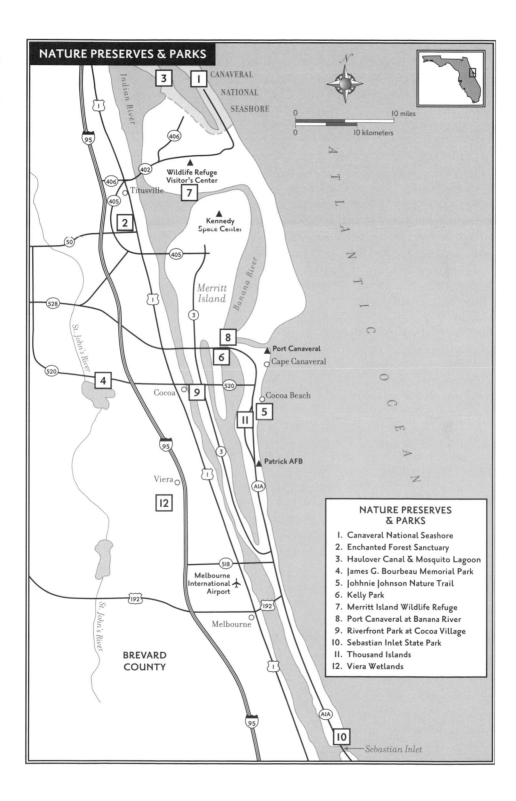

NATURE PRESERVES & PARKS

CANAVERAL NATIONAL SEASHORE

Indian River

Wildlife Refuge Visitor's Center

Titusville

Kennedy Space Center

Merritt Island

Banana River

Cocoa

St. John's River

Port Canaveral
Cape Canaveral

Cocoa Beach

Patrick AFB

Viera

Melbourne International Airport

Melbourne

ATLANTIC OCEAN

BREVARD COUNTY

St. John's River

Sebastian Inlet

0 — 10 miles
0 — 10 kilometers

NATURE PRESERVES & PARKS

1. Canaveral National Seashore
2. Enchanted Forest Sanctuary
3. Haulover Canal & Mosquito Lagoon
4. James G. Bourbeau Memorial Park
5. Johhnie Johnson Nature Trail
6. Kelly Park
7. Merritt Island Wildlife Refuge
8. Port Canaveral at Banana River
9. Riverfront Park at Cocoa Village
10. Sebastian Inlet State Park
11. Thousand Islands
12. Viera Wetlands

Kelly Park

321-455-1380

www.brevardparks.com

2550 N. Banana River Dr., Merritt Island 32952

Directions: Located at the south side of the Banana River, at the FL 528 and Banana River Dr. exit

Open: 7 AM–dark; boat ramp 24 hours

Admission: Free

Activities: Birding, boating, windsurfing

This popular all-purpose park is a stop on the Great Florida Birding Trail and a launching point for private and commercial boats. The shallow, protected cove along the Banana River has a small natural beach and catamaran/sailboard launch, and the area has acquired international acclaim with windsurfers. A scenic area near the lagoon has pavilions seating up to one hundred, volleyball courts, and a playground. Groups are advised to book the pavilions in advance. The large parking lot has plenty of spots for cars and boat trailers, but it still fills up quickly on weekends. Most facilities are ADA accessible. No pets. Alcohol is restricted to posted areas.

Port Canaveral at Banana River

321-783-7831

www.portcanaveral.org/recreation

FL 528 at Cape Canaveral

Directions: Exit into the port at George King Blvd. off FL 528

Open: Varies by activity

Admission: Free, except for $5 day parking fee at Jetty Park

Activities: Birding, boating, camping, cruising, fishing

Port Canaveral is a man-made inlet connecting the Atlantic Ocean and the Banana River, and locks at the port minimize the impact of tides on the river's water level. Small recreational boats, deep-sea fishing ships, large cruise ships, and commercial and military barges all ply the waters of the busy port. Marinas and launches in the port offer boaters quick access to the ocean, and three public waterside parks host recreational facilities: Jetty Park, Freddie Patrick Park, and Port's End Park. Observe posted security rules.

Thousand Islands

321-868-3252

www.ci.cocoa-beach.fl.us

Ramp Rd., Cocoa Beach 32931

Directions: From A1A, go west on Fifth St. S. Take a left on Brevard Ave., and then turn right on Ramp Rd.

Open: Daylight hours

Admission: Free

Activities: Boating, fishing, paddling

Ramp Road Park is the entry point to the Thousand Islands of Cocoa Beach, a group of about 50 unadorned mangrove islands located just south of FL 520 in the Banana River Aquatic Preserve. Shallow-water trails teem with manatees, dolphins, and birds, and paddlers will find this to be a very easy and enjoyable experience. The park has two ramps, picnic facilities, and a fishing dock.

Central Brevard

James G. Bourbeau Memorial Park
321-633-1874
www.brevardparks.com/nature
8195 King St. (FL 520), Cocoa 32926
Directions: 5 miles west of I-95 on FL 520
Open: Daylight hours; boat ramp 24 hours
Admission: Free
Activities: Birding, boating, fishing, paddling

The winding St. Johns River flows south to north through Florida and forms much of the western border of Brevard County. Nature writer Bill Belleville describes the path of this liquid highway as "an indigo snake working its way through the tall rushes and reeds." Outdoor adventurers, boaters, and bass fishermen love gliding out on this American Heritage river, thick with sawgrass and alligators. This park, near the intersection of Lake Poinsett and FL 520, provides easy access to the river. Across the street, the Leroy Wright Recreation Area has additional parking for cars and boat trailers.

Riverfront Park at Cocoa Village
321-639-3500
www.cocoafl.org
Harrison Ave., Cocoa Village
Directions: West side of Indian River at FL 520
Open: Daylight hours
Admission: Free
Activities: Boating, fishing, family fun

Enjoy an outdoor break from shopping in Cocoa Village at this 10-acre recreational site bordering the Indian River. The area has an amphitheater, water feature, playground, boardwalk, and facilities for fishing and boat launching. Restrooms are ADA accessible.

Viera Wetlands
321-255-4328
South Central Wastewater Treatment Facility
Wickham Rd., Viera 32940
Directions: The entrance is off Wickham Rd., 2 miles west of I-95
Open: 7 AM–dusk
Activities: Birding, hiking

Right after sunrise is the best time to visit Viera Wetlands, a man-made habitat that attracts unique communities of birds. The dirt drive in front of the wastewater plant leads to the wetlands. The narrow 2-mile path is so close to the natural elements, it's easy to spot a bird and get a good photograph using your car as a blind. An observation tower overlooks the grassy prairies. Parking for hikers is available.

The Viera Wetlands is a haven for birders and photographers.

North Brevard

Canaveral National Seashore

321-267-1110
www.nps.gov/cana
308 Julia St., Titusville 32796 (local office)
Directions: Go east on FL 406/402 from Titusville
Open: Daylight hours
Admission: $7 per person
Activities: Birding, camping, fishing

Canaveral National Seashore is the longest stretch of undeveloped, unspoiled beachfront on Florida's east coast. Sunbathe, swim, surf, and fish along an ocean shore virtually unchanged from when it was inhabited by ancient settlers. From the refuge, enter on FL 402. Playalinda Beach, at the southern end, is accessible from FL 402, where a paved road leads to several parking areas with restroom facilities. There are no other amenities. Eight magnificent vistas in the lagoon and dunes are great spots to view plants and wildlife, as well as the Kennedy Space Center launch complexes. Wheelchair access is available at parking lot 8. For more information on the beaches, see the Beaches and Surfing chapter.

Enchanted Forest Sanctuary

321-264-5185
www.nbbd.com/godo/ef/
444 Columbia Blvd., Titusville 32780
Directions: North side of FL 405; 0.5 mile west of US 1
Open: Daily 9–5
Admission: Free
Activities: Birding, trails

Long a local favorite, the Enchanted Forest Sanctuary was acquired by the Environmentally Endangered Lands (EEL) program in 1990 and is their flagship preserve in Brevard County. The Management and Education Center has hands-on exhibits and interpretive displays, as well as guided tours every Saturday morning at 10. Several short trails weave through the 428-acre park. Five uniquely different habitats host an abundance of wildlife. The operation is subsidized by donations and purchases from the charming gift shop, operated by the Friends of the Enchanted Forest. Call to schedule guided tours for groups. Pets, bikes, and smoking are prohibited. The parking lot, garden, and one trail are ADA accessible.

Haulover Canal & Mosquito Lagoon

321-861-0667
www.fws.gov/merrittisland
Merritt Island National Wildlife Refuge
Directions: US 1 or I-95 north to FL 406; 10.5 miles from visitors center
Open: Daylight hours; sections may close for space launches
Admission: Free
Activities: Birding, boating, fishing, paddling

The Haulover Canal links Mosquito Lagoon to the Indian River Lagoon and is an incredibly beautiful, peaceful waterway where birds, manatees, and dolphins mingle with boaters, paddlers, and fishermen. Paddling here is just a little more challenging than in the Thousand Islands at Cocoa Beach. A manatee observation deck is on the east side of FL 406, and a significant number of these docile creatures swim in the Haulover Canal year-round. The platform is ADA accessible. Mosquito Lagoon is aptly named, so bring bug repellent.

Merritt Island National Wildlife Refuge

321-861-0667
www.fws.gov/merrittisland
North Merritt Island
Directions: US 1 or I-95 north to FL 406; east over Indian River Lagoon
Open: Refuge is open during daylight hours; sections may close for space launches. The visitors center is open Mon.–Fri. 8–4:30, Sat. and Sun. 9–5; closed federal holidays.
Admission: Free
Activities: Birding, boating, fishing, paddling, trails

Unique Merritt Island National Wildlife Refuge is one of the most accessible natural habitats in America. When NASA acquired land to build a space center, 140,000 acres on north Merritt Island were set aside as a buffer and are protected by the U.S. Department of Interior as a national wildlife refuge and seashore. The many diverse habitats commingle and are home to more than five hundred species of wildlife and the highest number of endangered and threatened species found in any wildlife refuge. First-time guests should begin at the visitors center. From there, every area of the refuge is within a 15-mile drive. The visitors center and boardwalk trail are ADA accessible. See the sidebar later in this chapter for more information.

Kayaking at Haulover Canal

South Brevard

Sebastian Inlet State Park

321-984-4852

www.floridastateparks.org/sebastianinlet

9700 S. A1A, Melbourne Beach 32951

Directions: Located on A1A, 18 miles south of US 192

Open: 24 hours a day

Admission: $3 for single entry, $6 per vehicle up to eight people

Activities: Birding, boating, camping, fishing, paddling, trails

Water, wilderness, and sunshine are the backdrop for this strikingly beautiful inlet connecting the Atlantic Ocean with the Indian River Lagoon. This Florida state park is a popular and affordable recreational area with trails, campgrounds, a marina, and coves ideal for paddling. Anglers can choose from two fishing jetties extending into the Atlantic Ocean. Picnic tables, a playground, restrooms, bathhouses, showers, and a snack bar are available near the fishing jetties and beach. The nearby Sebastian Fishing Museum and McLarty Treasure Museum are fun family diversions. See the Beaches and Surfing chapter for more information about the 3 miles of beachfront.

BIRDING

Home to 32 Great Florida Birding Trail sites, Brevard County is definitely for the birds. Some settle here in great numbers and diversity; others rest while migrating south or stay just for the winter. With the success of the Space Coast Birding & Wildlife Festival (see the Seasonal Events section of the Culture chapter for information) over the last decade, the area has earned a reputation as one of the premier birding spots in the country. Individuals, families, and groups enjoy the outdoors, and the cost is minimal—just binoculars and a field guide gets you started. Experts may want to track favorites from among more than three hundred species in this area, and novices will enjoy making new feathered friends. All of the following sites are part of the Great Florida Birding Trail.

Jim Angy's Tips for Photographing Birds and Wildlife

Before your trip, study professional wildlife photos for setup and framing ideas.

Visit fishing piers and parks where wildlife is more accustomed to humans.

Shoot early in the morning when the light is good and will improve over time.

Be patient and observe the environment.

Get as close as possible without disturbing the bird or animal. Sit or crouch down, and avoid noises, eye contact, and quick moves. On driving paths, use your car as a blind.

Find a natural element to add contrast and perspective to the picture, like a spider web, tree branch, or flower.

Set your digital camera to continuous shooting mode to try to capture an action shot.

Use a macro lens for close-ups of small wildlife.

Turn off your cell phone.

Keep your distance when photographing alligators. They can quickly turn aggressive, especially around nests or during mating season.

Area wildlife information and photographs are available at Jim's Web site, www.stillnature.com.

Birding Hotspots

CAPE CANAVERAL & COCOA BEACH

Avocet Lagoon (www.portcanaveral.org; Port Canaveral locks). Audubon member Jason Frederick calls Avocet Lagoon a hidden jewel for birders. Follow Mullet Drive around to Port's End Park and stop to enjoy a view of the harbor from the observation tower. Continue on the same road to the locks at Port Canaveral, where flocks of white pelicans settle in the winter months. Plans are in the works for an observation tower to the east of the locks that will overlook the lagoon. Make sure you look for manatees and dolphins inside the locks.

Jetty Park (321-783-7111; 400 E. Jetty Rd., Port Canaveral 32920). In the early morning, hundreds of gulls, terns, and shorebirds roost on the beach, especially in fall and winter. The birds come and go throughout the day and settle back on the beach before sunset. Check offshore for rare seabirds.

Johnnie Johnson Nature Trail (321-868-1123; Lori Wilson Park, 1500 N. Atlantic Ave., Cocoa Beach 32931). The best time to visit here is between October and March, when migratory songbirds and shorebirds are present. Look for painted buntings and numerous warbler species.

BREVARD COUNTY

Black Point Wildlife Drive (321-861-0667; www.fws.gov/merrittisland; Merritt Island National Wildlife Refuge, North Merritt Island). Black Point Wildlife Drive is one of the premier birding spots in the country. The refuge has more than 330 species of birds, including wood storks and bald eagles, gulls, terns, sparrows, and raptors. A flock of roseate spoonbills provides a breathtaking sight. A birding guide and loaner binoculars are available at the visitors center, and field trips take place during peak times. Call ahead for reservations.

Canaveral National Seashore (321-267-1110; www.nps.gov/cana; 308 Julia St., Titusville 32796 [local office]). The undeveloped coast of the national seashore features an abundance of shorebirds, especially during the fall and winter. Elevated platforms provide a venue for scoping gannets and jaegers out at sea. Along the road to the beach there are ponds that attract wading birds and waterfowl.

North Tidal Pool (321-984-4852; www.floridastateparks.org/sebastianinlet/; Sebastian Inlet State Park, 9700 A1A, Melbourne Beach 32951). Early morning at the North Tidal Pool, before the crowds arrive, is a bonanza. The cove is a feeding ground for shorebirds and waders, such as American oystercatchers and reddish egrets. A nearby wooded area attracts woodpeckers and songbirds, and at dawn you may see a great horned owl.

Viera Wetlands (321-255-4328; South Central Wastewater Treatment Facility, Wickham Rd., Viera 32940). Thousands of ducks winter here—such as green- and blue-winged teals, mallards, and northern pintails. Black-necked stilts nest in spring and summer, and a bald eagle nest is visible from the road. Expect some surprises. The first U.S. sighting of a mangrove swallow was here.

Most Common Birds

Gulls frequent the shore in large numbers but are also seen inland, especially on cold or stormy days. Young birds are brownish; when mature, they all have gray backs and white bellies. To identify them, check their size and leg color. Look for three varieties of this common bird: the herring gull, the ringed-billed gull, and the laughing gull. Largest is the herring gull, with flesh-colored legs. The medium-sized ringed-billed gull has yellow legs and a black ring around its bill. The appropriately named laughing gull has a song call that sounds like a laugh. This small, red-legged gull has a handsome black head in summer.

Brown pelicans are found whereever there are fish and fishermen, but especially at the beaches and piers. Many are accustomed to beachgoers and won't fly away unless you get very close, and sometimes if you wait a few minutes, they'll preen and stretch their wings, making for some great photos. Their larger, attractive cousin, the **white pelican**, spends the winter in this area.

Along the water's edge, look for the **ruddy turnstone**, brown with a white stomach and orange legs, often turning over stones and shells looking for food. The beige and cream **willet** almost fades into the sand, while the **royal tern** steps out in a snow-white suit with a top hat of coal black feathers, black legs, and an orange beak. Children love chasing **sanderlings**, flocks of tiny birds that are constantly playing catch-me-if-you-can with incoming waves.

Elegant wading birds parade along the shallow ocean surf and the fringes of the intra-coastal waterways, using long, narrow beaks to poke for food in the moist ground. The majestic **great blue heron** is blue-gray, with slightly darker plumes on the head, and stands 4 feet tall. Two smaller varieties are the **little blue heron** and the **tricolored heron**. Like a bride at the altar, the **great egret** is a stately vision in white, with a veil of long wispy feathers that cover its back like a lace cape during breeding season. The **snowy egret** is a little shorter, with a black bill and legs, and feet resembling tiny golden slippers. The **reddish egret** (very rare in North America) has a burgundy head and neck.

Often seen in residents' yards, one of the most recognizable wading birds is the **white ibis**, with black-tipped feathers and a bright orange bill and legs. The **roseate spoonbill** has pink feathers and a beak in the shape of a paddle. The unique-looking, endangered **wood stork** has white feathers, black wing tips, and a bare-skinned, wrinkled black head and neck.

In the lagoon, look for **double-crested cormorant**, muddy brown or black with a pale orange sharply curved bill, and the **anhinga**, or snakebird, so nicknamed because in water the body is submerged, and only the small head and long, slender neck are visible. The **American coot** is often mistaken for a duck, but it's all black with a white triangular beak.

Two birds of prey, recognizable by their strong hooked beaks, stand guard along the Space Coast. **Bald eagles**, all black with a smooth white head and tail, and a 6- to 7-foot wingspan, are seen mostly in northern Brevard. The **osprey** is a little smaller than the eagle, with dark brown and white feathers on the back and head, white on the belly.

Resources

Great Florida Birding Trail (850-488-9478; www.floridabirdingtrail.com; 620 S. Meridian St., 5B4, Tallahassee 32399-1600). A collection of more than four hundred sites throughout the state selected for their excellent bird-watching or bird-education opportunities, the Great Florida Birding Trail is a 2,000-mile, self-guided highway trail. Trail maps identify state sites by region, and guides and pamphlets on a variety of birding topics are available for download from the Web site.

Space Coast Audubon Society (www.spacecoastaudubon.org; P.O. Box 1741, Cocoa 32923). Brevard County's largest all-volunteer environmental organization, the Space Coast Audubon Society maintains a checklist of local birds and hosts frequent field trips open to the public.

Space Coast Birding (www.spacecoastbirding.com). This Web site is a portal to vast amounts of birding information, both general and specific to this area.

Boating and Paddling

Getting out on the water is the perfect way to explore the area's natural elements, and there are marinas, ramps, and water access points all over the county. The following is just a small selection of the facilities and tours that will make it easy to cruise the lagoon.

All boats must have safety vests available, and boat renters should expect a thorough briefing on safety and regulations before they head out on the water. Be aware that it's against the law to drink and drive a boat. Anytime you head out on the water, it's a good idea to bring a jacket to offset the cooling combination of water spray and wind.

Paddling is another way to enjoy Florida's natural beauty. Quietly gliding through the calm lagoon waters is one of the most personal ways to experience its flora and fauna, and everyone from grade-school children to grandparents can learn in just a few minutes. Recreation kayaks have open seating like a canoe, and beginners may want to go with a partner in a two-seater the first time. Turning over is unusual, but it happens, and even if you stay in the boat, plan on you and your belongings getting wet. Consider taking a disposable camera; most outfitters will lock your car keys in their van so you don't risk dropping them in the water.

Marinas and Ramps

Cape Canaveral & Cocoa Beach

Banana River Marine
321-452-8622
1360 S. Banana River Dr., Merritt Island 32952

Located on the Banana River about 2 miles south of FL 520, this boatyard and storage facility provides storage and maintenance, specializing in boats 20 feet and longer. Slips for transient travelers are available. Boat ramp $5.

Cape Marina
321-783-8410
www.capemarina.com
800 Scallop Dr., Port Canaveral 32920

For boaters, this certified-clean marina and boatyard is a home away from home. Dock your boat for a day, a week, a month, or a season. The ships store carries groceries, souvenirs, and fishing supplies. Other amenities include rental berths, a do-it-yourself and full-service yard, cleaning and storage, and a fuel dock.

Freddie Patrick Park
Flounder Rd., Port Canaveral

Three double-wide ramps offer a convenient launch for larger boats and provide quick access to the ocean. Amenities include a restroom and boat and trailer parking. No fee.

Harbortown Marina Boatyard
321-453-0160
www.harbortownmarina.com
2700 Harbortown Dr., Merritt Island 32952

This full-service facility is located on the Barge Canal, 2.5 miles directly west of the deep-water Cape Canaveral inlet. Boats are stored inside and outside, and launched once each day. Day boaters can stop for maintenance, fuel, and a meal at the restaurant. Slips are available for monthly rentals, which include the use of laundry facilities and a pool.

Kelly Park
FL 528 and Banana River Dr., Merritt Island

Kelly park has a natural shoreline from which canoes and kayaks can be launched, and a four-lane lighted boat ramp and dock. The launch provides easy access to the north Banana River, where the entire area is a no-wake zone. The lockmaster will not open for paddlers; you must wait until a motorized boat approaches. Amenities include parking and restrooms. No fee.

Ports End Park
Near Canaveral locks, Port Canaveral

This double-wide boat launch provides the closest access to the Banana River through the locks. There are restrooms and boat and trailer parking. No fee.

Ramp Road Park
Ramp Rd., Cocoa Beach

This relaxing green space, a picturesque place to spend an afternoon enjoying a scenic view of the Thousand Islands, is located at the west end of Ramp Road. It has two boat ramps, a fishing dock, and picnic facilities.

Scorpion's New Port Marina
321-784-5788
www.scorpionmarine.com
960 Mullett Rd., Port Canaveral 32920

The marina provides full-service sales and storage, and the service facility is conveniently located for easy access to the ocean or the Banana River. Rack storage accommodates up to 40 feet, dockage up to 95 feet. Amenities include a ship's store, gas and diesel fuel, restrooms, and laundry facilities.

Sunrise Marina
321-783-9535
www.sunrisemarina.com
505 Glen Cheek Dr., Port Canaveral 32920

Service and fuel (diesel and unleaded) are available at this full-service marina, the closest to the Atlantic Ocean. A new facility stores boats from 15 to 40 feet. Call ahead on VHF channel 16 to arrange transient moorage. Fishing licenses are sold here.

CENTRAL BREVARD

Cocoa Village Marina
321-632-5445
90 Delannoy Ave., Cocoa 32922
ICW mile marker 897.5

Located in a protected basin at the north end of Cocoa Village, this first-class marina is a great stop for overnight or longer stays. Dockage is available up to 70 feet, and amenities include showers, laundry facilities, ice, wireless Internet, cable television, and a sauna. If you're just stopping for lunch in the village, your stay is complimentary. Be advised: They don't sell fuel.

James G. Bourbeau Memorial Park
321-633-1874
www.brevardparks.com
8195 King St. (FL 520), Cocoa 32926

The park has a dock and a two-lane public boat ramp, an airboat ramp, parking for 115 cars and boat trailers, a barbecue grill, and a pavilion. Here you'll have 24-hour access to the St. Johns River, and it's a stop along the Great Florida Birding Trail. Leroy Wright Recreation Area, directly across the road, has a launch for nonmotorized boats.

Lone Cabbage Fish Camp
321-632-4199
8199 King St. (FL 520), Cocoa 32926

Use the launch ramp, and purchase bait and tackle. This authentic Old Florida fish camp has a restaurant and airboat rides.

NORTH BREVARD

Bair's Cove
Haulover Canal, Merritt Island National Wildlife Refuge
321-861-0667
www.fws.gov/merrittisland
North Merritt Island

Encounter birds, manatees, and dolphins, as well as barges and yachts, in this intracoastal waterway connecting Mosquito Lagoon and the Indian River. A natural sandy beach launch for kayaks and canoes is at the end of the dirt road heading west across from the manatee viewing deck.

Eddy Creek
Canaveral National Seashore
386-428-3384, ext. 10
www.nps.gov/cana
308 Julia St., Titusville 32796 (local office)

There is an access launch available for motor and nonmotorized boats entering the south-ernmost part of Mosquito Lagoon. Amenities include parking and restrooms. There is a $7 fee to enter the national seashore.

Marina Park
Near US 1 and Garden St., Titusville, past Titusville Marina
There is a public nonmotorized boat launch and a two-lane boat ramp here. Open 7 AM–dark.

Parrish Park
Max Brewer Cswy. (FL 406, on the east side of the Indian River), Titusville
Has a public launch on south side for paddlers heading south on the Indian River.

Titusville Marina
321-269-7255
451 Marina Rd. (south of marker 27), Titusville 32796

This marina has 195 slips in a protected basin with floating docks. Transients are welcome. Ship's store, gas, and fuel.

SOUTH BREVARD

Inlet Marina
321-724-5424
www.sebastianinlet.com
9502 S. A1A, Melbourne Beach 32951

This full-service marina and gateway concessionaire is located about 1 mile north of Sebastian Inlet State Park. Boat slips are available for $20 per night or $300 per month. Rent small boats, a deck boat that accommodates six to eight passengers, or a pontoon boat with capacity for 10–11; half-day rates range from $99 to $169, and full day from $139 to $210. Launch from paved ramps: $5 for boats, $3 for canoes and kayaks. Canoes and kayaks are also available to rent.

Tours and Rentals

CAPE CANAVERAL & COCOA BEACH

Adventure Kayak of Cocoa Beach
321-480-8632
www.advkayak.com
Ramp Rd., Cocoa Beach

Enjoy a guided tour with Bill, a Brevard County native and experienced kayaker who shares both his knowledge and his love of the area. Choose a canoe or kayak; snacks, water, and dry bags for personal items are provided. Fun for novices and the experienced. For a two- to three-hour tour: adults $25, children 4–16 $15.

Brevard County Parks

321-868-1123
Ramp Rd., Cocoa Beach

A canoe tour of the Thousand Islands leaves at 9:30 AM on the fourth Friday of each month. Children must be at least four years old and accompanied by an adult. $5 per person for two hours.

Cocoa Beach Kayaking

321-784-4545
www.cocoabeachkayaking.com
Ramp Rd., Cocoa Beach

For a decade Kathleen Bennett has been leading guided nature tours out of Cocoa Beach with a focus on fun and education. Settle in a comfortable, stable two-seat touring kayak for an unforgettable paddle through the mangroves. She supplies hats, towels, polarized sunglasses, sunblock, and water. It's $25 per person for an estimated two-hour weekday tour.

Island Boat Lines

321-454-7414
www.islandboatlines.com

Climb aboard for two daily tours on a comfortable, covered pontoon boat, the *Miss Florida*. On the Thousand Islands cruise, the captain and narrator share entertaining local stories and information about area wildlife and birds. This cruise departs from Banana River Marine, 1357 Banana River Dr. on Merritt Island. To get there, turn left at the first light west of the FL 520 causeway. The other cruise, a sunset cruise, sails from Cape Marina, 800 Scallop Dr. in Port Canaveral. Bring your own cocktails and snack, and relax as you coast through the port lock west toward the Indian River via the Barge Canal. Call ahead for reservations. There are usually spots available for the same day. On-boat restrooms are available. $25 per person, with discounts for seniors, children, and military; children under five are free.

Island Watercraft Rentals

321-454-7661
www.islandwatercraftrentals.com
1872 E. FL 520 Cswy., Merritt Island 32952

Deck boats and pontoons are available to rent and are a fun option for families and groups wanting to explore the Banana River on their own or go waterskiing or tubing. An instructional briefing, life vests, fuel, and safety gear are provided. You bring personal gear and refreshments. Rates start at $150 for a half day. Call ahead for reservations. Boats dock at north side of FL 520 at the western intersection of the Banana River.

Ron Jon Watersports

321-799-8888
www.ronjons.com
4275 N. Atlantic Ave., Cocoa Beach 32931

Paddlers can rent one- and two-person kayaks, and rates start at $20 and $25 for four hours. Must be 18 or older to rent; a cash or credit card deposit is required.

Guests of Island Boat Lines embark on an ecotour through the Cocoa Beach Thousand Islands.

Space Coast Kayaking

321-784-2452

www.spacecoastkayaking.net

Ramp Rd., Cocoa Beach

Experienced kayakers Jim and Donna begin with a brief demonstration, and then lead the group out to explore the history and ecology of the Thousand Islands. Pick a regular or custom tour, such as a paddle and/or camp at Manatee Cove Park, sunset or moonlight outing, or an early summer, after-dark bioluminescence tour, when the water comes alive with sparkles of bright lights. Adults $30, children under 13 $15 for a two-hour tour. Price includes life jacket, sunscreen, and water.

Space Coast River Tours, Inc.

321-652-1052

www.spacecoastrivertours.com

Kelly Park

FL 528 and Banana River Dr., Merritt Island

Boating has been a lifelong passion for captains Mark and Michelle Anderson, who met on a sailing vacation and married two years later on a catamaran. Today they run the 42-foot *Blue Dolphin,* a comfortable pontoon boat with a retractable roof. Nature tours depart from Kelly Park and sail north into the Barge Canal, past Ski Island at the northernmost end of the Banana River, and into Port Canaveral. Sunset and special party tours can be arranged. Beer, wine, soda, and snacks are provided, and restrooms are available. $29 per person for adults, $25 for children 12 and younger.

Wild Side Tours

321-799-5495

Ramp Rd., Cocoa Beach

Capt. Skip McLean casts off at 10 every morning for a two-hour cruise through the nearby Thousand Islands. His pontoon-style boat, with a retractable roof and a restroom, accommodates up to 20 guests. Seats are often available for same-day bookings, but call ahead to reserve a spot.

CENTRAL BREVARD

Grasshopper Airboat Eco Tours

321-631-2990

www.airboatecotours.com

Lake Poinsett Rd., Cocoa (off FL 520, 0.5 mile west of I-95)

U.S. Coast Guard Master Captain Rick takes passengers for a thrill ride and ecotours on comfortable and stable state-of-the-art boats. Children ages seven and older are welcome. $35 for 90-minute ride; group rates are available. Launch is from Lake Poinsett Lodge and Marina, at the end of Lake Poinsett Rd.

Indian River Cruises

321-223-6825
www.indianrivercruises.com
Cocoa Village Marina
90 Delannoy Ave., Cocoa 32922

The wide stretch of the Indian River alongside the communities of Cocoa and Rockledge is a perfect spot for Brevard County's only sailing excursion. Captain Mark and First Mate Joe host a maximum of six guests on a personalized cruise aboard the *S/V Double ShAAfted*, a luxury 47-foot catamaran with staterooms, two heads, and a wide deck with comfortable chairs and a trampoline lounger. Sail at 11, 2, or just before sunset. Private dinner cruises can be arranged. $45 per person for two-hour tour.

Island Boat Lines

321-454-7414
www.indianriverqueen.com

Take a trip back in time aboard the fully restored *Indian River Queen*, a romantic triple-decker paddle-wheeler. Dinner and live musical entertainment set the stage for a sunset cruise down the Indian River. The cruise departs from the east end of the dock at Cocoa Village Marina, at 90 Delannoy Avenue in Cocoa. Catered charter excursions are perfect for family reunions, weddings, and other group functions. $40 per person, plus tax.

Twister Airboat Rides

321-632-4199
www.twisterairboatrides.com
FL 520 at St. Johns River, Cocoa

Coast Guard–certified deluxe airboats, which launch from Lone Cabbage Fish Camp (8199 King St.) in Cocoa, twist and turn at speeds up to 45 mph. Children ages 12 and older are welcome. For a 30-minute ride: adults $20, children $12. A minimum of four can book a longer ride for $45 for adults, $25 for children.

Adventure and alligators await passengers on a Twister Airboat ride on the St. Johns River.

Village Outfitters

321-633-7245
229 Forrest Ave., Cocoa 32922

Rent a kayak, or schedule a personalized paddling tour. Serious sportspeople will find clothing, hats, sunglasses, and gear such as coolers, bags, and binoculars here.

NORTH BREVARD

A Day Away Kayak Tours

321-268-2655
www.adayawaykayaktours.com

First-timers and experienced paddlers alike will enjoy Mike and Elizabeth's two-hour guided tour into the Haulover Canal and Merritt Island National Wildlife Refuge. Multiday, overnight, and more challenging tours can be custom planned. For an unforgettable experience, sign up for a moonlight paddle, or the bioluminescent night tour offered during the summer season. This is a great family experience. Children three and older are welcome, but consider the capability and patience of the child. $25–30 per person; reservations required. Single, double, and fishing kayaks are also available to rent. Fee includes paddle, life jacket, whistle, and equipment to secure boat to your car. $20 half day, $30 full day for single; $35 half day, $45 full day for double.

Blazing Paddles Kayak Adventures

321-890-9992
www.floridablazingpaddles.com

Jesse, the founder of Blazing Paddles, grew up in Brevard County, and after seeing the world with the U.S. Air Force, he has returned to a place he considers one of the most beautiful in the world. Hear his stories and experience nature at eye level on a two- to three-hour day or nigh paddle through the Merritt Island National Wildlife Refuge. Tours start at $30 per person.

Brevard Zoo

Leroy Wright Recreation Area
321-254-9453
www.brevardzoo.org

Trained naturalists are your guide on a two-hour ecotour through the Haulover Canal and Pine Island Conservation Park. $45 per person, $35 with your own kayak.

SOUTH BREVARD

Inlet Marina

321-724-5424
www.sebastianinlet.com
9502 S. A1A, Melbourne Beach 32951

Join a Florida naturalist and experienced guide on a two- or four-hour tour through this area of the Indian River Lagoon. Groups are limited to a maximum of four, so the tour can be very personalized toward the capabilities and interests of the paddlers. The fee is $35 per hour in addition to a boat rental fee. Rent single or double kayaks, or canoes, for two hours, a half day, or a full day; prices range from $18 to $45.

CAMPING AND RVING

Year-round pleasant weather and the stunning natural environment make the Space Coast a perfect spot for camping. Expect higher demand and higher rates during the winter months and holidays. Both the sun and the insects grow stronger in the summer, so be prepared with sunscreen and bug repellent.

Cape Canaveral & Cocoa Beach

Jetty Park Campground
321-783-7111, fax 321-783-5005
www.portcanaveral.org
400 E. Jetty Rd., Cape Canaveral 32920

Thirty-five-acre Jetty Park, located alongside the Port Canaveral Inlet and the Atlantic Ocean, is one of the best public campgrounds in Florida. Many vacationers have been repeat visitors for decades. Guests have access to beaches, restrooms, showers, a 1,200-foot fishing pier, refreshment stand, bait shop and convenience store, grills, picnic pavilions, a playground, volleyball courts, and a wooded bicycle path. Choose from rustic tent sites, RV sites with water and electric, and RV sites with water, electric, and sewer. Daily rates range from $30 to $40 during peak times and $24 to $31 for nonpeak, with discounts for Brevard County residents. Reservations may be made 90 days in advance for a two-night minimum to 21-night maximum stay. For $2 per night, dogs and cats less than 35 pounds are permitted for RV campers, but they're not allowed in most public areas.

Mango and Oak Manor
321-799-0741
190 Oak Manor Dr., Cape Canaveral 32920

Travelers with self-contained mobile units will find these two nearly adjacent beach town parks to be friendly, convenient, and affordable. Cape Canaveral beaches, Jetty Park, and the Port Canaveral restaurants are all located within a mile. Oak Manor is open for short-term rentals, with water, sewer, and electric included in the rate. Mango sites are leased by the month, and electric is metered and paid by the occupant. Small pets are welcome.

Central Brevard

Son Rise Palms RV Park
321-633-4335
www.sonrisepalmsrvpark.com
660 Tucker Ln., Cocoa 32926

Families might enjoy this small, quiet park, located near the Cocoa Expo Center. Palm and citrus trees dot this rural spot, which has 83 large, grassy sites with patios and concrete pads, each with full hookup and 30/50 amp. A bathhouse, pool, and laundry facilities are provided.

Space Coast RV Resort

321-636-2873, 1-800-982-4233
www.spacecoastrv.net
820 Barnes Blvd., Rockledge 32955

RV travelers looking for a community atmosphere might prefer this well-kept city park, located just a short distance from three golf courses, Space Coast Baseball Stadium, the Brevard Zoo, and shopping at Viera. Every site includes electric and sewer hookups, and a picnic table. Phone and cable are available. The resort provides restrooms and showers, a pool, and laundry facilities. Small pets are allowed.

North Brevard

Canaveral National Seashore

386-428-3384, ext. 10
www.nps.gov/cana
308 Julia St., Titusville 32796 (local office)

The National Park Service offers backcountry camping along the beach from November 1 through April 30, and year-round on designated islands in Mosquito Lagoon. Campsites are $10 per night, and a permit must be picked up in person from the information center located at the north end of the seashore near New Smyrna Beach. Advance reservations are required. The sites are very primitive and have no fresh water or sanitation facilities. Island sites are only accessible by boat, canoe, or kayak. Campers are advised to bring a cell phone and plenty of bug repellent.

Manatee Hammock Park

321-264-5083, fax 321-264-6468
www.brevardparks.com
7275 S. US 1, Titusville 32780

This 26-acre site, located on the banks of the Indian River about halfway between the Beachline Expressway and Titusville, offers 152 shaded RV spots with water, electric, and sewer, and 30 campsites with water and electric. Hot showers are available. Other amenities include laundry facilities, a fishing pier, and a small swimming pool.

Titusville KOA

321-269-7361, 1-800-562-3365
www.koa.com
4513 W. Main St., Mims 32754

KOA Kampers will be pleased to discover this location, a perfect base for exploring Merritt Island National Wildlife Refuge and Kennedy Space Center attractions. The shady, rural setting has a clubhouse, swimming pool, and convenience store; free wireless Internet; and bicycle rentals. Rent a tent or RV site, or reserve an air-conditioned cabin or lodge with a kitchenette and enough beds to sleep six (with your own linens). Pets are permitted, with restrictions for some large dogs.

South Brevard

Long Point Park

321-952-4532, fax 321-952-6306
www.brevardparks.com
700 Long Point Rd., Melbourne Beach 32951

This rustic camp is located near Sebastian Inlet. All sites have water and sewer; some also include electricity. The island campground fronts the Indian River, and campers can fish right from their front door. The 84.5-acre conservation spot has showers, laundry facilities, nature trails, a playground, and a swimming pond. Cross a bridge to Scout Island, where primitive camping is offered to groups.

Sebastian Inlet State Park Campground

Reserve through ReserveAmerica: 1-800-326-3521; 1-888-433-0287 for the hearing disabled
www.floridastateparks.org/sebastianinlet/
9700 A1A, Melbourne Beach 32951

Reservations are in demand for the 51 tent sites in this premier location, just a short walk from the Indian River Lagoon or the Sebastian Inlet beaches. The campground accommodates RVs up to 32 feet long, and it has has electrical hookups, fire rings with grills, picnic tables, full ADA-accessible restroom facilities, and a coin laundry. Pets are welcome. Reservations may be made up to 11 months in advance.

CRUISING

Port Canaveral is one of the world's most popular cruise ports, offering smooth sailing with straightforward directions, convenient parking, and an attractive, secure setting. Cruisers will be amazed at how quick and easy it is to get from the airport to the cruise terminals. Be prepared to show your cruise ticket when entering the parking area and at the terminal. Drivers can pull up to the ship to drop off passengers, but no one is allowed in the terminals without a cruise ticket. Parking is $12 per day for cars up to 20 feet in length and $24 for longer vehicles. (Many of the gaming cruises offer free parking, however; see the individual listings for details.)

Even if you're not going on a cruise, watching the mega cruise ships leave port is exciting. The ships are so close, you almost believe you can touch them. Waterside restaurants and bars along Glen Cheek Drive at the Cove all provide a front-row seat. Head to Jetty Park and take a walk on the pier, wave to departing cruisers, and let the children burn off some energy before dinner.

Multiday Cruises

Several world-renowned cruise lines offer multinight trips to the Bahamas, the eastern Caribbean, or Mexico's Gulf coast. Check with each company as to required identification or documentation and restrictions on what's allowed on the ship.

Carnival Cruise Lines

1-800-327-9501
www.carnival.com

Embark from Port Canaveral aboard one of the "fun" ships proudly sailing beneath the company's trademark red, white, and blue funnel. The largest is the *Canaveral Glory,* which offers seven-night trips to the Caribbean. The *Sensation* makes short jaunts to the Bahamas. Every ship features entertainment, a spa, and casinos.

Disney Cruise Line

1-800-939-2784
www.disneycruise.com

From the moment you enter the terminal, you're treated to first-class accommodations, entertainment, and guest service aboard the *Disney Magic* and *Disney Wonder.* Families will enjoy the no-gambling, no-smoking atmosphere. Separate areas and activities ensure a relaxing and romantic experience for adults. Everyone smiles as the departing horn blasts the opening bars of "When You Wish Upon a Star." Ships leave port for three- and four-night trips to the Bahamas and Castaway Cay (Disney's private island), or seven-night sails to the Caribbean.

Royal Caribbean International

1-800-327-6700
www.royalcaribbean.com

The majestic *Mariner of the Seas* is currently the largest ship at Port Canaveral and includes a rock-climbing wall, ice skating rink, and basketball court to keep you occupied on seven-night treks to the Caribbean. Climb aboard the smaller *Sovereign of the Seas* for a cruise to the Bahamas, including great entertainment, a fitness center, and a spa.

Gaming Cruises

Take a day or evening trip to nowhere aboard large, floating casinos that combine the thrill of gaming with an Atlantic cruise. Ships embark from Port Canaveral twice daily and offer all the favorite games, such as roulette, blackjack, craps, Caribbean stud poker, and slots. Reservations are recommended, but walk-ins are accepted if space is available. Dress is comfortable and casual. Be sure to bring a sweater or jacket even on hot summer evenings, because air over nighttime water can turn cool. Be aware that smoking is allowed inside the ships, and space on the outside decks may be limited.

Sterling Casino Lines

321-784-8558, 1-800-765-5711
www.sterlingcasinolines.com
Terminal 2, Port Canaveral

Ambassador II is the largest casino ship at the port, with five decks of games, entertainment, and a complimentary deli-style buffet. Cruisers must be at least 21 years of age. Follow exit signs for B terminals to cruise terminal 20, near Jetty Park. Admission, parking, and entertainment are free. Bus transportation can be arranged from many local hotels. Schedule: daily 11–4, evening cruises Fri. and Sat. 7 PM–1 AM, Sun. 7 PM–midnight.

The birds throw their own beach bon voyage party as the Disney Magic *leaves port.* John Anderson

Suncruz Casinos

321-799-3511, 1-800-474-3423
www.suncruzcasino.com
610 Glen Cheek Dr., Port Canaveral 32920

On the *Suncruz XII* you'll find four decks of fun, live entertainment, great food, and state-of-the-art slots and gaming tables. You must be 18 or older to gamble and 21 and up to consume alcoholic beverages; drinks are free while gaming. The ship departs from a berth at the Cove. Parking is free, and bus transportation is available from most local hotels. Departs daily at 11 AM and 7 PM for four- to six-hour cruises.

Combo Vacations

Couple a trip to the beach with a cruise from Port Canaveral for twice the vacation and twice the fun. Staying at the beach before your cruise is a relaxing way to start your trip. Many hotels participate in a cooperative program that lets you leave your car at the hotel, take a shuttle to the cruise terminal, and save money on port parking fees.

FAMILY FUN AND FITNESS

No matter what your age or fitness level, there are lots of convenient and exciting outdoor activities, many perfect for children. Visit the Port Canaveral locks or take a walk in the park at sunset. Stop by the Cocoa Beach recreation complex for an afternoon of swimming or tennis. The more adventurous might take a spin on a Jet Ski or windsurf. Everyone will enjoy a trip to the zoo or a baseball game.

Cape Canaveral & Cocoa Beach

Boom Fitness Center

321-868-2114
1355 N. Atlantic Ave., Cocoa Beach 32931

Short-term passes provide access to state-of-the-art equipment, a weight room, dance and exercise classes, a wet and dry sauna, and tanning beds. Child care is available. A 24-hour pass is $15; weekly pass, $49.

Calema Windsurfing

321-453-3223
www.calema.com
2550 N. Banana River Dr., Merritt Island 32952

The protected cove at Kelly Park is the perfect spot to try windsurfing. Everyone from the age of 8 to 80 can learn according to the folks at Calema. Surfers venturing into the windy channel follow in the tracks of professionals and Olympic competitors from around the world, who vie here each year in windsurfing championship races. Instructions and rentals are available. Private lessons are $50 per hour and include equipment. Rentals are $45 for three hours or $65 for the day. Rent a pedal kayak for the same rate.

Windsurfing on the Banana River

Cape Canaveral Recreation Complex
321-868-1226
7300 N. Atlantic Ave., Cape Canaveral 32920

Reserve tennis, racquetball, and shuffleboard courts up to a day in advance. Racquets are available for rent, and you can join drop-in classes such as yoga and Jazzercise. Open Monday–Friday 8 AM–9 PM, weekends and holidays 8–8. Court fee is 75 cents per hour.

Cocoa Beach Aquatic Center
321-868-3314
5000 Tom Warriner Blvd., Cocoa Beach 32931

This outdoor, heated Olympic-sized swimming pool, open year-round to the public, features adult swim laps, 1-meter diving board, jumbo water slide, and children's pool with shower umbrella and spray. Open Monday–Friday 9–7 (9–6 winter months), Saturday 9–5, Sunday 11–5. Fee: $2–3 for the day.

Cocoa Beach Parasail
321-212-8277
628 Glen Cheek Dr., Port Canaveral 32920

Get a bird's-eye view of the beach on a parasailing excursion. Single and tandem options are available, and you take off and land from the back of a boat. Photo packages capture the memory. Continuous flights are offered throughout the day from March through November; reservations are required. It's $65 for 800-foot flight and $60 for a 500-foot flight.

Cocoa Beach Skatepark

321-868-3238
1450 Minutemen Cswy., Cocoa Beach 32931

Visitors are welcome at this park, which features more than 32,000 square feet of smooth concrete in a mix of traditional and new configurations, such as bowls, pools, handrails, ledges, and stairs. The park opens at 1 PM daily, and skating continues under the lights until 9 each evening (10 PM on Saturday). Helmets are required and are available to rent or purchase. Admission is $3 per day.

Funntasia Fantasy Golf

321-799-4856
6355 N. Atlantic Ave., Cape Canaveral 32920

Two 18-hole miniature-golf courses wind through caves, streams, and waterfalls. Refreshments and an arcade are located inside. Open mornings at 10, 9 during the summer; closes Sunday–Thursday at 11, Friday and –Saturday at midnight. For 18 holes: adults $6.25, children and Seniors $5.25, children three and under free; play another 18 holes the same day for $3.

Manatee Sanctuary Park

321-868-1226
Thurm Blvd., Cape Canaveral 32920

A 380-foot boardwalk connects three decks along the edge of the Banana River. A large picnic pavilion, walking path, and restrooms are available. This is a popular spot for spotting manatees, especially in the morning. In the evening this quiet park offers a front-row seat for the sunset. Located on Thurm Boulevard, at the west end of Central Boulevard.

Wildlife Profile: Manatee

The manatee is a unique and popular resident of the Indian River Lagoon. The odd-looking, docile sea creatures were probably the beautiful sirens that ancient sailors dubbed mermaids, although it would take distance and an active imagination to make such a mistake. Manatees have a mermaid's flat, paddle-shaped tail, but it's attached to a gray, wrinkled body. An adult Florida manatee, a subspecies of the West Indian manatee, is about 10 feet long, weighs 1,000 pounds, and has whiskers and bad breath.

Florida's state marine mammal is commonly referred to as a sea cow because this strict vegetarian spends most of the day grazing on grasses in shallow rivers and estuaries. It resembles a walrus but is actually most closely related to the elephant. The manatee never leaves the water, but because it is a mammal it surfaces to take a breath every three to five minutes—with a noisy exhale.

The manatee is an endangered species but has no natural predators. Speedboats, plastic bags, and discarded fishing lines are its biggest threat. Area waters populated by manatees are designated no-wake zones so boaters can see and avoid the slow-moving swimmers. The manatee's reproductive process begins late and is infrequent, with a single birth every three to five years. Newborns are about 4 feet long and stay with their mother for two years.

Manatee *(Trichechus Manetus)* Jim Angy

The best way to see a manatee is from a pontoon boat, kayak, or canoe. Tour operators guide guests to areas where they like to feed. Their gray-brown skin blends with the water (hence the danger from boaters), so look for a tail flap as they propel forward or a snout poking upward. Manatees leave a swirling "footprint" as they meander close to the water's surface. Once located, they're often clearly visible in the water. They can turn and tumble but never jump like dolphins—and they are almost impossible to photograph. The best picture you'll have is the one planted firmly in your memory.

Space Coast Sightings: Manatee Park in Cape Canaveral, Port Canaveral locks, Cocoa Beach Thousand Islands, Haulover Canal, Crane Creek in Melbourne.

Port Canaveral Navigation Lock
Lock Park, at the end of Mullet Dr., Port Canaveral

In 1965 the U.S. Army Corps of Engineers built the Port Canaveral navigation lock to minimize the effect of tides and saltwater intrusion at this connection between the Atlantic Ocean and the Banana River. The size was larger than planned, to accommodate passage of the Saturn rocket stages on the way to Kennedy Space Center. Today the shuttle booster rockets follow the same path. A small park has been built alongside the lock, where you can watch boats make the transition between the waterways. The lock is equipped with a system to protect the manatees, dolphins, and pelicans that play in the contained area.

The Racquet Club of Cocoa Beach
321-868-3224
5000 Tom Warriner Blvd., Cocoa Beach 32931

This professional complex has 14 courts—2 with clay surface, 10 lighted—that may be reserved. Professionals are on staff, and lessons are available. The pro shop sells and rents equipment. Open Monday–Thursday 8–8, Friday–Sunday 8–noon. The fee for visitors is $4–8 for one-and-a-half-hour singles or two-hour doubles.

Surf & Ski Jetski Rentals
321-453-8900
1872 E. Merritt Island Cswy., Merritt Island 32952

The gentle Banana River is a great place for novices and experts to take a spin on a Jet Ski. Leave from the northwest intersection of the Banana River and FL 520. No reservations are necessary, but it's a good idea to call ahead and check on availability. Jet Skis seat up to three. You must be at least 21 to rent, but children can ride with an adult. Rates are $55 for a half hour and $90 for an hour, with a discount if you have a local hotel key. Life vests and instructions are included.

Traxx at Jungle Village

321-783-0595
8801 Astronaut Blvd., Cape Canaveral 32920

A pink elephant donned in giant sunglasses stands guard over this small amusement park, with bumper cars, go-karts, batting cages, a rock-climbing wall, arcade, and miniature-golf course. Open daily 10 AM–midnight. Adults $6.25, children and seniors $5.25, children three and under are free. Golfers can play a second round of 18 holes the same day for $3.

Brevard County

Ace of Hearts Horseback Riding

321-638-0104
www.aceofheartsranch.com
7400 Bridal Path Ln., Cocoa 32927

Lifelong horse lover Sandra Vann carved the Ace of Hearts Ranch out of the scrub so visitors could experience the unique Florida habitat at a leisurely pace. Knowledgeable guides lead one-hour ecotours on horseback through oak hammock, pine forest, palmettos, and wildflowers. Gentle horses accommodate riders over nine years of age, but smaller children can take a 15-minute pony ride. Rides are offered daily, but times vary based on season; reservations are required. Trail rides $25, pony rides $10. The ranch is located north of FL 528, about 25 miles from Cocoa Beach.

Spring training games at Space Coast Stadium are fun for all ages.

Baseball at Space Coast Stadium

321-633-9200

www.washingtonnationals.mlb.com, www.manateesbaseball.com

5800 Stadium Pkwy., Viera 32940

Every seat is a great seat in this red, white, and blue facility, which hosts Major League Baseball's Washington Nationals for spring training during March and the Brevard County Manatees, a minor league affiliate of the Milwaukee Brewers, in the summer. Spring training games are a great chance to see professional players in a small venue. Minor league season runs from April to August; $7 general seating tickets can be purchased on game day. Pose outside by a mock-up of a space shuttle donated by the Kennedy Space Center.

Brevard Zoo

321-254-9453

www.brevardzoo.org

8225 N. Wickham Rd., Melbourne 32940

Feeding the giraffe at Brevard Zoo. (My, what a long tongue you have!)

Experience wildlife in this unique zoo habitat, which takes you around the world. See primates, gazelles, rhinos, and giraffes from Africa; wallabies, kangaroos, and Indonesian fruit bats from Australasian; and monkeys, tapirs, and giant anteaters from the jungles of South America. Closer to home, the Wild Florida exhibit is a guaranteed spot to encounter alligators, red wolves, white-tailed deer, otters, and a bald eagle. Children will especially enjoy the interactive Paws-on Play Area and train ride through parts of the zoo. Twenty-minute guided kayak tours take visitors age five and older on an African safari or a journey through natural Florida wetlands. The zoo is wheelchair accessible and has wheelchair and stroller rentals, free parking, a snack bar, and a gift shop. Open daily 9:30–5. Adults $10.50, seniors $9.50, children 2–12 $7.50; kayak tours $5 per person. The zoo is located just off I-95 exit 191, near Viera.

Katabi Helicopter Tours
321-231-0802
www.katabihelicopters.com
6350 Horizon Dr., Titusville 32780

Experience the natural beauty of the Space Coast from a different perspective. Sgt. Mitch Young, a 20-year veteran of the Brevard County Sheriff's Office, conducts daily flights (depending on the weather) from the American Police Hall of Fame and Museum. Flight times range from a three-minute circle around the departing area and a look at the nearby Kennedy Space Center facilities to a 30-minute narrated ecotour from 3,500 feet in the air. A minimum of two passengers is required. Call for reservations; often same-day excursions are available. Operates 11–4. $25–153 per person.

FISHING

Water, water everywhere makes Brevard County the perfect place to get hooked on the idea of reeling in the perfect catch. Experienced fishermen and curious newcomers can mix a day in the sun with a great adventure. Port Canaveral is the starting point for deep-sea charters, which head about 20 miles out in the Atlantic to the Gulf Stream, where there are wahoo, sailfish, marlin, and dolphin. Closer in, captains may troll for kingfish, blackfin tuna, cobia, and barracuda. Larger fish, such as 40–100 pound yellowfin tuna, are found much farther out on "the other side" of the Gulf Stream. Bottom fishing is also productive offshore of Port Canaveral, with many species of snapper and grouper found in abundant wrecks and reefs.

Fish are plentiful on the quieter inland waters, such as the flats of the Banana River Lagoon, Mosquito Lagoon, and Indian River Lagoon. Fly-fishers travel from around the world to catch record redfish in the clear, shallow waters. Look also for sea trout, tarpon, and snook.

Because there are so many fishing spots in Brevard County, the following list concentrates on guides who are full-time, experienced, reputable, licensed captains working in the waters off Port Canaveral, the Banana River, northern Indian River Lagoon, and southern Mosquito Lagoon. Resources are included to help you locate guides in other areas, however. Stated fares usually include license, bait, and gear; refreshments and cleaning may be extra. The Canaveral Charter Captains' Association has these suggestions: Make your reservation as early as possible to get your desired date, confirm the time and meeting place with your captain a few days ahead, and remember that a tip of 10–20 percent is customary. Always bring a jacket and sunscreen; polarized sunglasses are suggested. A guided charter may be a little expensive, but it's worth the convenience and expertise you get for your money.

The catch of the day at Port Canaveral

Charters: Inland Flats

Backcountry Fly Fishing (321-267-9818; www.backcountryonfly.com; Mosquito and
Indian River Lagoons). Capt. John Turcot is passionate about fly fishing, and he guides in
north Brevard County with wisdom handed down through five generations. He has been
featured in several fishing and sport television shows and publications. Captain John specializes in sight fishing and uses a skiff and quiet push-pole approach.

　　Captain Doug Blanton (321-432-9470; www.sightfishing.com; Cocoa Beach and
Banana River Lagoon). Captain Doug is a full-time guide specializing in light tackle sight
fishing. Beginners and experts will enjoy a relaxing and productive fishing trip while
learning about the area from this lifelong Cocoa Beach resident and avid environmentalist.
Book a partial or full day and plan to leave just before sunrise. Maximum capacity is three
adults, or two adults and two children.

　　L/T Flat Fishing Charters (321-269-4568; 1-877-269-4568; www.ltflatsredfish.com;
Mosquito Lagoon, Indian River). Capt. Kelly Wiggins is a Titusville resident and has been
fishing these waters for 30 years. Half- and full-day charters, and night charters, are available; soft drinks and lunch are provided.

Mosquito Coast Fishing Charters (407-366-8085; 1-866-790-8081; www.irl-fishing.com; Mosquito Lagoon and Indian River Lagoon, Banana River Lagoon, Port Canaveral, Sebastian Inlet). Capt. Tom Van Horn specializes in near-shore coastal fishing at Port Canaveral and Sebastian Inlet and flats fishing in the lagoons. The former firefighter and writer for *Coastal Angler* magazine is a Florida native with a lifetime of fishing experience in the area.

Mosquito Lagoon Fly-Fishing Unlimited (321-795-9259 for Captain Scott; 386-479-3429 for Captain Nick; www.mosquitolagoonfly-fishing.com; Mosquito Lagoon and Indian River). Capt. Scott MacCalla and Capt. Nick Sassic are experienced sight guides who work together to provide local knowledge and state-of-the-art equipment and gear for fly-fishing or light tackle outings. Each boat has a one- to three-person capacity; two boats can be combined for families or larger groups.

Charters: Offshore

AA Sport Fishing (321-432-9839; 1-800-350-4482; www.aasportfishing.com; Cape Marina, 800 Scallop Dr., Port Canaveral 32920). The *Miss-N-Heather* and *Rendezvous* take up to six passengers out to the Gulf Stream or beyond to the other side. Capt. Barry Corzine heads up a team of experienced captains and crew. Catches are cleaned and packaged for you.

Bottom Dollar Charter Fishing (321-536-0802; www.bottomdollarcharterfishing.com; Sunrise Marina, 505 Glen Cheek Dr., Port Canaveral 32920). Capt. Brock Anderson has been operating fishing tours out of Port Canaveral since 1974, and his 38-foot boat accommodates one to six guests. He supplies tackle, bait, ice, rod and reel, and an icebox for your food and drinks; no hard liquor is allowed. Fish are cleaned at the dock. Children are welcome.

Cool Beans Fishing Charters (321-459-9766; www.coolbeanscharters.com; Sunrise Marina, 505 Glen Cheek Dr., Port Canaveral 32920). Book a private charter for up to four people. Capt. Tim Fletcher is a frequent tournament winner, holds fishing clinics for kids, and is a proponent of marine conservation and tagging programs.

Gettin There II Charters (321-631-5055; www.gettinthere.com; Cape Marina, 800 Scallop Dr., Port Canaveral 32920). Capt. Joe Fetro guides parties of six or fewer aboard the 28-foot *Bertram*, with two fighting chairs. Beginners are welcome. Fish are bagged and cleaned, and guests receive photos and a video of their trip.

Miss Cape Canaveral (321-783-5274; www.misscape.com; 670 Glen Cheek Dr., Cape Canaveral 32920). The *Miss Cape Canaveral* sails each morning at 8 for a full-day outing. Breakfast, lunch, and refreshments are provided. Captain, crew, and

Doug Blanton guides a sight fishing tour in the Banana River.

galley chef are all experienced and dedicated to delivering a pleasurable fishing experience. Seafarers of all ages are welcome on this party boat. The ship has a 150-person capacity; guests can relax in the air-conditioned lounge, galley, bar, and upper sundeck. An evening trip is offered from 7 to midnight.

Obsession Charters (321-453-3474; 1-888-347-4352; www.fishobsession.com; Sunrise Marina, 505 Glen Cheek Dr., Port Canaveral 32920). Pursue serious fishing, enjoy a party, or combine the two. The 33-foot *Obsession I* has room for six and offers half- and full-day packages. The 65-foot party boat *Ocean Obsession II* accommodates up to 70 passengers for an all-day outing, with food, beer, sodas, and a good time all included. Fare includes bait, fishing gear, and licenses.

Odyssey Charters (321-759-6022; www.fishingodyssey.com; Sunrise Marina, 505 Glen Cheek Dr., Port Canaveral 32920). The *Odyssey* is a 34-foot boat making full- and half-day trips near offshore, as well as blue-water excursions 60–100 miles out for big game sportfishing. Families and children are welcome; they have a capacity for six. Captains and crew have experience, expertise, and a love of ocean fishing.

Orlando Princess and Canaveral Star (321-784-6300; www.orlandoprincess.com; 650 Glen Cheek Dr., Port Canaveral 32920). This fleet, family owned and operated, offers half- and full-day trips, and a night shark fishing and party boat excursion. The *Orlando Princess* is a stable 80-foot catamaran with 1,900 feet of deck space. The *Canaveral Star* is a 65-foot fishing boat. Both boats have a comfortable, air-conditioned cabin. Every fishing trip includes lunch, beer and soda, rod, reel, bait, tackle, and fishing license.

Sea Legs (321-452-5315; 1-800-434-2057; www.atlanticdeepseafishing.com; Sunrise Marina, 505 Glen Cheek Dr., Port Canaveral 32920). Morning, afternoon, and full-day outings can be booked for one to six passengers on this charter with Capt. Floyd Curington, an experienced offshore fisherman. The 32-foot sportfishing boat has all the latest electronic and safety gear. Bring gallon-sized Ziploc bags and a cooler to store your catch.

Sea Leveler (321-794-3474; www.sealeveler.com; Sunrise Marina, 505 Glen Cheek Dr., Port Canaveral 32920). The *Sea Leveler*, a 30-foot Island Hopper, is designed to quickly get you out to the fish. You bring lunch and drinks; they supply everything else for half- and full-day trips, as well as evening shark fishing excursions. The crew is family-oriented and welcomes children. Spacious covered cockpits allow the entire party to fish at the same time, in or out of the sun.

Pier Fishing

Cocoa Beach Pier (321-783-7549; www.cocoabeachpier.com; 401 Meade Ave., Cocoa Beach 32931). No license is needed to fish from this popular pier. Rod and reel rentals are available; bait is for sale. Newcomers can get a brief lesson from the pier master.

Malcolm E. McLouth Fishing Pier (Jetty Park, 400 E. Jetty Rd., Port Canaveral 32920). Fish 24 hours a day for snook, Spanish mackerel, drums, and other sport fish off this lighted pier. Fish-cleaning tables with running water are provided, and the pier is ADA accessible. Sunrise Marina in Port Canaveral sells fishing licenses.

Port's End Park (www.portcanaveral.org; west end of Port Canaveral). Fish from the bulkheads at this 4-acre park, which has picnic tables and restrooms.

Ramp Road Park (Ramp Rd., Cocoa Beach). The dock at Ramp Road in Cocoa Beach has been voted the best fishing spot in the area by *Florida Sportsman* magazine.

Titusville Bridge and Causeway. In addition to being one of Florida's best locations for nighttime shrimping in the winter and spring, this is a popular spot to catch redfish, sea trout, black drum, and other fish. There are four bait and tackle shops within 2 blocks of the causeway to service anglers.

Surf Fishing

Capt. Doug Blanton (321-432-9470; www.sightfishing.com; Cocoa Beach). Catch fish the old-fashioned way: Follow the birds and cast into the ocean for whiting, pompano, snook, and other seasonal fish. Captain Doug brings everything needed for a surf-fishing expedition.

Fishing & Diving Center (321-783-3477; 6300 N. Atlantic Ave., Cape Canaveral 32920). Try surf fishing on your own with advice and gear from owner Rob. Open daily 7–6.

Resources

Angling Guide to Brevard County (www.research.myfwc.com). Produced by the Florida Fish & Wildlife Commission, this guide spells out all the rules and regulations regarding fishing in this area.

Coastal Angler Magazine (www.coastalanglermagazine.com). A resource for information on fishing, boating, and conservation along Florida's east coast waterways, including links to current fishing forecasts and an events calendar.

CruiseBrevard.com (www.cruisebrevard.com). Provides general information about the waters and fish in this area, along with a list of charter captains.

Fishing License (1-888-347-4356; www.wildlifelicense.com). If you're fishing without a guide, apply by phone or online to get a license within minutes. Florida residents may fish from land, piers, and docks without a license.

The Fly Fisherman (321-267-0348; 1114 S. Washington Ave. [US 1], Titusville 32780). In addition to being a first-rate outfitter, this store is a clearinghouse for checking on local conditions, finding a reputable guide, and picking up lessons or tips on fly-fishing, casting, and tying.

GOLF

Because of Florida's wide-open spaces and great weather year-round, golf is a favorite passion for residents and visitors. The course environments are a sanctuary for wildlife and particularly popular with sandhill cranes—tall, red-headed birds that are harmless and move slowly enough that you can get a great picture. Courses are usually open daily from sunrise to early evening, and most require guests to dress in appropriate golf attire: collared shirts, no denim or tank tops, and no metal spikes. Pricing is based on 18 holes and a cart, in peak season, which usually runs December through April. Expect discounts for off hours, seniors, or residents. Greens fees are broken down into the following categories:
Inexpensive: Under $25
Moderate: $25–50
Expensive: More than $50

Cape Canaveral & Cocoa Beach

Cocoa Beach Country Club
321-868-3351
5000 Tom Warriner Blvd., Cocoa Beach 32931
Price: Moderate

Dotted with 17 lakes and surrounded by the Banana River, three nine-hole courses are played in three 18-hole combinations. Each hole is named for one of the many species of birds you're likely to see on the course. Also keep your eyes open for dolphins, turtles, and the occasional alligator. Amenities include public driving range, putting greens, pro shop, club and cart rental, snack bar, and restaurant.

The Savannahs

321-455-1377
3915 Savannahs Trl., Merritt Island 32953
Price: Inexpensive

Consider walking this flat course set on a natural savanna, amid a hardwood forest and several lakes. Water and wetlands are a daunting factor on 13 of the holes. Amenities include a public driving range and a snack bar.

Central Brevard

Duran Golf Club

321-504-7776
7032 Stadium Pkwy., Viera 32940
Price: Expensive

Designed to be playable for golfers of all abilities, this semiprivate championship par 72, 18-hole course features plush-surface fairways and large, undulating greens. An equally well-maintained nine-hole, par 3, lighted course is open every night until 10. Amenities include a clubhouse with restaurant, lounge, and snack bar; driving range; and putting greens.

Turtle Creek Golf Club

321-632-2520
1279 Admiralty Blvd., Rockledge 32955
Price: Expensive

Fairways meander through pines, oaks, and palms on this 18-hole course. The friendly semiprivate club welcomes guests for daily play or to join special events such as the shootout held every Saturday at 11:30. Amenities include driving range, putting greens, rental clubs, restaurant, and bar.

North Brevard

La Cita Country Club

321-383-2582
777 Country Club Dr., Titusville 32780
Price: Moderate–Expensive

Experience the Old South at this semiprivate 18-hole, par 72 course, designed by Ron Garl and Lee Trevino to take advantage of the lakes, hills, and woods. Amenities include a restaurant and lounge, driving range, putting greens, and a pro shop.

Walkabout Golf & Country Club

321-385-2099
3230 Folsom Rd., Mims 32754
Price: Moderate

This course is a little out of the way, but it has become one of the more popular in north Brevard. Perry Dye designed the 18-hole championship course, along with LPGA star Jan Stephenson, and it is an undulating landscape with lakes and native vegetation. There is a bonus 19th hole—a par 3 green shaped like the continent of Australia. Amenities include a snack bar, driving range, and putting greens.

South Brevard

Aquarina Country Club

321-728-0600
7500 S. A1A, Melbourne Beach 32951
Price: Moderate

Across from the ocean and alongside the Indian River, this semiprivate Audubon-certified 18-hole midlength course combines habitat stewardship with a great golf experience. Two tees are set on docks overlooking wetlands. Amenities include a driving range, putting greens, pro shop, and snack bar.

Spessard Holland

321-952-4530
2374 Oak St., Melbourne Beach 32951
Price: Inexpensive

Ocean breezes and distracting views create challenges on this Arnold Palmer Signature 18-hole, par 67 public course, tucked between the Atlantic Ocean and the Indian River. There is only one par 5, so accuracy is an advantage. Amenities include a mini driving range, putting greens, and a snack bar.

HIKING, BIKING, AND RUNNING

Outdoor exercise will never be more enjoyable than it is in Florida. The terrain is flat, the temperature is pleasant, and the scenery is captivating, so enjoy making a jaunt on foot or bike a part of your vacation experience. Lots of walkers hit the beach at sunrise and sunset. The sand at low tide is a perfect surface for a run or bike ride. A bike path/sidewalk is built on the east side of A1A, but because of all the intersecting driveways, pedestrians and bikers have to really be alert. Other paths might be more appealing.

Pedestrian and Bicycle Routes

The **FL 520 Causeway** has a wide, paved, safe path running along its south side. Begin at the small Banana River Bridge, where you'll often see dolphins. Take a leisurely stroll part of the way, or a more challenging 10-mile workout if you go across the river and back.

Merritt Island National Wildlife Refuge

Refuge Visitor Information Center

Most accessible areas of the wildlife refuge are with a 10-mile radius, and first-time visitors will appreciate the orientation and information provided at the visitors center. The center's interpretive exhibits and habitat models provide an excellent overview of the habitat and its residents, and movies and programs are often held in the small auditorium. The center is about 5 miles east of US 1 in Titusville. To get there, stay on FL 406 as it merges to the right into FL 402.

Foot Trails

Five walking trails are identified on the refuge map, and the shortest is a 0.25-mile picturesque walk behind the visitors center. The raised boardwalk path, which meanders through oak and palm hammocks, includes a gazebo for resting and is ADA accessible. Other trails range from 0.75 mile up to the 5 mile Cruickshank Trail and Tower.

Black Point Wildlife Drive

Allow about an hour to follow this 7-mile, one-way loop and self-guided tour through diverse habitats teeming with wildlife. Everywhere you look there are great photo opportunities. Take shots from your car, or stop at one of the many parking pullovers. The least active season is the summer, but you will almost always see alligators basking in the sun. Portable restrooms are located along the drive.

Haulover Canal and Manatee Observation Deck

The Haulover Canal is a narrow, short, serene passage connecting Mosquito Lagoon and the Indian River Lagoon. Motorboats can launch from nearby Blair's Cove, but it's most popular with paddlers. The ADA-accessible parking area and observation deck are great places to see manatees, especially during the spring and fall.

A **1.5-mile loop through Port Canaveral** runs from Jetty Park to Port's End Park and to the Cove. Access is from N. Atlantic Avenue. If you want to watch the cruise ships head out or grab lunch at one of the Port restaurants, this is a nice bike ride.

Merrit Island National Wildlife Refuge is an ideal backdrop for exploring nature at ground level.

Minutemen Causeway from A1A to the Banana River is a short and scenic 2-mile round trip.

Athletic Events

Health First Triathlon
www.healthfirsttri.com
Eau Gallie

Two courses are offered for this scenic race held the first weekend in October—Olympic distance and sprint distance. Olympic competitors will swim for 1.5K, bike 40K, and run 10K. Sprint participants swim 0.25 mile, bike for 15.9 miles, and run 3.5 miles. The race begins and ends at Pineapple Park, at the northwest intersection of the Indian River and FL 518 in Eau Gallie, and all routes are set in that vicinity, including a breathtaking and challenging bike route across both the Pineda and Eau Gallie Causeways; the run starts and finishes with the Eau Gallie Causeway.

Reindeer Run

www.capecanaveral.gov
Cherie Down Park, Cape Canaveral

Start the holiday season off with a quick 5K family run from Cherie Down Park. Refreshments are served, Santa joins the race, and many participants dress in seasonal colors. The Race starts at 8 AM on the second Saturday in December and finishes early enough that you can still put in a few miles at the mall.

Space Coast Runners Marathon and Half-Marathon

www.spacecoastmarathon.org
Cocoa Village

Held the last weekend in November, this is the oldest marathon in Florida and runs along the Indian River on a mostly shaded flat course. A 5K run/walk leaves from the Cocoa Library on Saturday morning. Race-day Sunday begins at Cocoa Riverfront Park.

Surf the Sand 8K Beach Run

www.brevardparks.com
Lori Wilson Park, Cocoa Beach

On the second Saturday in May, runners get going at 8 AM to start this fun run in the sun, sand, and surf.

Tours and Rentals

Pampered Bicycle Tours

321-759-3433
www.pamperedbiketours.com

Serious bikers can arrange a concierge vacation that includes everything needed to experience the habitat and history of the Space Coast from a bicycle. Transportation to and from the airport, lodging, meals, top-quality bicycles, water bottles, helmets, and guided tours are all included. Group size is limited to 8 to 12 participants. Plenty of free time is available for nonbiking fun. Tours last six days and five nights, from Sunday to Friday, and are $1,575 per person; custom tours and day trips can be arranged. Call for reservations.

SALONS AND SPAS

After a day at the beach or before heading home or embarking on a cruise, consider some pampering.

La Bella Spa

321-453-1510
www.labellaspa.com
3505 N.Courtnay Pkwy., Merritt Island 32953

Rejuvenate your mind, body, and soul at Brevard County's most elegant destination spa. Located just minutes from the beach, La Bella offers a complete menu of personal services, including hair care, nail treatments, waxing, facials, massages, and reflexology. Call for an appointment.

Lady Jays Tanning Salon & Boutique

321-783-0093
5675 N. Atlantic Ave., Cocoa Beach 32931

Six tanning beds offer a quick way to get a beautiful glow. For even faster results, try the UV-free Mystic spray tanner. Located in the Cornerstone Plaza Shopping Center, they open daily at 9 in the winter and 10 in the summer.

Ocean Reef Spa

321-777-4100
www.cpmelbourne.com
Crowne Plaza Melbourne Oceanfront Resort and Spa
2605 N. A1A, Indialantic 32903

Relaxation and serenity surround you at this luxury spa, located inside the Crowne Plaza resort. Services range from massages, facials, and body wraps to hair and nail treatments. Private treatment rooms and experienced, attentive staff promise a wonderful escape.

Shore Thing of Cocoa Beach

321-223-6371
www.shorethingofcocoabeach.com

Treats yourself or the young lady in your life to cornrows, plaits, or wraps woven with an assortment of beads and charms. The price can quickly add up, so ask before the braiding begins. This service is provided at area boutiques, the Doubletree Hotel gift shop, and by the Holiday Inn pool.

Spa Nirvana

321-784-5772
1727 N. Atlantic Ave., Cocoa Beach 32931

By blending diverse cultural influences and calming decor, Dr. Rachel Fornes has created an oasis of peace and bliss in the heart of Cocoa Beach. Call for an appointment for personal services including massage therapy, facials, waxing, reflexology, and nail care.

8

Shopping

Buried Treasures

For many, a vacation isn't complete without the pleasure of unearthing unusual and fun treasures to take home as mementos. On the Space Coast, expect to discover resort fashions, bathing suits, and souvenirs, along with some unexpected finds, such as a shark's tooth in a dinosaur shop and a 6-foot-tall Mai Tiki carved from a cabbage palm.

The shopping venues in this chapter are organized geographically, then by type of shop, and there are several retail clusters with shops and restaurants within walking distance of one another. Many of these stores are small and locally owned. Artists often sell their works in cooperatives or other locations such as hotels and coffee shops, making it easy to find original art, jewelry, music, books, and decor. If you need to ship your purchases back home, see the Information chapter for businesses that can help you.

Grab your GPS, get your bearings, and head out for the hunt. X marks the spot of the famous Ron Jon Surf Shop, a distinctive blue, yellow, orange, and turquoise art deco surf palace near the corner of A1A and FL 520. Consider a side trip to the museums listed in the Culture chapter—they feature unusual and affordable merchandise, and sales proceeds help support their operations. Enjoy the adventure!

Cape Canaveral & Cocoa Beach

Most of the stores at the beach are on or near A1A and are easy to find and have a breezy seaside ambience. If you're in the mood for some mall shopping or just want to get out of the sun for a few hours, head to the **Merritt Square Mall** (321-452-3270; www.merrittsquaremall.com; 777 E. Merritt Island Cswy., Merritt Island 32952), located on FL 520 just 5 miles from Cocoa Beach. It features Macy's, JCPenney, Dillard's, and Sears; more than 80 specialty shops; a fast-food court; an arcade; and the Cobb Merritt Square 16 Cinema.

BEACH GEAR

See the Beaches and Surfing chapter for information on buying and renting beach gear.

LEFT: *Nautical Decor at Woods and Water in Cocoa Village*

BOOKS

Barnes & Noble Booksellers

321-453-8202
www.barnesandnoble.com
780 E. Merritt Island Cswy., Merritt Island 32952

This bookstore and café, located across the street from the Merritt Square Mall, is a convenient and cool retreat after a day in the sun. They carry an extensive collection of space-related publications. Head to a room in the the back filled with selections for infants through young adult, with interactive toys and small-sized tables and chairs.

Books-A-Million

321-453-5177
www.booksamillion.com
777 E. Merritt Island Cswy., Merritt Island 32952

Books, small gifts, cards, and a huge selection of magazines fill this store. They also have a children's section with movies for sale. The Jo Muggs Café offers a variety of drinks and snacks. Enter from parking lot or from inside the Merritt Island Mall.

CLOTHING, SHOES, AND ACCESSORIES

Beall's Outlet

321-784-4555
www.beallsoutlet.com
190 Canaveral Plaza Blvd., Cocoa Beach 32931

Bargain shoppers will find racks of discounted brand-name women's clothing, including T-shirts, swimsuits, and golf apparel, and a full line of men's casual fashion. A Beall's Outlet home decor shop is located two doors down.

Flirt

321-783-2626
4265 N. Atlantic Ave., Cocoa Beach 32931

The young and daring will find brief and glitzy swimsuits, casual clothes, club outfits, short shorts, and high heels.

Mar Chiquita Swimwear

321-784-2626
1 N. Atlantic Ave., Cocoa Beach 32931

Fit and stylish young women will find a great selection of bathing suits and beachwear at this tiny, hip storefront, located just 1 block from the beach at the Minutemen Causeway.

Moniques Boutique

321-799-4412
320 N. Atlantic Ave., Cocoa Beach 32931

Sift through stylish and fashionable clothes, and add pizzazz with the perfect belt, scarf, purse, or bauble. Top it off with a popular red hat.

Nearly Barefoot Sandals

321-784-2244
350 N. Atlantic Ave., Cocoa Beach 32931

Local owners and tennis buffs Eileen and Maggie have amassed a collection of sandals for every occasion, from a day at the beach to a night on the town, featuring name brands such as NAOT, Sperry, and Nautica. Also look for tennis attire, purses and hats, and novel jewelry handcrafted by Tanya.

Patchington's

321-783-6691
2051 N. Atlantic Ave., Cocoa Beach 32931

This Florida-based private label brand offers upscale resort and cruise wear in tropical colors, and sold as separates. New-age polyester clothing is washable and wrinkle-proof for easy travel.

Shady Characters Sunglass Emporium

321-783-4244
25 S. Atlantic Ave., Cocoa Beach 32931

Capture a cool look with a selection from the newest and best assortment of sunglasses on the beach.

Shobha's Boutique

321-784-4441
2031 N. Atlantic Ave., Cocoa Beach 32931

Shobha's, which offers brand-name casual wear and more than two thousand bathing suits (including tan-through, long torso, and mastectomy choices), is the perfect stop for stylish women beyond the bikini years. Accessorize with cover-ups, beach bags, and jewelry.

Susan's Birkenstock Shoes

321-799-9858
227 W. Cocoa Beach Cswy., Cocoa Beach 32931

Slide into a comfortable pair of shoes, clogs, or sandals, from respected names such as Birkenstock, Mephisto, Ecco, Teva, and La Plume.

GALLERIES

Another Planet Glassworks

321-784-0631
114 N. Brevard Ave., Cocoa Beach 32931

Claudia and Steve Beckworth design and craft eye-catching glass and fused glass decorative pieces and jewelry.

Loco for Coco

321-783-0500
3185 N. Atlantic Ave., Cocoa Beach 32931

Chocolate is the featured creation in this cozy showcase for local artists, with an eclectic collection of wall decorations, jewelry, candles, and soaps. Delectable handmade chocolates are available individually or in made-to-order gift boxes.

Mai Tiki Studio & Gallery

321-783-6890
251 Minutemen Cswy., Cocoa Beach 32931

Wayne Coombs was in high school when he carved his first tiki from a piece of sabal palm wood. Thirty years later, carving tropical art remains his passion. For a distinctly Cocoa Beach experience, stop by the studio, where Wayne and other artists sculpt the now world-famous statues, available from 18 inches to an imposing 6 feet tall. Any size can be shipped.

R|K Studio

321-863-3325
17 N. Orlando Ave., Cocoa Beach 32931

Just through the looking-glass door is Rachel Kercher's wonderland, where the designer fuses layers of glass and creates sparkling works in vivid, deep tones. Commission large window or door pieces, or select from smaller items such as starfish night-lights, picture frames, and a stunning collection of jewelry. Surfboard-shaped incense holders reflect the studio's beach environment.

GIFTS AND SOUVENIRS

Ann Lia Gift Shop

321-783-2323
38 S. Atlantic Ave., Cocoa Beach 32931

For more than 50 years, this small emporium has been a favorite of Cocoa Beach residents and visitors, who stop for its souvenirs, space memorabilia, beachwear, sundries, and ornaments, along with the selection of books and toys for children. Paintings and photographs of the area, wildlife sculptures, and handcrafted Ironwood pieces are also featured. A unique choice are the vintage toys and decor from the *I Dream of Jeannie* days.

The Dinosaur Store

321-783-7300
299 W. Cocoa Beach Cswy., Cocoa Beach 32931

Children absolutely love visiting this one-of-a-kind science and nature store, which has an authentic collection of dinosaur teeth and claws, fossil shark teeth, and dinosaur reproductions. Educational toys and books are also available. Mom will find vivid jewelry crafted from gemstones and amber specimens.

Exotic Shells and Gifts by Eleanor

321-783-0848
1 S. Atlantic Ave., Cocoa Beach 32931

Eleanor has a huge selection of shells and ornaments made from shells, as well as costume jewelry, hanging decorations, lamps, and nautical-themed art.

Many different varieties of seashells are for sale at Exotic Shells and Gifts by Eleanor. Eileen Callan

Irish Shop

321-784-9707
5675 N. Atlantic Ave., Cocoa Beach 32931

Top of the morning to you! Owners John and Mary Nolan will help you find a pot of gold at the end of the rainbow with traditional products from Ireland, such as Belleek china, Galway crystal, Claddagh jewelry, scarves and throws, and wedding and baby gifts. The shop is located in Cornerstone Plaza.

The Perfect Gift and Florist

321-799-4438
6550 N. Atlantic Ave., Cape Canaveral 32920

Owner Shirley Nelson Brown stocks a wonderful assortment of gifts and edible treats. Her specialty is creating flower arrangements and one-of-a-kind gift baskets. Call for delivery to cruise staterooms when ships are in dock at Port Canaveral.

Trinity
321-783-8499
5675 N. Atlantic Ave. #112, Cocoa Beach 32931

This shop, in Cornerstone Plaza, is devoted exclusively to religious items, including greeting cards, framed blessings, First Communion gifts, jewelry, and statues.

Twombly's Nautical Furniture
321-783-8610
101 Manatee Ln., Cocoa Beach 32931

Joe Twombly is a locally grown surfer who was a 2000 inductee into the East Coast Hall of Fame. For more than 30 years he has gained a following as a nautical furniture designer. His deep cast resin seashell tables and other decor are known throughout the country. The shop and studio are combined. A small number of items are ready to go, but most are custom orders.

Sports and Surfing

Cocoa Beach Surf Company
321-799-9930
4001 N. Atlantic Ave., Cocoa Beach 32931

This new, bright surf complex has three stories of hip, fun merchandise, such as Body Glove and Life is Good, in juniors, misses, and men's sizes, as well as a large selection of sandals, flip flops, and water shoes for children and adults. They also carry gear and accessories for surfing and other water sports. Open daily from 8 AM to 11 PM. See the Beaches and Surfing chapter for more information.

Jetty Park Bait & Tackle Shop
400 E. Jetty Rd., Cape Canaveral 32920

This small general store carries basics such as sunscreen, hats, and towels. Snacks, cold drinks, beer, small coolers, ice, and souvenirs are also available. The bait side of the house supplies most fishing needs.

Matt's Bicycle Center
321-783-1196
166 N. Atlantic Ave., Cocoa Beach 32931

Matt Molnar is a community advocate for biking and bike safety. Buy or rent a bicycle, purchase apparel and accessories, and get sound advice on maintaining your bike in good form.

Natural Art Surf Shop
321-783-0764
2370 S. Atlantic Ave., Cocoa Beach 32931

At their shop located along the south Cocoa Beach stretch, Deb and Pete Dooley provide surfboards and local surfing information. The couple makes boards under the name Natural Art, shapes the boards and sends them out to be finished, and sells them wholesale. They also accept custom orders. See the Beaches and Surfing chapter for more information.

Deb Dooley assists customers at Natural Art Surf Shop. Eileen Callan

Ocean Sports World

321-783-4008
3220 S. Atlantic Ave., Cocoa Beach 32931

This sporting gear shop in south Cocoa Beach carries equipment to get you on the waves or the river, including surfboards, kayaks, wave skis, kiteboards, and paddleboards. Watch surfboards being shaped, or order a custom board under the Island or Slater brand. See the Beaches and Surfing chapter for more information.

Quiet Flight Surf Shop Inc.

321-783-1530
109 N. Orlando Ave., Cocoa Beach 32931

Select a board from the showroom, or order one custom made at the Cape Canaveral factory, and find swimwear, wetsuits, and beach accessories. See the Beaches and Surfing chapter for more information.

Ron Jon Surf Shop

321-799-8888
www.ronjons.com
4151 N. Atlantic Ave., Cocoa Beach 32931

Since 1963, Cocoa Beach visitors have made a stop at this flagship site of the most famous surf shop in the world. The megastore is open 24/7 and promises it has the best selection of surf, skate, swim, and beach essentials on earth. Spread over 2 acres, it has a huge selection of tropical fashions and accessories, racks of bathing suits, and Ron Jon souvenir merchandise. See the Beaches and Surfing chapter for more information.

Ron Jon Surf Shop is open 24 hours a day. Courtesy Ron Jon Surf Shop

Surfet's Surf Shack

321-868-3021
www.surfet.com
165 N. Orlando Ave., Cocoa Beach 32931

Hit the waves in style with boards, supplies, and accessories from this surf shop, catering to girls and women with bikinis, sandals, tops, and hats, as well as lightweight training boards for beginners. See the Beaches and Surfing chapter for more information.

Sundries and Extras

All Strung Out

321-783-4550
46 N. Brevard Ave., Cocoa Beach 32931
Crafters will find yarn galore for knitting and crochet; beads, baubles, and buttons; and fabrics and fibers. Look for chitin, a yarn made from shrimp and crab shells blended with other materials.

Cocoa Beach Winery

321-783-4701
5675 N. Atlantic Ave., Cocoa Beach 32931

Drop by this tropical paradise in Cornerstone Plaza for a selection of sweet wines made from Florida fruits, as well as candies and CDs. Wines may be sampled.

Cocoa Beach Harley-Davidson

321-799-2221
3688 N. Atlantic Ave., Cocoa Beach 32931

Bikers will discover a great selection of apparel, accessories, and gifts themed to the Harley-Davidson style and trademark, including fun fashions and functional riding gear.

The Corner Tattoos and Body Piercing

321-783-8287
112 Dixie Ln., Cocoa Beach 32931

For more than a decade, trained and experienced professionals have been providing beachgoers with creative body art applied in a sanitary environment. Conveniently located right behind the Surfing Hall of Fame, it is open daily 11–11. Must be 18 or older, or with a parent, to enter the shop.

CVS

321-784-0503

Walgreens

321-799-9112

Located next to each other at the corner of A1A and FL 520, both are open 24 hours for convenient shopping for basic beach needs, forgotten personal products, medicines, and prescriptions. Both sell photo supplies and offer quick service on film development or downloading memory-card photos to a CD.

Fairvilla

321-799-9961
500 Thurm Blvd., Cape Canaveral 32920

Spice up a romantic weekend with an assortment of adult toys and games, sexy clothing, costumes, and paraphernalia. The megastore is bright and designed to ensure a comfortable but adventurous shopping experience.

Wine-Oh!

321-784-4298
220 N. Atlantic Ave., Cocoa Beach 32931

In keeping with the mix of international gourmet restaurants located in downtown Cocoa Beach, Mary McNeal has brought together unique and hard-to-find wines from around the world. Microbrewed beer is also available, as well as meats, cheeses, crackers—and serving accessories to complement your experience.

Central Brevard: Historic Cocoa Village

It's difficult to tell where art ends and merchandising begins at this attractive, relaxing, and dog-friendly outdoor marketplace. Yesterday's riverside trading post has blossomed into a landscape of colorful shops interspersed with benches, fountains, and outdoor art. If shopping is part of your vacation itinerary, this is your destination.

The tree-lined streets of historic Cocoa Village Roger Scruggs

ANTIQUES AND COLLECTIBLES

Almost Antiques Mall & Factory Street Market

321-639-8992
625 Florida Ave., Cocoa 32922

This turquoise and yellow warehouse on the outskirts of Cocoa Village holds an unstructured collection of antiques, housewares, furniture, and books, plus an outside garden setting for patio and yard furnishings and decor.

Antiques and Collectibles Too

321-632-9924
115 Harrison St., Cocoa 32922

Browse through an eclectic assortment of Highwaymen paintings, primitives, vintage holiday decorations, toys, and jewelry, as well as pottery, glassware, and furniture from liquidated estates.

Horsefeathers Antiques and Gifts

321-638-4054
14 Oleander St., Cocoa 32922

Enjoy a nostalgic display of vintage jewelry, dolls, fine porcelain, glassware, painted ponies, and unique gifts.

CLOTHING, SHOES, ACCESSORIES

Coco's

321-433-0403
402 Brevard Ave., Cocoa 32922

Unique jewelry made from turquoise, citrine, amber, ceramics, and pearls is displayed next to T-shirts, hats, jackets, travel bags, and candles in this mercantile marvel.

Downtown Divas

321-433-0727
411 Brevard Ave., Cocoa 32922

Take a cruise, enjoy a night on the town, or just make a statement while wearing this daring metropolitan-style women's clothing.

Frankly My Dear

321-631-3327
404A Brevard Ave., Cocoa 32922

This ladies' boutique carries fashions for mature ladies of all sizes, along with Onex shoes, Mary Francis Bags, and Lunch at the Ritz jewelry.

Green Apples

321-635-8728
111 Harrison St., Cocoa 32922

A bright setting blends perfectly with a fun, upscale collection of contemporary and comfortable women's clothing and accessories made from natural fibers—wrinkle-resistant and perfect for warm climates. Stylish jewelry, bags, belts, hats, and shoes are also available.

Mangos Fashion Boutique

321-639-3292
319 Brevard Ave., Cocoa 32922

Mix and match casual pants, skirts, shirts, and jackets in bright fabrics, then add jewelry, belts, shoes, and a bag. Featured labels are Salaam, Pure Handknit, Cut Loose, and Cactus, as well as Me Too and Naughty Monkey shoes.

Rare Essentials
321-633-6211
415 Brevard Ave., Cocoa 32922

Women's clothing, gifts, and accessories from the Vera Bradley and Brighton lines are the specialty of this establishment.

Sadie's for Infants and Children
321-639-6662
643 Brevard Ave., Cocoa 32922

Find stylish maternity wear; soft, attractive baby apparel, cribs, and bedding; and bags, bears, and classic books to start the little one off in style.

Season Tickets Boutique
321-690-1919
301 Brevard Ave., Cocoa 32922

Appropriately located directly across from the Cocoa Village Playhouse, this well-respected shop has been helping the women of Brevard County step out in fashion for nearly two decades with an unusual selection of international fashions, evening wear, sports and business clothes, shoes, and handbags.

VernaFlora Boutique
321-636-5532
403 Brevard Ave. #3, Cocoa 32922

Pamper yourself with a mix-and-match selection of fine lingerie in juniors, misses, and plus sizes, along with jewelry, natural cosmetics, and aromatherapy products.

World of Fashions
321-631-7222
206 Brevard Ave., Cocoa 32922

Here you'll find international and tropical fashions that were designed for world travel—or simply wear them to bring a distant part of the world to your own backyard.

CRAFTS

Knit and Stitch Inc.
321-637-8997
15 Stone St., Cocoa 32922

This store carries a complete line of needlework kits, instruction books, and supplies, and it's a great place to get ideas for your next project.

Space Coast Crafters
321-632-6553
410 Brevard Ave., Cocoa 32922

Pick up some great ideas for creating memorable pieces, or purchase already-completed handmade dolls, jewelry, woodcarvings, and ceramic pieces.

Tatan Ka Beads
321-636-4104
234 King St., Cocoa 32922

Make your own jewelry with beads from distant lands, such as the Czech Republic, Africa, Ireland, Japan, and China, as well as Swarovski crystals, semiprecious stones, turquoise, pearls, and shells.

GALLERIES

Art Vue Galerié
321-637-2787
225 King St., Cocoa 32922

The village's largest gallery showcases tropical art by more than 60 Florida artists. Browse among paintings and sculptures, pottery and photographs. Decorators will enjoy the unique furniture selection. Look carefully for unusual creations, such as handmade soaps and CDs featuring local musicians. As a bonus, Red Hat ladies will find a generous selection of clothing and accessories.

The Black Dog Gallery
321-631-6890
404D Brevard Ave., Cocoa 32922

Lori's shop will feel familiar as soon as you step through the door because her amusing paintings on wood are scattered throughout the village. The gallery is named for Myria, Lori's black Belgian shepard, her companion when the gallery and studio opened more than 10 years ago. A golden-toned King Charles holds court these days, while visitors browse and chuckle at the amusing and eclectic mix of original paintings, furnishings, jewelry, and other works. Lori specializes in custom-made pet storyboards.

Sundancer Gallery
321-631-0092
6 Florida Ave., Cocoa 32922

Owner John McCarthy, of Blackfoot descent, carries on in the tradition of generations of Indian reservation traders at this Southwestern-style post. Most of the Native American art and artifacts are created and produced by tribes throughout North America, and each month a new artist is featured. The gallery also serves as a Brevard County gathering place for local Native Americans and others interested in learning about the culture and partipating in special events.

A King Charles spaniel welcomes visitors to the Black Dog Gallery.

GIFTS & SOUVENIRS

Annie's Toy Chest
321-632-5890
405 Brevard Ave., Cocoa 32922

Once upon a time, there were small, enchanting shops brimming with delightful toys for young boys and girls. This magical emporium harkens back to that time and will bring out the child in you. They carry collectible dolls, including Madame Alexander.

Bath Cottage
321-690-2284
425 Brevard Ave., Cocoa 32922

Create a world of relaxation and comfort with a selection of soaps, bath salts, lotions, essential oils, and other pampering products from Crabtree and Evelyn, Tyme, and Lady Primrose.

Candles by G
321-638-4131
402 Brevard Ave., Cocoa 32922

Try their longer-burning Bean Pot candles, made from soybeans. Wick cutters and decorative gifts are also available.

Gingerbread House
321-639-4694
15 Oleander St., Cocoa 32922

Here is a wonderful eclectic collection of crafts, gifts, collectibles, home decor, stained glass, and oil paintings, along with lots of Florida-themed items.

Handwerk Haus
321-631-6367
401 Brevard Ave., Cocoa 32922

Traditional craftwork, figurines, and fine collectibles adorn this charming old-world shop.

Pear Tree
321-632-5432
310A Brevard Ave., Cocoa 32922

Franz porcelain and an SPI gallery collection of sea life in brass and marble are featured, along with wall art, oil candles, garden flags, and greeting cards.

The Strawberry Patch
321-632-5991
423 Brevard Ave., Cocoa 32922

A Victorian-themed selection of candles, vases, and glasswork for the home is sold, along with watches, very unusual greeting cards, and jewelry.

The Toy Box

321-632-2411
419 Brevard Ave., Cocoa 32922

Come in and peek at the large selection of dollhouses—in kits or preassembled—and miniature furnishings and decor.

The Village Gourmet

321-636-5480
19 Stone St., Cocoa 32922

Buy something for yourself or a friend from the unique collection of dishes, platters, and every kind of gadget for the kitchen, as well as a fine collection of wine and all the necessary utensils to outfit your bar. Custom gourmet gift baskets can be shipped.

HOME AND GARDEN

Rendez-Vous & Something Different

321-633-0113
121 Harrison St., Cocoa 32922

Browse through a cornucopia of upscale, European-design home furnishings, including vases, floral arrangements, lamps and shades, custom-made pillows, bedding, quilts, duvet covers, draperies, and local art.

Travis Hardware Store

321-636-1441
300 Delannoy Ave., Cocoa 32922

Repeat visitors to Cocoa Village usually find their way to this friendly old-fashioned hardware store, where you can just browse or get help from the knowledgeable staff to find exactly what you need. Mac "Travis" Osbourne is the fourth generation of his family to operate this business, which opened in 1885 at the peak of the steamboat era. Today the store supplies nuts and bolts for the crawler that carries the Space Shuttle on its long, slow trek to the launch pad.

Ventana al Mundo

321-633-5151
210 Brevard Ave., Cocoa 32922

Decorate your home with pieces from this window to the worlds of Peru, Nicaragua, and Mexico, including pottery, pewter, candles, and handblown glass.

Woods and Water

321-433-2077
204 Brevard Ave., Cocoa 32922

Sportsmen and boaters will love this oceanful of nautical home decor, such as WELCOME ABOARD life preservers, lighthouses, ship's wheel lamps, and books about Florida birds and wildlife.

Jewelry

Bailey's Jewelry
321-632-3752
310 Brevard Ave., Cocoa 32922

This store will repair your jewelry or install a new watch battery. You can buy a Seiko watch or clock, or look over their consignment and estate jewelry.

Contemporary Concepts
321-632-9505
216 Brevard Ave., Cocoa 32922

The coral Bellaire Arcade is a perfect spot for this avant-garde shop, featuring handcrafted jewelry. Enjoy wearable art such as ear sweeps, which slip into a single pierced hole and playfully climb up your ear.

Jon's Fine Jewelry
321-631-0270
215 Brevard Ave., Cocoa 32922

Designer Jon Miller creates stunning custom jewelry pieces. Select from the showcase or have diamonds and colored gemstones set or reset into classic styles.

Sundries and Extras

Freida's Kritter Boutique
321-639-8206
116 Harrison St., Cocoa 32922

Follow the paw prints—and bring your pet along if you like—to a pint-sized marketplace of toys, apparel, sunglasses, bandanas, and other goodies for the pampered pooch.

Nature's Haven
321-632-1221
602 Brevard Ave., Cocoa 32922

Owner Doreen invites you to try a holistic approach to healing the body and spirit with aromatherapy from natural, organic, and botanical products and oils. Books and music soothe the mind. She also carries a small selection of apparel in natural fibers and hosts weekly workshops and occasional Sunday-afternoon concerts by local musicians.

Old Time Photo
321-961-2202
404C Brevard Ave., Cocoa 32922

Adults play dress-up at this unusual shop. Pick a costume, maybe a cowboy, gangster, pirate, or roaring '20s dancer, and a color or sepia-toned memento will be ready in minutes.

Central Brevard: The Avenue Viera

The Avenue Viera

321-242-1200

www.viera.com

Viera 32940

Conveniently located off I-95, the Avenue Viera is a regional marketplace encompassing more than 60 department and specialty stores, 10 restaurants, coffee and ice cream stops, a 16-screen movie theater, and a park for special events or just relaxing amid fountains and plants. Some of the many shops here include: Coldwater Creek, Ann Taylor Loft, Glad Rags, Jos. A. Banks, Chico's, Old Navy, and Lane Bryant for clothing and accessories; Justice for young teen girls and Baby Gap for children; Bombay, World Market, Yankee Candle, and Bed, Bath & Beyond for the home; Liz Claiborne Shoes, Motherhood Maternity, Pacific Sunwear, and Wine Styles; and Belk department store for fashions and more.

The fountain is an oasis amid the shops at the Avenue Viera.

North Brevard: Downtown Titusville

Stores in downtown Titusville mirror the environment. Historic, turn-of-the-20th-century buildings have been restored, and many have been converted to antiques emporiums. Galleries display the themes and colors of nature, and sport shops prepare adventurers with equipment and information about recreation on the Indian River Lagoon.

Antiques and Collectibles

Accents

321-790-7805
1113 S. Washington Ave., Titusville 32780

In addition to the silver, crystal, artifacts, and jewelry found in many antiques shops, this small house has unique offerings such as primitives and items more geared toward men, such as fishing tackle, tools, decoy ducks, and pocket knives.

Banana Alley Antiques

321-268-4282
106 Main St., Titusville 32796

The steady tick-tock of an assortment of wind-up clocks accompanies visitors while they browse through estate jewelry, china, silver, and collectibles. Look for the banana sign hanging over the door.

Dusty Rose Antique Mall

321-269-5526
1101 S. Washington Ave., Titusville 32780

Dusty Rose Antique Mall

For more than 25 years, Dusty Rose has built a loyal following of antiques lovers throughout central Florida. More than 40 dealers share 7,000 square feet of air-conditioned space, providing variety in product and a steady change of inventory. The mall is located on US 1 as it divides into two one-way roads and is about a mile before historic downtown Titusville.

Inventory
321-269-7175
305 S. Washington Ave., Titusville 32780

A dripping can of Sherwin Williams paint hangs over the door of this restored hardware store turned antiques mart. Owners Jon and Terri Eberhart have a delightful collection of vintage furniture, local handcrafted goods, baskets, fabrics, linens, toys, and Pyrex kitchenware.

River Road Mercantile
321-264-2064
219 S. Washington Ave., Titusville 32780

Dixie operates this quaint storefront, where the collectibles of four dealers represent a varied assortment of kitchen, glassware, vintage textiles, toys, dolls, and more. The garden center features yard implements and decorations.

GALLERIES

Gallery OCOCO
321-385-2598
107 Broad St., Titusville 32796

This showcase gallery features an original and innovative collection of works from more than 20 local artisans, including clay bowls and beads, glass vases, candleholders, watercolors, and hand-painted cards. Jewelry maker Vivian Lacerte runs the gallery, and her daughter, potter Rhea Lacerte, is the primary contributor.

Vessels in Stoneware
321-720-0783
113 Broad St., Titusville 32796

Oregon native Jo Chapman uses a midrange firing temperature to infuse pottery with trendy, vivid tones of periwinkle, plum, and sage. Her specialty is utilitarian stoneware for the home, such as dinnerware and ovenware, serving dishes, wine coolers, and olive-oil dipping plates. Small berry bowls with drain holes are a beautiful and practical way to store and serve fruit.

SPORTS

Action Bait & Tackle
321-264-0996
425 Garden St., Titusville 32796

Open daily and conveniently located near the bridge leading to Merritt Island National Wildlife Refuge, this small and friendly shop sells fishing gear and live bait.

Captain Hook's Bait & Tackle

321-268-4646
103 Max Brewer Memorial Pkwy., Titusville 32780

This is the last stop for bait and fishing goods before heading over the causeway to the Merritt Island National Wildlife Refuge. They carry a full line of fishing equipment, as well as navigational maps and some last-minute supplies.

Wildlife Profile: Alligator

After existing more than 150 million years and surviving the cataclysmic disaster that drove its dinosaur cousins to extinction, the American alligator species was nearly done in by love—the public's love for purses, belts, shoes, wallets, and other goods made from exotic alligator hide. In the late 18th century, naturalist William Bartram wrote of seeing so many alligators in the St. Johns River "it would have been easy to have walked across on their heads had the animals been harmless." A hundred years later, the population was significantly depleted, and the state stepped in to protect the species and reverse the decline.

The adaptable American is the official reptile of Florida, a curious, reclusive star in the state's ecological drama. These cold-blooded creatures spend long hours basking in the warm sun near canals, rivers, lagoons, and even ponds on the golf course. A shovel-shaped snout is trimmed with teeth; bulging eyes sit high on the head and scan for prey while the gator floats just beneath the water's surface. The hide is dark, scaly, and bony—reminiscent of prehistoric roots. The largest reptile in North America, the alligator is usually at least 8 to 10 feet long as an adult, including a thick powerful tail that propels it through the water and sideswipes adversaries. Alligators creep slowly across the ground on stubby, webbed appendages but can move *very* quickly if provoked.

American alligator (Alligator mississippiensis) Jim Angy

Make no mistake, these normally timid creatures are the wildest of wildlife, and when mating or protecting their young, or when harassed, they can quickly become aggressive. It's illegal to feed alligators because they'll lose their fear, and the chance of an attack on humans or pets increases. The risk is so great that once an alligator has been fed, it will be captured and killed. For your protection and theirs, keep your distance as you admire these fascinating and fearsome survivors.

Space Coast Sightings: Black Point Wildlife Drive at the Merritt Island National Wildlife Refuge, St. Johns River airboat tour, Wild Florida exhibit at Brevard Zoo.

The Fly Fisherman
321-267-0348
1114 S. Washington Ave. (US 1), Titusville 32780

Inside this impressive store, knowledgeable and helpful staff guide novice and experienced fishermen in selecting equipment and services. As the name suggests, fly-fisherman will find tackle, line, weights, rods, and reels, and custom rigging. Conventional fishing gear is also available. Clothing, hats, sunglasses, maps, books, and a large selection of kayaks round out the inventory.

Design your own rigging with the help of The Fly Fisherman.

Skeeter Lagoon Bait & Tackle
321-383-2001
450 Garden St., Titusville 32796

Owner Rich grew up in Titusville and is an avid Indian River fisherman. Look for the blue and yellow building just east of the railroad tracks and stop by for bait, tackle, equipment, rod repair, reel cleaning, and spooling service—or just to hang out and talk about fishing.

SUNDRIES AND EXTRAS

Frontenac Flea Market
321-631-0241
5605 N. US 1, Cocoa 32927

Bargain hunters can make a day of it exploring acres of booths and enjoying special events at this outdoor marketplace, located about halfway between FL 528 and Titusville. It's open every Friday and Saturday.

Jim's Dollhouses & Gifts

321-267-4995
329 S. Washington Ave., Titusville 32796

Kits and preassembled dollhouses in a variety of styles are available in this small specialty store, along with an extensive collection of miniatures to furnish and accessorize.

Prop'a Place Hobby Shop

321-267-5999
329 S. Washington Ave., Titusville 32796

Enthusiasts who enjoy assembling aviation and boating vehicles will find kits for both here. Ready-to-fly remote-control planes and flight-simulation software are also available.

South Brevard: Main Street Melbourne

Stroll through the restored area of old Melbourne and enjoy a glimpse at what this avenue was like at the turn of the 20th century. Antiques and bric-a-brac vie for your attention, along with contemporary furnishings and miniskirts. This is the place to find that one-of-a-kind souvenir for yourself or gift for someone back home. Many of the shops are open on Friday evening but are closed on Sunday.

ANTIQUES AND COLLECTIBLES

The Antique Mall

321-951-0151
806 E. New Haven Ave., Melbourne 32901

Poke around inside and discover a selection of furniture, vintage dishes, and eclectic finds, including art.

Betty's Antiques

321-951-2258
2001 Melbourne Ct., Melbourne 32901

Betty specializes in estate sales, especially furniture, silver, jewelry, and glassware, and is a licensed appraiser.

Finder's Keepers

321-676-5697
809 E. New Haven Ave., Melbourne 32901

Thirty dealers are represented in this cooperative of children's toys, kitchen items, vintage scarves, knives and swords, furniture, books, chandeliers, and imported woodcarvings from Indonesia.

Nostalgia, Inc.
321-722-9963
908 E. New Haven Ave., Melbourne 32901

Betty Boop greets you at the front door as you step back into an earlier time at this shop, with extensive displays of genuine collectibles and quality reproductions, along with figurines, accessories, nostalgic novelties, home and office furnishings, and wall hangings.

Seldom Scene
321-768-8442
724 E. New Haven Ave., Melbourne 32901

More than 40 dealers are part of this antiques mall, with a vast assortment of collectibles, furniture, and artifacts sharing 5,000 square feet of uncluttered space.

CLOTHING, SHOES, AND ACCESSORIES

Albatross
321-723-2270
924 E. New Haven Ave., Suite 101, Melbourne 32901

Men and women will discover tropical and stylish Tommy Bahama brand clothing and watches, perfect for watching time go by, at this sophisticated shop located in the Railroad Emporium.

Baby Patch
321-676-7590
800 E. New Haven Ave., Melbourne 32901

For nearly 20 years this adorable shop has been outfitting pampered Brevard babies with layettes, unique gifts and toys, furniture, and decor.

The Flop Shop
321-724-6740
820 E. New Haven Ave., Melbourne 32901

Step through the door and into a world of colorful footwear and Crocs in a variety of styles for adults and children—everything from truly casual to flops sprinkled with bling.

The Gauzeway
321-723-0334
818 E. New Haven Ave., Melbourne 32901

Bright, breezy cloth is spun into delicate gauze skirts, tops, pants, and capris, all 100 percent cotton and made with natural fibers and dyes. Distinctive handmade jewelry by Treska complements the outfits.

Albatross sells tropical wear for men and women.

Isabella's Ladies Apparel
321-952-4489
845 E. New Haven Ave., Melbourne 32901

Fashionable formal wear in traditional and daring designs, perfect for a special occasion, is available here. An entire wedding party can be accommodated with choices in bridal gowns, wedding party dresses, and accessories.

Mirabella's
321-725-4983
909 E. New Haven Ave., Melbourne 32901

Find playful, unique resort wear, jewelry, and accessories, with brand names such as Downtown Divas, Flax Flax, and Lily Pad.

Orchid Beach Clothing Company
321-723-8008
826 E. New Haven Ave., Melbourne 32901

Come in and see the wide range of colors and styles of Fresh Produce sportswear and belts, bags, and jewelry.

GALLERIES

Mud Flats Pottery & Gallery
321-951-1310
826 E. New Haven Ave., Melbourne 32901

Drawing inspiration from the natural world, nationally recognized potter Sue Tuttle molds decorative clay vessels fused with texture, patterns, and colors influenced by Asian and African cultures. The gallery features her own creations as well as handmade works from around the country, including photographs, baskets, small oils, and jewelry.

GIFTS AND SOUVENIRS

The Chandlery
321-726-0192
911 E. New Haven Ave., Melbourne 32901

Enhance the warmth of your home with candles and home fragrance accessories, such as oil lamps, scented candles, and decorative holders. Select from a full line of wedding candles and a rotation of seasonal selections.

Christmas Cottage
321-725-0270
1002 E. New Haven Ave., Melbourne 32901

Capture the holiday spirit any day of the year as you browse through seasonal collectibles, decorations, and gifts.

Mud Flats Pottery & Gallery has creations for every budget.

Creative Energy

321-952-6789
835 E. New Haven Ave., Melbourne 32901

Aromatherapy fills the air and sets the mood for exploring new age gifts for the mind, body, and soul, including books, music, jewelry, clothing, lotions, and oils.

East Coast Winery

321-409-8400
827 E. Strawbridge Ave., Melbourne 32901

Florida wines are featured in gift baskets and accessories sold here; try a sample before your purchase.

The Flying Corkscrew

321-956-0026
901 E. New Haven Ave., Melbourne 32901

Choose a ready-made gift basket or fill your own with wines, accessories, microbrews, and sweets for your favorite gourmet.

Heart Strings

321-724-0111
802 E. New Haven Ave., Melbourne 32901

Forty craftspeople create unique, handmade works, including aluminum and wood wind chimes, ceramics, jewelry, cloth dolls, and hand-painted bowls and dishes.

Indian River Soap

321-723-6464
804 E. New Haven Ave., Melbourne 32901

The natural, wholesome skin products, soaps, soy wax candles, bath accessories, and gifts sold here are all made locally.

Lord Ravenswood Hall

321-768-8369
909 E. New Haven Ave., Melbourne 32901

Enjoy the flavor of olde England with comedy videos, bone china teacups, teapots and cozies, sweets and biscuits, and more imports from across the pond.

Melwood Creek Tea Company

321-722-0107
2013 Melbourne Ct., Melbourne 32901

High ceilings and rustic wood floors add to the old-world charm of this shop, featuring a "varie-tea" of brews by the cup and more than a hundred varieties to take home, as well as accessories and gifts.

Sea Things

321-768-0204
924 E. New Haven Ave., Suite 103, Melbourne 32901

Owner Jeanne sells big and little seashells near the seashore, along with other nautical home decor.

JEWELRY

Jessups

321-724-2201
912 E. New Haven Ave., Melbourne 32901

This family-owned store, which carries both estate and new fine jewelry, is also Melbourne's oldest licensed pawnbroker. They feature real roses dipped in gold, jewelry boxes, and guitars.

Just for You Estate Jewelry

321-768-2636
829 E. New Haven Ave., Melbourne 32901

In addition to fine antique and estate items, the store has a complete line of Vera Bradley purses, watches, and belts.

SPORTS

Harry Goode's Outdoor Shop

321-723-4751
1231 E. New Haven Ave., Melbourne 32901

Harry Goode, a member of one of Melbourne's founding families, opened this sporting goods store in 1946 with the motto, "fish more, live longer." Stop by for fishing supplies, paraphernalia, assistance, and a smattering of tall tales. Located at the intersection of the Indian River and Crane Creek.

SUNDRIES AND EXTRAS

Pinede Harley-Davidson

321-259-1311
6030 N. US 1, Melbourne 32940

This full-service complex offers maintenance, parts, sales, and rentals, as well as a calendar of local rides. They are located about 15 miles from the beach, but if you're a biker visiting the area, you may have an interest or need to visit.

Russian House, Inc.

321-733-5929
822 E. New Haven Ave., Melbourne 32901

Discover the beauty of Russian jewelry, giftware, collectibles, dolls, and toys. Russian translation, interpretation, and language lessons are also available.

Schading International Fine Oriental Rugs

321-951-7560
830 E. New Haven Ave., Melbourne 32901

This gorgeous selection of imported Anatolian, Persian, Pakistani, Afghani, Indian, and Chinese rugs, made from silk, wool, and cotton, are all heirloom quality, hand knotted, and personally selected.

Cocoa Beach Library   Cassidy Dianne Neary

9

INFORMATION

Practical Matters

In the years between 1950 and 2000, the population of Brevard County grew from about 25,000 to nearly 500,000—a phenomenal increase that reflects the magnetic draw of the area. Visitors often return to settle in Brevard County, and residents enjoy the wealth of natural and recreational resources as much as the visitors. This listing of practical information should be useful to both, and it includes the following topics:

Ambulance, Fire, Police, and Coast Guard
Area Codes, City Halls, and Zip Codes
Banks
Bibliography
Celebrations
Chambers of Commerce
Handicapped Services
Hospitals and Clinics
Late-Night Food and Fuel
Mail and Shipping
Media
Real Estate
Road and Marine Services
Visitor Resources
If Time is Short

AMBULANCE, FIRE, POLICE, AND COAST GUARD

In Brevard County, three phone numbers connect you to assistance, information, and referral to the appropriate agency.

Dial 911 for medical and other emergencies, and an operator will immediately route you to ambulance, fire, local police, Brevard County Sheriff, Florida Highway Patrol, or Coast Guard Search and Rescue.

Dial 211 to reach the Brevard County Help Line, where trained counselors are available 24 hours a day to provide information or referral on local governmental, health, or social services, including disaster planning information.

Dial 511 for traffic reports.

Other important numbers:
Poison Control: 1-800-222-1222.
Sexual Assault Victim Services Rape Crisis Hotline: 321-784-4357.

AREA CODES, CITY HALLS, AND ZIP CODES

The area code for all of Brevard County is 321. For metropolitan Orlando the area code is 407, and you must dial all 10 digits to place a call. An elected board of commissioners governs Brevard County, which has a population of nearly half a million. Many services are provided at the county level, but individual municipalities retain local controls and are the best resource for specific community information.

City Hall	Phone	Zip Code
Brevard County	633-2000	32940
Cape Canaveral	868-1230	32920
Cocoa	639-7550	32922
Cocoa Beach	868-3235	32931
Indialantic	723-2242	32903
Indian Harbour Beach	773-3181	32937
Malabar	727-7764	32950
Melbourne	727-2900	32901
Melbourne Beach	724-5860	32951
Palm Bay	952-3400	32907
Palm Shores	242-4555	32940
Rockledge	690-3978	32955
Satellite Beach	773-4407	32937
Titusville	383-5775	32796
West Melbourne	727-7700	32904

BANKS

The following are banks in the Cape Canaveral and Cocoa Beach area. Most have links to national or regional banking systems and are part of automatic teller networks.

Bank of America, 430 Brevard Ave., Cocoa Beach 32931; 321-635-1900.
Bank of America, 82 N. Atlantic Ave., Cocoa Beach 32931; 321-783-2444.
Bank of America, 4300 N. Atlantic Ave., Cocoa Beach 32931; 321-783-2455.
Coastal Bank, 1701 N. Atlantic Ave., Cocoa Beach 32931; 321-868-3580.
RCB Centura Bank, 4350 N. Atlantic Ave., Cocoa Beach 32931; 321-868-6060.
Sunrise Bank, 5604 N. Atlantic Ave., Cocoa Beach 32931; 321-784-8333.
SunTrust, 150 Cocoa Isles Blvd., Cocoa Beach 32931; 321-799-2203.

BIBLIOGRAPHY

Aerospace

Anderson, Eric, and Joshua Piven. *The Space Tourists Handbook*. Philadelphia: Quirk Books,

2005. Space adventurers will appreciate this handy reference on preparing for suborbital and orbital flights, including the now-available zero-gravity flights.

Barbree, Jay. *Live from Cape Canaveral*. New York: HarperCollins Publishers, Inc., 2007. For
fifty years veteran NBC News reporter and Brevard County resident Jay Barbree has
covered America's manned space flight. Now he shares his inside stories about the
astronauts, and the adventure and evolution of the space program.

Faherty, William Barnaby. *Florida's Space Coast: The Impact of NASA on the Sunshine State*.
Gainesville, Fla.: University Press of Florida, 2002. The story of America's space exploration told through the recollections of the people who built the spaceport.

Glenn, John, and Nick Taylor. *John Glenn a Memoir*. New York: Bantam Books, 1999. The life
story of the man who would be at the center of man's journey into space, becoming the
first, and later oldest, to fly into orbit.

Hawking, Stephen. *The Illustrated A Brief History of Time*. New York: Bantam Books, 1996.
The best-selling book on the nature of the universe has been updated and combined
with amazing visual displays. In 2007 Hawking experienced space on a zero-gravity
flight from Cape Canaveral spaceport.

Kranz, Gene. *Failure is Not an Option: Mission Control from Mercury to Apollo 13 and Beyond*.
New York: Berkley Books, 2000. Former flight director for NASA gives a behind-the-
scenes account of the people and work critical to the success of space launches, including the successful recovery efforts that saved *Apollo 13*.

Wendt, Guenter, and Russell Still. *The Unbroken Chain*. Burlington, Ontario, Canada:
Apogee Books, 2001. This autobiography of the last man seen by crews before lifting
into space from Cape Canaveral from 1967 through 1989 provides insight into the culture and challenges of the manned-flight program.

Wolfe, Tom. *The Right Stuff*. New York: Bantam Books, 2001. A look at the first astronauts,
space pioneers, and heroes who "were willing to set on top of an enormous Roman candle" and wait for the fuse to be lit.

Biography and Reminiscence

Lindbergh, Anne Morrow. *Gift from the Sea*. New York: Random House, 1991. This timeless
classic of reflection centered on a solitary trip to the seashore and a collection of
seashells has been enjoyed and shared by generations of women since it was first published in 1955.

Rawlings, Marjorie Kinnan. *Cross Creek*. New York: Touchstone, 1996. This Pulitzer
Prize–winning novelist left New York to settle a homestead in a wild stretch of central
Florida. The tale ends with a trip down the St. Johns River and a discussion of man's
relationship with the land.

Environment and Natural Sciences

Alden, Peter, Rick Cech, and Gil Nelson. *National Audubon Society Field Guide to Florida*.
New York: Alfred A. Knopf, 2004. This fit-in-a-backpack guide provides an overview of
Florida's natural history and detailed descriptions of flora and fauna.

Belleville, Bill. *River of Lakes: A Journey on Florida's St. Johns River*. Athens, Ga.: University of
Georgia Press, 2000. Central Florida resident and nature writer Belleville rediscovers the
wonder and beauty of nature on a paddle trip along the full length of the St. Johns River.

Katz, Cathie. *The Nature of Florida's Beaches*. St. Petersburg, Fla.: Great Outdoors Publishing
Co., 2001. This popular book, written and illustrated by a local environmentalist and sea-

bean aficionado, is often carried by local bookstores; an enjoyable and easy-to-read guide.
———. *The Nature of Florida's Waterways*. Melbourne Beach, Fla.: Atlantic Press, 1996. Learn about the birds, marine life, and plant systems of Brevard County's estuaries.
Littler, Mark Masterton, and Diane Scullion Littler. *Waterways & Byways of the Indian River Lagoon: Field Guide for Boaters, Anglers & Naturalists*. Washington, D.C.: Offshore Graphics, Inc., 2005. Boaters, anglers, and naturalists will appreciate the intricate view of each section of the Indian River Lagoon, along with photos and descriptions of plants and animals in the region.
Whitney, Ellie, D. Bruce Means, and Anne Rudloe. *Priceless Florida*. Sarasota, Fla.: Pineapple Press, 2004. A paperback, coffee table reference guide to the state's natural ecosystems and native species includes discussion on coastal estuarine waters, sea floors, and the ocean.

Fiction

Argo, Don. *Canaveral Light*. Cocoa, Fla.: Chapin House Books, 2001. An award-winning and best-selling novel centered around the conflicts and interactions of Florida pioneers and Native Americans during the Seminole Wars.
Dorsey, Tim. *Stingray Shuffle*. New York: HarperCollins, 2003. This laugh-out-loud story blends murder, mayhem, and drugs with the history of Florida and the east coast railroad. Other books by Dorsey are equally irreverent and entertaining.
Gear, Kathleen O'Neal, and W. Michael Gear. *People of the Lightening*. New York: HarperCollins, 2003. The Gears are both writers and archaeologists. This historical novel is set eight thousand years ago in pre-Columbian North America and is woven with fact and fiction from the Windover Pond discovery in north Brevard.
Hemingway, Ernest. *The Old Man & the Sea*. New York: Scribner, 2003. This classic work by Hemingway is the definitive fishing tale.
Hurston, Zora Neale. *Their Eyes Were Watching God*. New York: HarperCollins, 2006. Hurston was born and raised in Eatonville, outside Orlando, and lived in Eau Gallie for several years. Her fictional story of the life of a proud, independent black woman was first published in 1937 and is a classic of African American literature.
Pratt, Theodore. *The Barefoot Mailman*. Port Salerno, Fla.: Florida Classics Library, 1993. A mail carrier in the mid-19th century walks a 100-mile route along the sands of Florida's Atlantic coast.
Rawlings, Majorie Kinnan. *The Yearling*. New York: Simon Pulse, 1988. Pulitzer Prize–winning novel tells the story of a young boy growing up in remote central Florida in the early 20th century.
Smith, Patrick D. *A Land Remembered*. Sarasota, Fla.: Pineapple Press, 1984. Merritt Island resident Smith penned this story, which begins in 1858 and follows three generations of the MacIvey family as they go from dirt-poor Crackers and cowboys to land barons. Winner of the Florida Historical Society's Tebeau Prize as the Most Outstanding Florida Historical Novel.

History

Gannon, Michael. *Florida: A Short History*. Gainesville, Fla.: University Press of Florida, 1996. Since its publication, this comprehensive and easy-to-read book by University of Florida professor Gannon has become a respected and quoted reference of the state's history.

Hiller, Herbert L. *Highway A1A: Florida at the Edge.* Gainesville, Fla.: University Press of Florida, 2005. Take a ride from the past to the present down Florida's famous beachside highway, including a 38-mile stretch through Brevard County.

Mormino, Gary R. *Land of Sunshine, State of Dreams.* Gainesville, Fla.: University Press of Florida, 2005. Mormino weaves the influences of citrus, land development, tourism, technology, and America's continuing fascination with the beach into an entertaining social history of modern Florida.

Parrish, Ada Edmiston, A. Clyde Field, and George Leland Harrell. *Images of America: Merritt Island and Cocoa Beach.* Charleston, S.C.: Arcadia Publishing, 2003. Photographs and stories document the settlement and growth of these Brevard County communities during the early and mid-20th century.

Hobbies and Special Interests

Arnov, Boris, and Susan Jyl Feldmann. *Fish Florida. Saltwater.* Houston, Tex.: Gulf Publishing Co., 1998. A guide on where and how to catch more than 35 varieties of sport fish.

Hardister-Heumann, Darlene. *The Southern Sass Cookbook: It's All in the Sass.* Apopka, Fla.: Palm Crews Printing, 2005. Recipes for Southern favorites such as fried chicken, biscuits, and peach cobbler are presented with healthier, but still tasty, ingredients and preparation tips.

Wynne, Nick. *Southern Cooking: A Man's Domain.* Cocoa, Fla.: Chapin House Books, 2006. Recipes for down-home Cracker dishes such as catfish, okra, biscuits, and Hoppin' John, a stew of black-eyed-peas and rice.

Pictorial

Gorn, Michael, and Buzz Aldrin. *NASA: The Complete Illustrated History.* London: Merrell Publishers, 2005. The story of space exploration from the early 20th century to the present, told through photographs, personal stories, and technical illustrations.

Monroe, Gary. *The Highwaymen.* Gainesville, Fla.: University Press of Florida, 2001. Learn the history of young African American artists who sold their works on roadsides along the Indian River Lagoon in the 1950s and '60s, and enjoy color photo plates of selected works.

Moran, John. *Journal of Light: The Visual Diary of a Florida Nature Photographer.* Gainesville, Fla.: University Press of Florida, 2004. Prize-winning photographer Moran has beautifully captured the best of Florida; essays weave together philosophical observations and photographic technique.

Young People

Crane, Carol. *S is for Sunshine: A Florida Alphabet.* Chelsea, Mich.: Sleeping Bear Press, 2000. An illustrated alphabet designed to introduce children to the wonders of Florida—like the alligator, which can stay underwater for an hour.

Dunham, Montrew, and Meryl Henderson. *Neil Armstrong: Young Flyer.* New York: Aladdin Paperbacks, 1996. Follow astronaut Armstrong from his days as a young boy to becoming the first man on the moon.

Farndon, John, and Tim Furniss. *1000 Facts on Space.* New York: Barnes & Noble Publishing, Inc., 2006. This complete overview of space, from the big bang theory to a history of space technology, is perfect for curious middle and high school students.

Gamble, Adam, and Red Hansen. *Good Night Florida.* Yarmouth, Mass.: Our World of Books, 2006. A board book for young children that captures highlights of the state.

Hammond, Roger, and Steve Weaver. *Those Peculiar Pelicans.* Sarasota, Fla.: Pineapple Press, 2005. Children are introduced to one of Florida's most familiar birds in an easy-to-read book.

Hixon, Mara Uman, and Steve J. Harris. *Turtles Way: Loggy, Greeny & Leather.* Melbourne Beach, Fla.: Canmore Press, 2005. An accurate and entertaining story of sea turtles perfect for toddlers and preschoolers.

Lithgow, John, and Ard Hoyt. *I'm a Manatee.* New York: Simon & Schuster Books for Young Readers, 2003. Grade school children will enjoy this imaginative and informative book about a young boy's dream of being a manatee.

Check Out from the Local Library

Ball, Jim, Roz Foster, Douglas Hendriksen, and Vera Zimmerman. *History of Brevard County: Photographic Memories.* Stuart, Fla.: Southeastern Printing Co., Brevard County Historical Commission, 2001. Photographs and stories reflect each era of life in Brevard County, from steamboat captains and citrus barons to community leaders.

Kjerulff, Georgiana Greene. *Tales of Old Brevard.* Melbourne, Fla.: The Kellersberger Fund of the South Brevard Historical Society, Inc., 1972. An informal history focused on southern Brevard and based on letters, journals, and interviews with early settlers.

Rabac, Glenn. *The City of Cocoa Beach: The First Sixty Years.* Winona, Minn.: Apollo Books, 1986. Follow along as the author tracks the fast-paced growth of the city and provides insight into the people and times.

Sansom, Dixie, Rachel Moehle, and Rosalind Postell. *Staying the Course: Port Canaveral—the First 50 Years.* Cocoa, Fla.: Wolf Jessee Paquin Communications, 2003. Follow along on the evolution of Port Canaveral from a mud bank with a fishing pier to a world-class seaport.

Shofner, Jerrell H. *History of Brevard County: Volume 1.* Stuart, Fla.: Southeastern Printing Co., Brevard County Historical Commission, 1995. A comprehensive look at the history of the area, told in stories and photographs. Volume 2 was published one year later.

Thurm, Ann Hatfield. *History of the City of Cape Canaveral.* Cape Canaveral, Fla.: City of Cape Canaveral, 1994. Thurm, at one time the city's historian, records the early settlement and development of Cape Canaveral from its incorporation in 1962.

Verne, Jules. *From the Earth to the Moon.* Philadelphia, Pa.: Xlibris Corp., 2001. Written in 1865, this early entry to the science fiction genre provides details on designing and launching a space vehicle. Verne's lunar launch pad was based in Florida.

Von Braun, Dr. Wernher. *Space Frontier.* New York: Holt, Rinehart and Winston, 1971. Space buffs will learn about rocketry, man's journey into space, and the future possibilities from the man considered the architect of space exploration.

CELEBRATIONS

The beaches of Florida's Space Coast are an ideal location for family reunions, weddings, anniversaries, and other celebrations. Planners can help blend lodging, dining, and recreation to create a perfect stay for your small or large gathering.

Doubletree Oceanfront Hotel (321-783-9222; www.cocoabeachdoubletree.com; 2080 N. Atlantic Ave., Cocoa Beach 32931). The staff at the Doubletree Hotel make all the arrangements for a celebration you'll always remember. Facility choices include the beach, pool deck, or elegant ballroom. The planning and service will be exceptional for intimate events or sit-down dinners for 300.

Dream Beach Weddings (321-271-0908; www.dreambeachweddings.com). Imagine exchanging vows against a backdrop of blue sky, soft breezes, and rolling surf. Relax and let the folks at Dream Beach Weddings guide you through every wedding planning detail—flowers, location, limousines, photographers, and more.

Radisson Resort at the Port (321-784-0000; www.raddison.com/capecanaveralfl; 8701 Astronaut Blvd., Cape Canaveral 32920). Planners at this resort work with large groups or small private parties to ensure an event or wedding that is memorable. Wedding ceremonies can be performed indoors or in a tropical garden setting.

Rainbow Connection Tours (321-453-3233; www.rctours.net). Linda May, Faye Gallant, and a team of travel experts are available to plan and escort customized excursions for visitors—on the Space Coast or throughout the central Florida area. They make all the arrangements. Wedding planning, including cruise ship ceremonies, is one of their specialties.

Sun Touched Weddings (321-258-7122; www.suntouchedweddings.com). Michael Howard, founder of Sun Touched Weddings, is a Cocoa Beach native who specializes in intimate beachside weddings and can provide everything you need for a casual barefoot-on-the-beach event or a formal gathering. Michael is also a professional photographer and offers beach portrait packages for a lasting memory of your vacation.

Sunward Tours (321-453-0704; www.sunwardtours.com; P.O. Box 1511, Cape Canaveral 32920). Tour and event coordinators David and Margaret Bodchon serve as your concierges, tailoring an itinerary exactly to your time and budget.

CHAMBERS OF COMMERCE

Cocoa Beach Area Chamber of Commerce, 400 Fortenberry Rd., Merritt Island 32952; 321-459-2200; www.cocoabeachchamber.com.

Florida Puerto Rican/Hispanic Chamber of Commerce, 2293 Aurora Rd., Melbourne 32935; 321-752-1003; www.fprhcc.org.

Greater Palm Bay Chamber of Commerce, 4100 Dixie Hwy. NE, Palm Bay 32907; 321-951-9998; www.palmbaychamber.com.

Melbourne–Palm Bay Area Chamber of Commerce, 1005 E. Strawbridge Ave., Melbourne 32901; 321-724-5400; www.melpb-chamber.org.

Titusville Area Chamber of Commerce, 2000 S. Washington Ave., Titusville 32796; 321-267-3036; www.titusville.org.

HANDICAPPED SERVICES

Space Coast hotels, restaurants, and recreational providers do a great job of catering to those with special physical needs. Florida law requires that dogs assisting disabled visitors be allowed in restaurants. All businesses must provide handicapped parking, so remember to pack your permit. When making reservations or planning an outing, call ahead to confirm what's available. There may be some limitations, especially in older buildings, but in general, disabled visitors will find themselves able to enjoy every facet of a fun vacation. Here's just a small sample of what to expect.

Art's Shuttle (783-2112) has a van with a motorized wheelchair lift; all Space Coast Area

Transit buses are similarly equipped. Kennedy Space Center Visitor Complex (449-4444) is set up for full accessibility for mobility-, hearing-, and seeing-impaired guests. Lori Wilson Park and the Johnnie Johnson Nature Trail have ADA-compliant parking, restrooms, playground, boardwalk, trail, and dune crossovers. Specially designed beach wheelchairs are available at Canaveral National Seashore, Jetty Park, and Sebastian Inlet State Park. Boat and fishing tour guides are happy to accommodate the needs of all passengers, but let them know in advance.

HOSPITALS AND CLINICS

Cape Canaveral Hospital (321-799-7111; 701 W. Cocoa Beach Cwsy., Cocoa Beach 32931). Emergency room open 24 hours. Part of the Health First system, which provides a medical referral line at 321-434-2300.

Cape Canaveral Hospital

Health First Physicians Walk-in Clinic (321-868-8313; 105 S. Banana River Blvd., Cocoa Beach 32931). Minor illnesses and injuries are treated at this clinic, conveniently located just off A1A about 1 mile south of FL 520. They participate in many insurance plans and accept several major credit cards. Open Monday–Friday 8 AM–7:30 PM, Saturday 9–4, and Sunday 9–1.

Holmes Regional Medical Center (321-434-7000; 1350 S. Hickory St., Melbourne 32901). Physicians are on duty at this 24-hour emergency room, which has a level II trauma center and air ambulance service. Part of the Health First system.

Palm Bay Community Hospital (321-434-8000; 1425 Malabar Rd., Melbourne 32907). Emergency room open 24 hours. Part of the Health First system.

Parrish Medical Center (321-268-6111; 951 N. Washington Ave., Titusville 32796). Emergency room open 24 hours.

Wuesthoff Medical Center–Melbourne (321-752-1200; 250 N. Wickham Rd., Melbourne 32935). Emergency room open 24 hours. Part of the Wuesthoff Health system.

Wuesthoff Medical Center–Rockledge (321-636-2211; 110 Longwood Ave., Rockledge 32955). Emergency room open 24 hours. Part of the Wuesthoff Health system.

LATE-NIGHT FOOD AND FUEL

The beach communities get quiet late in the evening, especially on weekdays. Many bars remain open until 2 AM and will serve some food. Here are some other locations where food, snacks, and gas are available 24 hours a day.

Cape Canaveral

Circle K (gas and groceries), 7700 N. Atlantic Ave.; 321-799-2173.
McDonald's Restaurant (fast food, 24-hour drive-through), 8780 Astronaut Blvd.; 321-784-5520.
Race Trac (gas and groceries), 8899 Astronaut Blvd.; 321-784-3444.

Cocoa Beach

Denny's Restaurant (food), 1245 N. Atlantic Ave.; 321-783-4005.
Dunkin Donuts (fast food), 5810 N. Atlantic Ave.; 321-784-0426.
McDonald's Restaurant (fast food/drive-through), 3920 N. Atlantic Ave.; 321-783-3450.
7-11 Food Stores (groceries), 190 E. Cocoa Beach Cswy.; 321-784-3267.
7-11 Food Stores (gas and groceries), 6770 N. Atlantic Ave.; 321-784-6050.
Speedway/Sunoco (gas and groceries), 102 S. Orlando Ave.; 321-784-4223.

MAIL AND SHIPPING

U.S. Post Office, Cape Canaveral (321-783-3163; 8700 Astronaut Blvd., Cape Canaveral 32920). Open 9–5 weekdays, 9–noon Saturday. Lobby open 24 hours.
U.S. Post Office, Cocoa Beach (321-783-2544; 500 N. Brevard Ave., Cocoa Beach 32931). Open 9–5 weekdays, 9–noon Saturday. Lobby open 24 hours.
Pak Mail (321-799-9905; 8501 Astronaut Blvd., Cape Canaveral32920). Open: Monday–Friday 9–5:30, Saturday 10–3.
The UPS Store (321-799-3030; 2023 N. Atlantic Ave., Cocoa Beach 32931). Open Monday–Friday 8–6, Saturday 9:30–2.

MEDIA

Magazines and Newspapers

Florida Today (321-242-3500; www.floridatoday.com; P.O. Box 419000, Melbourne

32941). Brevard County's primary newspaper publishes daily, along with weekly and biweekly local publications. The Friday edition includes a special supplement showcasing activities during the upcoming week. The Web site provides space launch updates, including a journal detailing progress during the final countdown hours.

Hometown News (321-242-1013; www.hometownnewsol.com; 1102 S. US 1, Fort Pierce 34950) Informative weekly newspaper offers timely information about community events. The edition featuring Cape Canaveral and Cocoa Beach is distributed each Friday.

Orlando Sentinel (407-240-5000; www.orlandosentinel.com; 633 N. Orange Ave., Orlando 32801). This daily paper is available at most outlets in Brevard County or by subscription and is a good resource for central Florida news, as well as information on activities and events in the Orlando area.

Space Coast Business (321-591-2670; www.spacecoastbusiness.com; P. O. Box 410901, Melbourne 32941) Monthly magazine provides insight and information about Brevard business and professional activities. Subscriptions and back issues are available online.

Space Coast Chronicle (321-773-3800; www.spacecoastchronicle.com; P. O. Box 33248, Indialantic 32903) Monthly publication highlighting news about Brevard County people, places, and events is available at retail and service locations, as well as the libraries.

Space Coast Living (321-541-1014; www.sclmagazine.com; 1900 S. Harbor City Blvd. Suite 323, Melbourne 32901) Monthly magazine celebrates the arts, interests, and activities popular with residents of Brevard County—a great way to get to know the area. Magazine is available at major bookstores.

Radio Stations

WAIA-FM 107.1 (321-953-9942; Melbourne). Contemporary music and current hits.
WBVD-FM 95.1 (321-733-1000; Melbourne). R&B, hip-hop.
WFIT-FM 89.5 (321674-8140; Melbourne). Jazz, bluegrass, folk; NPR programming.
WHRK-FM 102.7 (321-984-1000; Rockledge). Country.
WLOQ-FM 103.1 (407-647-5557; Winter Park). Jazz.
WLRQ-FM 99.3 (321-733-1000; Cocoa). Light rock favorites.
WMEL-AM 920 (321-254-1199; Melbourne). Talk radio, news, and sports.
WMFE-FM 90.7 (407-273-2300; Orlando). Classical, NPR programming.
WMIE-FM 91.5 (321-632-1000; Cocoa). Christian contemporary music.
WMMB-AM 1240 (321-733-1000; Melbourne). Talk radio, news, and sports.
WPIO-FM 89.3 (321-267-3000; Titusville). Alternative Christian music and talk.
WTKS-FM 104.1 (407-916-7800; Maitland). Edgy talk radio and rock.
WWKA-FM 92.3 (407-298-9292; Orlando). Country.

Television Stations

Cape Canaveral, Cocoa Beach, and most of Brevard County are served by cable provider Bright House Networks.

BPS TV Channel 9 (321-633-1000; Viera). Brevard Public Schools, educational.
NASA TV Channel 15 (202-358-0001; Washington, D.C.). Space launches and news.
NEWS13 Channel 13 (407-513-1313; Orlando). Twenty-four-hour local news and weather.
WESH TV Channel 2 (407-645-2222; Winter Park). NBC affliliate.
WFTV TV Channel 7 (407-841-9000; Orlando). ABC affliliate.

WKMG TV Channel 6 (407-521-1200; Orlando). CBS affiliate.
WMFE TV Channel 24 (407-273-2300; Orlando). PBS affiliate.
WMJV TV Channel 22 (321-259-5544; Melbourne). Religious.
WOFL TV Channel 3 (407-644-3535; Lake Mary). FOX affiliate.
WOTF TV Channel 43 (321-254-4343; Melbourne). Spanish-language programming.

REAL ESTATE

Visitors to the area often decide to invest in vacation property or relocate as year-round or seasonal residents. Single-family homes are available, but condominiums will be more affordable and require less maintenance when buying in the beach areas. As a reference, new residents must apply for auto registration and tags within 10 days after starting work or enrolling children in school and obtain a Florida driver's license within 30 days after the beginning of such employment or enrollment.

Melbourne Area Association of Realtors, 1450 Sarno Rd., Melbourne 32901; 321-242-2211; www.maar-fl.org.

Space Coast Association of Realtors, 105 McLeod St., Merritt Island 32953; 321-452-9490; www.space321.com.

ROAD AND MARINE SERVICES

Call these numbers for emergency service 24 hours a day.

Automotive
A Beeline Towing & Auto Service, 321-799-9893.
AAA Membership Emergency Road Service, 1-800-222-4357.
Atlantic Towing & Service, 321-452-3377.
Spaceport Amoco in Cape Canaveral, 321-784-5228.

Marine
Sea Tow Port Canaveral, 321-868-4900.
Towboat US Port Canaveral, 321-783-5600.

VISITOR RESOURCES

Here are some organizations with resources that may be helpful to you in planning your vacation and enjoying your stay.

Brevard County Parks and Recreation (321-633-2046; www.brevardparks.com). The easy-to-navigate Web site contains a comprehensive listing of parks, current events, and summer camps, requirements for booking pavilions.

Canaveral Port Authority (321-783-7831, 1-888-767-8226; www.portcanaveral.org; P.O. Box 267, 445 Challenger Rd., Cape Canaveral 32920). Review their Web site for updates on recreational activities at the port and links to restaurants and vendors.

Cocoa Beach Area Chamber of Commerce Tourist Information Center (321-454-2022; 8501 Astronaut Blvd., Suite 4, Cape Canaveral 32920). Features materials and displays on lodging, dining, and activities, including online terminals and assistance with booking hotels. Open 10–4 daily.

Cocoa Beach Vacation Guide (www.cocoabeachnow.com). This Web site, operated by the Cocoa Beach Hotel & Motel Association, is a great portal to businesses in the area.

Cocoa Village (www.cocoavillage.com). The site includes a comprehensive directory and photo gallery of businesses in historic Cocoa Village.

Florida Space Coast Office of Tourism (321-433-4470, 1-877-572-3224; www.space-coast.com; 430 Brevard Ave., Suite 150, Cocoa 32922). Stop by their office in Cocoa Village, or request a vacation-planning brochure by phone or from their Web site.

Melbourne Main Street (321-724-1741; www.downtownmelbourne.com; 1908 Municipal Ln., Melbourne 32901). This Web site consolidates information for the shops, restaurants, entertainment, and special events in downtown Melbourne.

North Brevard Business Directory (www.nbbd.com). Refer to this comprehensive Web site for information on businesses and activities in Titusville and the north Brevard community.

If Time is Short

For many Space Coast visitors, their first visit to central Florida consists of days spent at the theme parks or on a cruise, and time is limited. The beach, of course, is the star attraction, so enjoy taking in the sunrise, wading in the shallow surf, or sitting in the sun with a good book. Beyond that, here is a list of my personal favorites, each with something extra special that will make you love the area and impatient to return for a longer stay.

Cape Canaveral & Cocoa Beach

Lodging

Beach Place Guesthouses (321-783-4045, fax 321-868-2492; www.beachplaceguesthouses.com; 1445 S. Atlantic Ave., Cocoa Beach 32920). Perfect for a calming retreat, with a nearly private beach and comfortable accommodations.

Best Western Oceanfront Hotel (321-783-7621, 1-800-962-0028, fax 321-799-4576; www.bestwesterncocoabeach.com; 5500 Ocean Beach Blvd., Cocoa Beach 32931). One of the best locations on the beach, the hotel is near the Cocoa Beach Pier and within walking distance of several restaurants.

Radisson Resort at the Port (321-784-0000, 1-800-333-3333, fax 321-784-3737; www.radisson.com/capecanaveralfl; 8701 Astronaut Blvd., Cape Canaveral 32920). An ideal location for a precruise overnight stay. Relax and play by the pool, have dinner at the Flamingo restaurant, and then board a quick shuttle to the ship the next day.

Cultural Attractions

East Coast Surfing Hall of Fame Museum (321-799-8840; www.ecsurfinghallandmuseum.org; 4275 N. Atlantic Ave., Cocoa Beach 32920). For a truly unique experience, stop by this homage to surfing and learn how area surfers influenced it.

Heidi's Jazz Club (321-783-4559; www.heidisjazzclub.com; 7 N. Orlando Ave., Cocoa Beach 32931). This cozy nightspot offers quality jazz in a contemporary club setting.

Redhead Martini and Cigar Bar (321-799-1616; 626 Glen Cheek Dr., Port Canaveral 32920). Begin the evening with a martini and a front-row seat for the parade of departing cruise liners. When the Disney ship appears, Mickey Mouse mitts are passed around to wave with flair.

BEACHES

Cocoa Beach Pier (321-783-7549; www.cocoabeachpier.com; 401 Meade Ave., Cocoa Beach 32931). Like a trip to a seaside mall, everything you need for a fun day at the beach is in one convenient location.

Jetty Park (400 E. Jetty Rd., Cape Canaveral 32920). If time is extra short but you would like to experience the beach, take a walk on the shore of Jetty Park or on the 1,200-foot fishing pier. Time your visit to catch the cruise ships leave at about 5 most evenings.

Ron Jon Surf Shop (321-799-8888; www.ronjons.com; 4151 N. Atlantic Ave., Cocoa Beach 32931). Capture the essence of the beach and surfing experience at this Cocoa Beach landmark, open 24 hours a day to easily fit into any travel schedule.

RECREATION

Island Boat Lines (321-454-7414; www.islandboatlines.com). Take a short break from the beach and experience the wildlife and wonder of the Banana River Lagoon aboard a pontoon boat tour.

Space Coast Kayaking (321-784-2452; www.spacecoastkayaking.net; Ramp Rd., Cocoa Beach). Offers leisurely kayak paddles through the Thousand Islands.

DINING

Atlantic Ocean Grille (321-783-7549; Cocoa Beach Pier, 401 Meade Ave., Cocoa Beach 32931). Glass walls ensure a beautiful ocean view as you enjoy breakfast, dinner, or Sunday brunch.

Cactus Flower (321-452-6606; 1891 E. Merritt Island Cswy., Merritt Island 32952). Authentic Mexican food and friendly service make this an enjoyable evening. Come for happy hour and stay for dinner on the riverside deck.

Fishlips Waterfront Bar & Grill (321-784-4533; 610 Glen Cheek Dr., Port Canaveral 32920). This Port Canaveral seafood restaurant has indoor and outdoor seating, and delicious dishes prepared and presented with style.

Central Brevard

Brevard Zoo (321-254-9453; www.brevardzoo.org; 8225 N. Wickham Rd., Melbourne 32940). The Wild Florida exhibit is a sure opportunity to see much of the wildlife in this area, and the park is great fun for all ages. Couple your visit with lunch or dinner at Pizza Gallery & Grill at the Avenue Viera (see the Restaurants and Food Purveyors chapter for more information).

Cocoa Village is just a short drive from the beach. Pick up a map at any gallery and embark on a self-guided tour of the areas that interest you most. Don't miss the the Black Dog Gallery (404D Brevard Ave.), Boatyard Studio (118 Harrison St.), and the Clay Studio (116B Harrison St.) Take a break for breakfast, lunch, or dinner at Ossorio's (316 Brevard Ave.), a charming restaurant in the heart of the village. Call ahead and reserve a spot with Indian River Cruises (321-223-6825) for a romantic sunset sail down the Indian River.

Twister Airboat Rides (321-632-4199; www.twisterairboatrides.com; FL 520 at St. Johns River, Cocoa). Adventurers of all ages will enjoy a uniquely Florida trek, and an almost-guaranteed chance to see alligators, with Twister Airboat Rides, which leave from Lone Cabbage Fish Camp (8199 King St.) in Cocoa. See the Recreation chapter for more information.

North Brevard

Black Point Wildlife Drive (321-861-0667; www.fws.gov/merrittisland; Merritt Island National Wildlife Refuge, North Merritt Island). In an hour or two, drive around the circular road, where there's a good chance you'll see exotic birds, alligators, and other wildlife. If time permits, make a side trip to the Manatee Observation Deck, about 5 miles farther up the road.

Dixie Crossroads (321-268-5000; 1475 Garden St., Titusville 32796). While in north Brevard, include a stop at this popular, fun, and affordable eatery with an extensive seafood menu, including the house specialty, rock shrimp.

Kennedy Space Center Visitor Complex (321-449-4444; www.kennedyspacecenter.com; NASA Parkway, Merritt Island 32899). Kennedy Space Center is a must-see stop on a visit to Florida's Space Coast, but you need several hours to really enjoy your experience.

South Brevard

The **Eau Gallie** section of Melbourne, by the riverfront, is about a 30-minute drive from Cocoa Beach, much of it along scenic A1A. Within 2 blocks you can explore the Brevard Art Museum (321-242-0737; 1463 Highland Ave.), Fifth Avenue Art Gallery (321-259-8261; 1470 Highland Ave.), and the James Wadsworth Rossetter House (1760 Highland Ave.). Nosh & Ganache (1540 Highland Ave.) is perfect for a relaxed lunch on the patio.

General Index

Lodging by Price

Inexpensive: Up to $100
Moderate: $100 to $150
Expensive: $150 to $200
Very Expensive: More than $200

Cape Canaveral

Moderate
Country Inns & Suites by Carlson, 46

Moderate-Expensive
Radisson Resort at the Port, 52–53
Expensive
Residence Inn by Marriott, 53
Royal Mansions, 57

Expensive-Very Expensive
Canaveral Towers Resort, 56
Cape Winds Resort, 56

Very Expensive
Ron Jon Cape Caribe Resort, 54

Cocoa Beach

Inexpensive
Dolphin Inn, 47

Inexpensive-Moderate
La Quinta Inn, 51
Luna Sea Bed & Breakfast Motel, 51–52
Pelican Landing Resort, 52
Sea Aire Motel, 54–55
South Beach Inn, 55
Surf Studio Beach Resort, 55

Moderate
Beach Island Resort, 44
Comfort Inn & Suites, 45–46
Days Inn Cocoa Beach, 46–47
Fawlty Towers Resort Motel, 48
Four Points by Sheraton, 48–49
Holiday Inn Express Hotel & Suites, 50
Seagull Beach Club, 58

Moderate-Expensive
Best Western Oceanside Hotel, 45

Courtyard by Marriott Cocoa Beach, 46
Hampton Inn, 49
Hilton Cocoa Beach Oceanfront, 49
Ocean Landings Resort & Racquet Club, 57
Oceanside Inn, 52
Ola Grande Condominiums, 57

Expensive
Beach Place Guesthouses, 44–45
Cocoa Beach Club Condominiums, 56
Doubletree Oceanfront Hotel, 47–48
Holiday Inn Cocoa Beach-Oceanfront
    Resort, 49–50
Inn at Cocoa Beach, The, 50–51
Resort on Cocoa Beach, The, 53–54
Wakulla Suites, 55–56

Very Expensive
Discovery Beach Resort, 47

Indialantic

Moderate
Tuckaway Shores, 61

Moderate-Expensive
Windemere Inn by the Sea, 61

Melbourne

Moderate
Holiday Inn & Conference Center, 59

Moderate-Expensive
Crane Creek Inn Waterfront Bed &
    Breakfast, 60–61

Expensive-Very Expensive
Crowne Plaza Melbourne Oceanfront, 58
    Very Expensive
Old Pineapple Inn, The, 61
Mims

Moderate
Dickens Inn Bed & Breakfast, 60

Dining by Price

Inexpensive:	Up to $15
Moderate:	$15 to $25
Expensive:	$25 to $35
Very Expensive:	$35 or more

Cape Canaveral

Inexpensive-Moderate
DiLorenzo's, 107–8
La Fiesta, 111

Moderate
Kelsey's Pizzeria, 111
Taste of Goa, 118
Zachary's Family Restaurant, 119

Expensive
Flamingos at the Radisson Hotel, 109
Mangroves, 112
Ron Jon Surf Grill, 114

Cocoa

Inexpensive
Café Flamant, 119–20
Lone Cabbage Fish Camp, 121
Madison's Café, 122

Inexpensive-Moderate
Ossorio, 123

Moderate-Expensive
Cara Mia Riverside Grill, 120–21
Murdock's Bistro and Char Bar, 123
  Expensive-Very Expensive
Black Tulip, 119

Very Expensive
Café Margaux, 120
Ulysses Prime Steakhouse, 124

Cocoa Beach

Inexpensive
Barrier Jack's, 105
Boston Beef and Seafood, 105
Eagle's Nest Sports Bar and Grill, 108

Simply Delicious Café and Bakery, 116
Sunrise Cafe, 117
Taco City, 118

Inexpensive-Moderate
Boardwalk, The, 105
Cape Codder, The, 106
Oh Shucks Seafood Bar, 112–13
Omelet Station, The, 113
Sonny's Real Pit Par-B-Q, 116–17

Moderate
Anacapri Pizzeria, 104
Azteca Two, 104–5
Bunky's Raw Bar and Seafood Grille, 105–6
Captain J's Ocean Deck Restaurant, 106–7
Captains Grill, 107
Italian Courtyard, 110–11
Lobster Shanty & Wharfside, 111
Pita Garden, 113
Roberto's Little Havana, 113–14
Siam Orchid, 115
Slow and Low Barbeque Bar & Grill, 116
Sunset Café Waterfront Bar & Grill, 117
Thai Japanese, 118

Moderate-Expensive
Atlantic Ocean Grille, 104
Atlantis Bar and Grill, 104
Coconuts on the Beach, 107
Durango's Steak House, 108
Florida's Seafood Bar & Grill, 109
Marlins Good Times Bar and Grill, 112
Shark Pit Bar and Grill, 114–15
Yen-Yen, 119

Expensive
Surf Bar and Grill, The, 117–18

Expensive-Very Expensive
Heidelberg Restaurant, 110
Three Wishes, 118–19

Very Expensive
Gregory's, 109
Mango Tree, The, 112
Silvestro's, 115–16